Praise for Italian Wine For Dummies

"Bravo to Ed and Mary! This book shows their love for Italy, the Italian producers, and the great marriage of local foods with local wines. Here is a great book that presents information without intimidation."
— Piero Selvaggio, VALENTINO Restaurant

"Mary and Ed share a great passion for Italian wines. They frequently visit Italy, taste the latest wines, explore vineyards and cellars, and meet with wine-makers. In *Italian Wine For Dummies,* they have taken their vast knowledge of the subject and presented it in a very readable, clear, entertaining format that should appeal to anyone interested in wine."
— Angelo Gaja, Owner of the Gaja Winery

"The esteem in which I hold the authors of *Italian Wine For Dummies* is boundless. I have known Ed and Mary, individually and as a team, for over 50 years and am able to say that I have yet to encounter more knowl-edgeable guides to the ins and outs of Italian wine. I was honored when they asked me to write the fore-word to their *Wine For Dummies* and thrilled to be endorsing this very important book, written with infi-nite skill and passion equal to that of the most committed Italian winemaker."
— Piero Antinori, Proprietor, Marchesi Antinori Winery, Florence, Italy

"It is not an easy task to decipher the beautiful and complex world of Italian wines. Mary Ewing-Mulligan and Ed McCarthy have long understood and negotiated this world. In their newest book, *Italian Wine For Dummies*, in a very organized fashion and with great love and passion for the subject, they offer readers a blueprint for a true understanding and enjoyment of Italian wines. A must-have book for anyone who is serious about Italian wines. Cin cin."
— Lidia Bastianich, Restaurateur (Felidia, Becco, Lidia's K.C., Lidia's Pittsburgh), Cookbook Author *(Lidia's Italian American Kitchen),* and TV Host *(Lidia's Italian Table)*

Praise for French Wine For Dummies

"The best way to sift through this informative tome is to pour yourself a big glass of Haut Brion, sit back, and enjoy. Whether you are an avid collector or wine novice, this book offers an extensive resource in an accessible format."

> — Charlie Trotter, Acclaimed Chef and
> Award-Winning Restaurant Owner
> and Author

"Helping people to love wine is worthy of encouragement. Congratulations to Mary Ewing-Mulligan and Ed McCarthy for your book about one of the greatest treasures of France: the vineyards. This book is an invitation to discover the bountiful wine regions, each different from one another, and is an homage to the beauty and uniqueness of the delicious wines they produce. I am convinced that your readers will enjoy reading this book, and I am sure they will enjoy tasting the wines you praise. I propose a toast: to the joy of reading and to your good health! (Santé)"

> — Georges Duboeuf, Les Vins Georges
> Duboeuf

Praise for Wine For Dummies

"[McCarthy and Ewing-Mulligan] have accomplished the almost impossible feat of writing a book about wine that both novices and connoisseurs will love because it's fun to read and crammed with authoritative information."

> — *Wine & Spirits* magazine

"BUY THE BOOK . . . [*Wine For Dummies*] is well organized, packed with information, and filled with reader-friendly graphics . . ."

> — *Food and Wine* magazine

Italian Wine
FOR
DUMMIES®

by Mary Ewing-Mulligan MW
and Ed McCarthy

Hungry Minds™

Best-Selling Books • Digital Downloads • e-Books • Answer Networks
e-Newsletters • Branded Web Sites • e-Learning

New York, NY ◆ Cleveland, OH ◆ Indianapolis, IN

Italian Wine For Dummies®

Published by:
Hungry Minds, Inc.
909 Third Avenue
New York, NY 10022
www.hungryminds.com
www.dummies.com

Library of Congress Control Number: 2001091998

ISBN: 0-7645-5355-0

Printed in the United States of America

10 9 8 7 6 5 4

1O/ST/QV/QS/IN

Distributed in the United States by Hungry Minds, Inc.

Distributed by CDG Books Canada Inc. for Canada; by Transworld Publishers Limited in the United Kingdom; by IDG Norge Books for Norway; by IDG Sweden Books for Sweden; by IDG Books Australia Publishing Corporation Pty. Ltd. for Australia and New Zealand; by TransQuest Publishers Pte Ltd. for Singapore, Malaysia, Thailand, Indonesia, and Hong Kong; by Gotop Information Inc. for Taiwan; by ICG Muse, Inc. for Japan; by Intersoft for South Africa; by Eyrolles for France; by International Thomson Publishing for Germany, Austria and Switzerland; by Distribuidora Cuspide for Argentina; by LR International for Brazil; by Galileo Libros for Chile; by Ediciones ZETA S.C.R. Ltda. for Peru; by WS Computer Publishing Corporation, Inc., for the Philippines; by Contemporanea de Ediciones for Venezuela; by Express Computer Distributors for the Caribbean and West Indies; by Micronesia Media Distributor, Inc. for Micronesia; by Chips Computadoras S.A. de C.V. for Mexico; by Editorial Norma de Panama S.A. for Panama; by American Bookshops for Finland.

For general information on Hungry Minds' products and services please contact our Customer Care department; within the U.S. at 800-762-2974, outside the U.S. at 317-572-3993 or fax 317-572-4002.

For sales inquiries and resellers information, including discounts, premium and bulk quantity sales and foreign language translations please contact our Customer Care department at 800-434-3422, fax 317-572-4002 or write to Hungry Minds, Inc., Attn: Customer Care department, 10475 Crosspoint Boulevard, Indianapolis, IN 46256.

For information on licensing foreign or domestic rights, please contact our Sub-Rights Customer Care department at 212-884-5000.

For information on using Hungry Minds' products and services in the classroom or for ordering examination copies, please contact our Educational Sales department at 800-434-2086 or fax 317-572-4005.

Please contact our Public Relations department at 212-884-5163 for press review copies or 212-884-5000 for author interviews and other publicity information or fax 212-884-5400.

For authorization to photocopy items for corporate, personal, or educational use, please contact Copyright Clearance Center, 222 Rosewood Drive, Danvers, MA 01923, or fax 978-750-4470.

Hungry Minds is a trademark of Hungry Minds, Inc.

About the Authors

Mary Ewing-Mulligan and **Ed McCarthy** are two wine lovers whose stars crossed at an Italian wine tasting in New York City's Chinatown in 1981, leading to personal and professional partership. Besides co-authoring seven wine books, they've taught hundreds of wine classes together, visited nearly every wine region of the world, run five marathons, and raised ten cats. Together, they've amassed more than half a century of professional wine experience.

Mary grew up in Pennsylvania and graduated from the University of Pennsylvania. Immediately after college, she took a position at the Italian Trade Commission, where she dicovered her love of wine and of Italy, and began sharing that passion with other Americans. She is now president of International Wine Center, a New York City wine school where she teaches classes mainly for wine professionals; she's also wine columnist for the *NY Daily News*. Mary's proudest credential is being America's first female Master of Wine (MW), one of only 18 MW's in America and 233 worldwide.

Ed, a New Yorker, graduated from City University of NY with a Master's degree in psychology. He taught high school English as his day job, all the while working part time in wine shops to satisfy his passion for wine. He began writing about wine in 1985, and in 1995 co-authored, with Mary, the best-selling *Wine For Dummies;* in 1999, he went solo as author of *Champagne For Dummies,* a topic in which he's particularly keen. He and Mary share a wine column in *Nation's Restaurant News,* and he also writes for *Wine Enthusiast Magazine* and *Underground Wine Journal.* Ed and Mary are both Certified Wine Educators (CWE).

Mary and Ed admit to leading thoroughly unbalanced lives in which their only non-wine pursuits are jogging and picnicking in the Alps — when they find the time. At home, they wind down to the tunes of Bob Dylan and Neil Young, in the company of their feline roommates, Léoville, Pinot, Brunello, Dolcetto, Clicquot, and Black & Whitey.

Dedication

We dedicate this book to the memory of Sheldon Wasserman, whose passion for Italian wine, conveyed through his writings and his always-opinionated voice, led so many Americans to discover Italy's wines and believe in them.

Acknowledgments

Italian wines were Mary's first love and Ed's second (after French) when we became a team. Every journey we've taken to Italy since then has only deepened our feelings about Italian wines, Italian food, the wonderful people, and Italy itself. And so our first acknowledgment is to the people of Italy: Thank you for making us feel so welcome and so special. We truly love you — especially our dear Italian friends in Piedmont. We always look forward to our next trip "home."

We thank the creative genius, CEO John Kilcullen — who's been known to enjoy a good glass or two of Italian wine — for making the *For Dummies* books the phenomenal success that they are. We sincerely thank Publisher Jennifer R. Feldman for giving us the "green light" on *Italian Wine For Dummies*. And thanks to Senior Editor Linda Ingroia — we know that you've been looking forward to this book as much as anyone! Really special thanks to our project editor Mary Goodwin for putting up with us for two books in a row. You're truly a saint. Both Linda and Mary managed to perform a minor miracle by getting us to finish this book on time!

Could we have had a better technical reviewer for this book than the Professor, Dr. Ed Beltrami? We couldn't have trusted anyone to catch our errors more than the scholarly *Dottore*. Thanks to Steve Ettlinger, our agent, who brought us to Hungry Minds, Inc., in the first place, and who knows enough not to bother us with phone calls when we're busy writing.

We're grateful for the support of our colleagues at International Wine Center, Linda Lawry and May Matta-Alliah, who sustained our absence while we wrote this book. Finally, to Elise McCarthy, E.J. McCarthy, and his wife Bernadette, and to Cindy McCarthy Tomarchio and her husband David — thanks for your continual encouragement and support.

Publisher's Acknowledgments

We're proud of this book; please send us your comments through our Online Registration Form located at www.dummies.com.

Some of the people who helped bring this book to market include the following:

Acquisitions, Editorial, and Media Development

Project Editor: Mary Goodwin

Senior Acquisitions Editor: Linda Ingroia

Assistant Acquisitions Editor: Erin Connell

Technical Editor: Dr. Ed Beltrami

Editorial Manager: Pam Mourouzis

Editorial Assistant: Jennifer Young

Cover Photos:
© Bill Bettencourt/Food Pix

Production

Project Coordinator: Maridee Ennis

Layout and Graphics: Amy Adrian, Kelly Hardesty, Joyce Haughey, Jacque Schneider, Julie Trippetti

Proofreaders: Andy Hollandbeck, Susan Moritz, Marianne Santy, TECHBOOKS Production Services

Indexer:
TECHBOOKS Production Services

General and Administrative

Hungry Minds Technology Publishing Group: Richard Swadley, Vice President and Executive Group Publisher; Bob Ipsen, Vice President and Group Publisher; Joseph Wikert, Vice President and Publisher; Barry Pruett, Vice President and Publisher; Mary Bednarek, Editorial Director; Mary C. Corder, Editorial Director; Andy Cummings, Editorial Director

Hungry Minds Manufacturing: Ivor Parker, Vice President, Manufacturing

Hungry Minds Marketing: John Helmus, Assistant Vice President, Director of Marketing

Hungry Minds Production for Branded Press: Debbie Stailey, Production Director

Hungry Minds Sales: Michael Violano, Vice President, International Sales and Sub Rights

Contents at a Glance

Introduction *1*

Part 1: The Big Picture of Italian Wine *7*
Chapter 1: Born to Make Wine 9
Chapter 2: Grapes from Near and Far 15
Chapter 3: The Language of the Label 27

Part 11: The Wine Regions of Northern Italy *35*
Chapter 4: The Wines of Piedmont 37
Chapter 5: Other Northwest Regions 77
Chapter 6: North-Central Italy 89
Chapter 7: Northeastern Italy 109

Part 111: The Wine Regions of Central Italy *141*
Chapter 8: The Wines of Tuscany 143
Chapter 9: The Wines of Central Italy 175

Part 1V: The Wine Regions of Southern Italy *203*
Chapter 10: The Wines of Southern Italy 205
Chapter 11: Sicily and Sardinia 233

Part V: The Part of Tens *251*
Chapter 12: Ten Commonly-Asked Questions
about Italian Wines 253
Chapter 13: Ten Common Italian Wine Myths Exposed 259

Part V1: Appendixes *265*
Appendix A: Pronunciation Guide to Italian Wine
Names and Terms 267
Appendix B: Italian Wine Vintage Chart: 1980 to 1999 271

Index *273*

Table of Contents

Introduction *1*

    About This Book 1
        Part I: The Big Picture of Italian Wine 2
        Part II: The Wine Regions of Northern Italy 3
        Part III: The Wine Regions of Central Italy 3
        Part IV: The Wine Regions of Southern Italy 3
        Part V: The Part of Tens 4
        Part VI: Appendixes 4
    Icons Used in This Book 4

Part 1: The Big Picture of Italian Wine *7*

    Chapter 1: Born to Make Wine **9**

    Wine to Boot 9
        From the Alps to almost Africa 10
        Diverse conditions, diverse wines 12
    Italian Wine Styles Today 12
        The Italian prototype 13
        Red, white, and beyond 14

    Chapter 2: Grapes from Near and Far **15**

    Italy's Curious Varieties 15
        Native talents 16
        Immigrants and migrants 16
    The Major Grapes 17
        Reds aplenty 17
        Over-achieving whites 22

    Chapter 3: The Language of the Label **27**

    The Name Game 27
        The DOC calls 28
        Non-DOC/G wines 29
        Putting faith in the DOC 32
    Common Wine Label Words 33

Part II: The Wine Regions of Northern Italy 35

Chapter 4: The Wines of Piedmont 37

The Majesty of Piedmont 37
    The wines of Piedmont 39
    The grapes of Piedmont 40
Wines of the Alba Area 41
    Barolo 42
    Barbaresco 47
    Barbera, Dolcetto, and Nebbiolo of Alba 52
    Roero and Roero Arneis 55
    Other DOC wines of Alba 56
    Visiting the Alba-Asti area 58
The Wines of Southeastern Piedmont 60
    Asti DOCG 61
    Barbera d'Asti 63
    Other varietal wines 64
    Gavi DOCG 67
    Other wines of Piedmont's southeast 68
Northern Piedmont 69
    Carema and Caluso 70
    Vercelli and Novara hills wines 71
Other Piedmont Wines 75

Chapter 5: Other Northwest Regions 77

Alpine Valle d'Aosta 77
    Red wines from cool climes 79
    Regional and varietal wines 80
Liguria: The Riviera 83
    Liguria's vineyards and wines 84
    Ligurian wine producers 88

Chapter 6: North-Central Italy 89

Lombardy Has It All 89
    The Valtellina: Nebbiolo's most austere face 91
    Oltrepó Pavese: Sparkling wines and more 93
    Franciacorta: Sparklers with style 95
    Lake Garda's vineyards 98
    Other Lombardy DOC wines 99
Emilia-Romagna: One Region, Really Two 100
    Emilia's beloved Lambrusco 101
    The hillside wines of Emilia 103
    The wines of Romagna 106

Chapter 7: Northeastern Italy 109

Trentino-Alto Adige: One Region, Two Cultures 109
    The wines of Alto Adige 112
    The wines of Trentino 116
Veneto: Verona to Venice 118
    Verona's major wines 120
    Wines of the Central Hills 127
    Wines of eastern Veneto 130
Friuli-Venezia Giulia: The Great White Way 133
    The wines of Friuli 135
    Other Friuli DOC wines 140

Part 111: The Wine Regions of Central Italy 141

Chapter 8: The Wines of Tuscany 143

The Big Picture of Tuscany 143
The Land of Chianti 147
    The range of Chianti wines 147
    Chianti Classico 148
    Chianti 153
    Pomino, San Gimignano, and other
        Chianti neighbors 156
Monumental Montalcino 159
    Brunello di Montalcino 160
    Other wines of Montalcino 162
The "Noble Wine" of Montepulciano 164
    Other Montepulciano DOC wines 165
    Montepulciano-area producers 166
Carmignano 166
Super-Tuscan Wines — The Winds of Change 167
Tuscany's "Hot" Coast 170
    Bolgheri 170
    Val di Cornia 171
    Grosseto's new frontier 171
Other Tuscan Wines 173

Chapter 9: The Wines of Central Italy 175

Umbria: The Inland Region 175
    Orvieto 177
    Torgiano 179
    Sagrantino di Montefalco 180
    Umbria's other DOC wines 180
    Recommended Umbrian wineries 183

Marches, on the Adriatic 183
    Verdicchio 183
    Rosso Cònero and Rosso Piceno 185
    Marche's other DOC wines 186
    Marche wines to buy 188
Mountainous Abruzzo 188
    Abruzzo's vineyards and wines 189
    Abruzzo wines worth buying 192
Forgotten Molise 192
    Molise's two DOC wines 193
    The lone Molise wine producer 193
Latium: Rome's Region 194
    Frascati and company, from Rome's hills 195
    Northern Latium wines 198
    Latium's South Coast 199
    Southeast Latium 200
    Latium wine producers 202

Part IV: The Wine Regions of Southern Italy 203

Chapter 10: The Wines of Southern Italy 205

Campania: Revival Begins 205
    The wines of Avellino 208
    Wines of the coastal hills and islands
        around Naples 210
    Southern Campania 212
    Campania's northern hills 213
    Campania wines worth buying 215
Apulia: Italy's Wine Barrel 215
    The Salento Peninsula 217
    The "Trulli" district 221
    Central Puglia 222
    The northern plains 223
    Recommended Puglia producers 224
Mountainous Basilicata 225
    Aglianico del Vulture 226
    Basilicata brands to buy 226
Rugged Calabria 226
    Cirò 227
    Other Calabrian wines 228
    Calabrian wines to buy 231

Chapter 11: Sicily and Sardinia **233**

Sicilia Leaves the Past 233
   Sicily's vineyards and wines 234
   A Sicilian wine shopping list 243
Sardinia Stands Alone 243
   Sardinia's vineyards and wines .244
   Sardinian wines to seek 250

Part V: The Part of Tens *251*

**Chapter 12: Ten Commonly-Asked Questions
about Italian Wines** **253**

Why Are Italian Wines So Much Better with Food? 253
What Are Super-Tuscan Wines? 254
Why Does the Italian Government Tell Producers
   How to Make Their Wines? 254
What's the Difference Between DOC
   and Non-DOC Wines? 255
What's the Best All-Purpose Italian Red Wine? 255
Isn't Southern Italy Too Hot for Making Wine? 255
Which Are Better: "Traditional" or "Modern"
   Italian Wines? 256
What Are Barriques, and Why Are They Controversial? 256
Why Do Italian Wines Have Such Strange Names? 257
Why Are Italian Wines Less Prestigious
   Than French Wines? 257

**Chapter 13: Ten Common Italian Wine
Myths Exposed** **259**

Chianti Is an Inexpensive, Commercial Wine 259
Italian Wines Should Be Enjoyed with Italian Food 260
Pinot Grigio Is One of Italy's Best Wines 260
Italy's Best Wines Are All Red 260
Marsala Is Cooking Wine 261
White Italian Wines All Taste Alike 261
Non-DOC Wines Are Better Than DOC Wines 262
Spumante Is Sweet 262
Soave and Valpolicella Are Low-Quality Wines 262
Montepulciano d'Abruzzo and Vino Nobile di
   Montepulciano Are Made from the Same Grape 263

Part VI: Appendixes *265*

   **Appendix A: Pronunciation Guide to Italian Wine
   Names and Terms** ....**.267**

   **Appendix B: Italian Wine Vintage
   Chart: 1980 to 1999** ....**.271**

Index *273*

Introduction

● ●

*A*t this moment in time, Italy is the most exciting wine
country on earth. The quality of the wines has never
been higher, and the range of wines has never been broader.
Nor have more types of Italian wines ever been available outside of Italy.

The quality of Italy's wines has been growing steadily for about
two decades. Now, finally, the message has leaked beyond the
small cult of wine lovers who have loyally followed Italian
wines, and into the mainstream of America's wine conscious-
ness. You can now find Italian wines in three-star French restaurants. California wineries are trying their hand with Italian
grape varieties and Italianate wine styles. New York City even
boasts two all-Italian wine shops.

Although Italy's wines are more desirable and more available
than ever, they're no more comprehensible. In fact, the prolif-
eration of new wines and new wine zones has made Italian
wine an even more confusing topic than it's always been. (All
the obscure grape varieties, complicated wine blends, strange
wine names, and restrictive wine laws — observed or
circumvented — make Italian wines just about the most
challenging of all to master.) Yet comprehensive, up-to-date
reference books on Italian wines simply weren't available in
English. *Italian Wine For Dummies* changes all that.

About This Book

When we planned this book, we had two goals in mind. First,
we wanted to share our passion for Italy's wines (and the land
and people who make them). We adore Italian wine. We've visited Italy's wine regions at every opportunity for more than 20
years; each visit has deepened our fascination with the array
of wines Italy makes — and the country's rich potential. We'd
love to turn you on to the excitement.

Our second goal was to provide straightforward, clear, comprehensive information that wine drinkers could turn to again and again as they delve ever deeper into the amazing universe of Italian wines. Our earlier books, such as *Wine For Dummies,* published by Hungry Minds, Inc., couldn't possibly do justice to the vast topic of Italian wines. Every time that our students or our readers asked us where they could find out more about Italian wines, we became frustrated that we had nowhere to send them. We decided that we had to fill the void.

We chose a regional approach for discussing Italian wines because in a country as diverse as Italy, very few general statements about wine hold true before individual realities of regional cultures, climates, and grape varieties rear their heads. In describing Italy's wine regions, we place special emphasis on wines that are widely available in markets such as the U.S., and wines of superior quality. But we also mention wines that are more difficult to find, and even wines that you won't find anywhere except Italy. We cover all these wines in the interest of thoroughness, to give you the complete picture of each region's wines. When you flip through the pages of this book, and your eyes fall on the names of wines you've never heard of, we hope you'll consider that a positive aspect of the book rather than unnecessary detail.

To gain the most comprehensive understanding of Italian wines, read *Italian Wine For Dummies* from the beginning — that is, don't skip the first three chapters. (And be sure to check out the useful information on the Cheat Sheet.) If you already know something about Italy's wines, you can go directly into the regional chapters.

Our discussions about individual regions begin with general information about the region, then proceed to cover the region's most important wines — either the highest quality wines, or the wines that are most widely available. Information about less important wines comes toward the end of each regional section. If you're interested mainly in Italy's major wines, you can skip the details about the minor wines. We've divided this book into five parts, which we describe here.

Part 1: The Big Picture of Italian Wine

In this part, we make whatever generalizations are safe to make about Italy's wines as a group. Chapter 1 discusses the intricately-contoured lay of the land in Italy. It also provides a broad overview of the styles of wine made in Italy, and puts us out on a limb describing the prototypical white and red Italian wine (as if!). In Chapter 2, the litany of strange names begins: Italy's major grape varieties; although we devote a whole chapter to this topic, new names join the litany throughout the book. Chapter 3 explains one of the most complicated aspects of Italian wines: the laws under which they exist, and how they're named. It also defines the most common label terminology.

Part 11: The Wine Regions of Northern Italy

This part describes the wines from Italy's very important northern regions: Piedmont (Chapter 4), Lombardy and Emilia-Romagna (Chapter 6), and Trentino-Alto-Adige, Veneto, and Friuli-Venezia-Giulia (Chapter 7). Chapter 5 covers the relatively minor regions of Aosta Valley and Liguria. We'd venture a guess that half the Italian wines you see in shops come from the regions covered in this part.

Part 111: The Wine Regions of Central Italy

Of that other half of Italian wines you're likely to see in wine shops, a huge percentage come from Tuscany, the very major region that occupies Chapter 8. That's where you meet Chianti, for example, and discover why some Tuscan wines are called "Super." Chapter 9 covers the whole remainder of Central Italy — the wines of Umbria, Latium, Marche, Abruzzo, and Molise. Some of Italy's best values live here.

Part IV: The Wine Regions of Southern Italy

Italy's southern regions are hot — figuratively as well as literally. Puglia, Campania, Basilicata, and Calabria — all discussed in Chapter 10 — are making their best wines in 4,000 years (not that we've technically been able to verify that). What's more, some of these wines are amazing values, especially if your favorite wine words are "red" and "powerful." Italy's two huge islands, Sicily and Sardegna, are equally "happening" these days; they share Chapter 11.

Part V: The Part of Tens

If there are 50 ways to leave your lover, there are definitely ten major misunderstandings about Italian wines, and ten burning questions you always wanted to ask. Chapter 12 tackles the ten questions, such as whether Super-Tuscans are better than DOC wines. Chapter 13 explodes the myths: Italian wine *doesn't* only go with Italian food, for example.

Part VI: Appendixes

If only everyone spoke Italian, Italy's wines would be so much easier to talk about and order in restaurants. Until then, Appendix A to the rescue: Here we give you an alphabetized pronunciation guide to Italian wine terms and wine names. Appendix B is a Vintage Chart to guide you in your wine choices.

Icons Used in This Book

We're not trying to turn you into a winemaker or an Italian politician, but some technical issues are important to understanding Italy's wines — depending on how deeply you want to understand them, of course. Where you see this icon, feel free to skip the information that follows.

Advice and information that makes you a wiser Italian wine drinker is marked by this bull's-eye so that you won't miss it.

When you see this sign, you know that you're in the territory of a common misunderstanding about Italy's wine. We alert you to help prevent confusion.

Some issues in wine are so fundamental that they bear repeating. Just so you don't think we repeated ourselves without realizing it, we mark the repetitions with this symbol.

Wine snobs practice all sorts of affectations that can make other wine drinkers feel inferior. When we discuss wines or issues that are fodder for snobs, we alert you with this icon, so that you won't fall prey.

To our tastes, the wines we mark with this icon are bargains because we like them, we believe them to be of good quality, and their price is low compared to other wines of similar type, style, or quality.

Unfortunately, some Italian wines have very limited distribution, and you won't find them just anywhere. We mark such wines with this icon, and hope that your search proves fruitful.

Part I
The Big Picture of Italian Wine

In this part . . .

1f ever a country was born to make wine, it's Italy. The land is covered with hillsides, just begging for grapevines. And what grapevines they are! Ancient varieties, native varieties, French and Spanish varieties, internationally-popular varieties, and unpronounceable (to foreigners) varieties — together making every type of wine under the sun. It's no wonder that Italy — along with France — has been the world leader in wine production since ancient times.

Italy has so many wines that you could spend a (happy) lifetime mastering Italian wine. These first few chapters set you on that journey, explaining Italy's natural wine resources, its grape varieties, and its wine laws so that you can glimpse the big picture of where you're headed.

Chapter 1

Born to Make Wine

● ●

In This Chapter

▶ A leader of the pack

▶ Forty centuries of winemaking experience

▶ Italy's wine diversity formula

▶ The trend toward quality

● ●

*W*hen most people think of Italy, they think of food. (History, art, or fast cars might be other associations — but food would have to be right up there, near the top of the list.)

As central as food is to Italy's personality, so is wine. For most Italians, wine *is* food, no less essential to every meal than bread or family. Wine, in fact, *is* family, and community, because nearly every Italian either knows someone who makes wine or makes wine himself.

Wine to Boot

The Italian peninsula, with its fan-like top and its long, boot-like body, has the most recognizable shape of any country on earth. But its recognition exceeds its actual size. Italy is a small land; the whole country is less than three-quarters the size of California.

Despite its small size, Italy's role in the world of wine is huge:

✔ Italy produces more wine than any other country on earth, in many years. (When Italy isn't the world's number one wine producer, it's number two, behind France.) Italy's

> annual wine production is generally about 1.5 billion gallons, the equivalent of more than 8 billion bottles! Nearly 30 percent of all the world's wine comes from Italy.
>
> ✓ Italy has more vineyard land than any other country except Spain. Vines grow in every nook and cranny of the peninsula and the islands.
>
> ✓ Italy boasts dozens of native grape varieties, many of which are successful only in Italy.
>
> ✓ Italy produces hundreds of wines — nearly 1,000 different types, we'd say.

Although the land called Italy has a long, proud history, the country became a unified nation only in 1861, and has existed in its present form only since 1919, when the Austro-Hungarian Empire ceded certain northern territories to Italy after World War I. Politically, Italy today consists of 20 regions, similar to states — 18 on the mainland and two islands; these 20 political regions are also Italy's wine regions. (Figure 1-1 shows Italy's 20 regions.) Because of the country's relative youth, diverse cultures exist in different parts of the country, and regional pride runs stronger than national pride. Italy's wines reflect these diverse cultures.

From the Alps to almost Africa

When we think about Italy's shape, location, and topography, we have to chuckle at the improbability of it all. Italy starts in the Alps but ends fairly close to Africa; it has a long, long seacoast but very little flat land; it has three major mountain ranges dividing it from other countries and segregating its regions from one another. Italy has everything, all together, in a small package of disjointed pieces that's isolated from everything around it. (Was the Creator playing a hoax?)

The mountain ranges are the Alps in the northwest, separating Italy from Switzerland and France; the Dolomites, actually part of the Alps, separating northeastern Italy from Austria; and the Apennines, starting in the northwest and running like a spine down the Italian boot, separating the regions of the east coast from those of the west.

Figure 1-1: Italy's 20 wine regions.

Italy's major expanse of flat land is the Po River Valley, which begins in western Piedmont and extends eastward until the Po empties into the Adriatic Sea just north of Emilia-Romagna's border with the Veneto (see Figure 1-1). Most of Italy's rice, grain, maize, and fruit crops come from this area; the rest of the country grows olive trees, garden vegetables, and, of course, grapes. In most of Italy, you can't travel five miles without seeing vines.

Wine from Day One

Grape growing is an historic occupation in Italy. When Phoenician traders arrived in Puglia 4,000 years ago, wine already existed there. The Etruscans grew wine grapes in Central Italy from the 8th to the 4th century B.C. By the 3rd century B.C., grapes grew in much of today's Italy, and the Romans get credit for dispersing the vine throughout western Europe.

Diverse conditions, diverse wines

What makes Italy an ideal and unique territory for growing grapes is precisely its improbable combination of natural conditions:

- ✔ The range of latitudes creates a wide variety of climatic conditions from north to south.

- ✔ The foothills of the mountains provide slopes ideal for vineyards, as well as higher altitudes for cool climate grape growing.

- ✔ The varied terrain — seacoast, hills, and mountains — within many regions provides a diversity of growing conditions even within single regions.

- ✔ The segregated nature of the regions has enabled local grape varieties to survive in near isolation.

When it comes to wine production, Italy's odd situation is a formula for variety (and a formula for confusion on the part of those trying to master Italian wines!). Different grape varieties make different wines in different regions. And the same grape variety makes different wines in different parts of a single region. In a nutshell, that's why Italy makes so many different wines.

Italian Wine Styles Today

Wine is so universally accepted within Italy, and so ubiquitous, that most Italians traditionally took it for granted. This casual attitude has changed somewhat in recent years, but it has taken its toll: Although Italy has some great, great wines, these wines haven't enjoyed nearly the prestige of France's top wines. (That situation is only now beginning to change.) And, considering how many wines Italy makes, only a small percentage are widely available in U.S. wine shops. The silver lining is that some of Italy's wines are still fairly inexpensive.

Italian wine producers today are more serious about their wine than they have ever been, and the quality of Italian wine is at an all-time high. (Recent excellent vintages have only helped.) As producers experiment with new techniques in their vineyards and wineries, new styles of Italian wine are emerging, and the traditional styles are improving. As a result, Italian wines today are more varied than ever. Congratulations on choosing a great time to discover Italian wine!

The Italian prototype

The fundamental style of Italian wine derives from the fact that Italians view wine as a mealtime beverage; a wine's first responsibility is to go well with food. The prototypical Italian red or white wine has the following characteristics:

- ✔ High acidity, which translates as crispness in the whites, and firmness in the reds (high-acid wines are very food-friendly)

- ✔ No sweetness

- ✔ Fairly subdued, subtle aromas and flavors (so as not to compete with food)

- ✔ Light to medium body (although many full-bodied wines do exist)

If you imagine such a wine, you can understand that it's a wine without illusions of grandeur, a straightforward beverage that might not win a wine competition but is a welcome dinner companion.

Variations on the prototype in recent years have included some of the following characteristics:

- ✔ More concentrated flavor and slightly fuller body, due to greater ripeness in the grapes (thanks to improved vineyard practices)

- Smoky or toasty aromas and flavors from small oak barrels

- Fruitier aromas and flavors — although the wines are still much less fruity than, say, the typical Californian or Australian wine

Red, white, and beyond

About two-thirds of all Italian wine is red. Every region makes red wine, even the cool northern regions and especially the South. But Italy makes plenty of white, too — particularly Northeast and Central Italy. Rosé wine is only a minor category.

Italy's production of sparkling wine is considerable, especially in the North. Italian sparkling wines include sweet styles, such as Asti, and fully dry styles. Dessert wines are a serious specialty of some regions. These sweet wines include wines from grapes dried after the harvest (to concentrate their sugar); wines from late-harvested grapes affected with "noble rot" (Chapter 16 of *Wine For Dummies,* 2nd Edition, by us, published by Hungry Minds, Inc., explains noble rot); and wines that are fortified with alcohol to preserve their natural sweetness.

We describe specific red, white, rosé, sparkling, and dessert wines from Italy in Chapters 4 through 11.

Chapter 2

Grapes from Near and Far

● ●

In This Chapter

▶ Native varieties galore

▶ French grapes at home in Italy

▶ Four celebrity red varieties

▶ Italy's notorious white grape

● ●

*W*e remember an episode of the 1970's television game show, *The $64,000 Question,* in which a policeman, whose hobby was wine, was asked to name a particular Sicilian white grape variety. Now *that's* a tough question, we thought. In those days, few wine lovers could name the grape that makes Chianti, let alone some obscure Sicilian white grape. (The answer was Inzolia.)

Times have changed: Today, Sangiovese, the main grape variety of Chianti, has a fairly high profile among wine geeks. As for the rest of Italy's grape varieties . . . well, maybe times haven't changed so much after all. The varieties that make most of Italy's wines are still obscure, behind-the-scenes characters that play their part without recognition or acclaim. This is their story.

Italy's Curious Varieties

An astounding number of wine-grape varieties grow in Italy. Besides varieties that are indigenous to Italy, Italian vineyards grow most of the world's major red grapes, and many of the world's major white grapes. To a large extent, the vast diversity of Italian wines is due to the enormous range of grapes that grow throughout the peninsula and the islands.

Native talents

Most of the varieties that make Italian wines are native Italian varieties that don't grow much, or don't grow well, outside of Italy. Like most wine-grape varieties, they have multi-syllabic, foreign, difficult-to-pronounce names — and their names are all the more foreign to wine drinkers because they generally don't appear on wine labels. (Most Italian wines are named for the place where the grapes grow rather than for the grapes; Chapter 3 explains Italy's wine-naming protocol.)

Some of Italy's native varieties, such as Sangiovese, Barbera, and Trebbiano, grow more or less throughout the country. But many varieties occupy vineyards only in certain parts of Italy, or are limited to a single region; for example:

- ✔ Nebbiolo is planted only in certain parts of Piedmont and Lombardy, in northwestern Italy.
- ✔ Verdicchio grows mainly in the Marche region.
- ✔ Lambrusco is a specialty of the Emilia area of Emilia-Romagna.
- ✔ Negroamaro and Primitivo grow almost exclusively in Puglia.
- ✔ Nero d'Avola grows mainly in Sicily.

Immigrants and migrants

Besides native Italian varieties, Italy also grows many French varieties, as well as a few varieties that are native to Germany, Austria, and Spain.

Some of these non-indigenous varieties have grown in parts of Italy for more than 100 years. Cabernet Sauvignon, Merlot, Cabernet Franc, the Pinot family of grapes (Pinot Noir, Pinot Gris, and Pinot Blanc), and Riesling are members of this group.

Italy also has some varieties that are relative newcomers, introduced into the country by a few progressive wineries in a spirit of experimentation; Viognier and Syrah are examples. This group of grape varieties is small, however, because Italian winemakers can find plenty of material for experimentation within their own country.

What has happened in the past two decades, rather than the mass importation of internationally-famous grape varieties into Italy, is a migration of major varieties from one part of Italy to another. Cabernet Sauvignon, for example, has been a major player in two northeastern regions, Trentino-Alto Adige and Friuli-Venezia Giulia, for generations; now, it figures prominently in many Tuscan wines. Similarly, Chardonnay has grown in the Northeast for several decades but now appears all over Italy.

The migration of Cabernet and Chardonnay within Italy is indicative of another trend: the increasing importance of internationally-known varieties. This trend exists for two reasons:

- Italian producers have sought to validate themselves and earn recognition by making wines from grape varieties that the outside world considers prestigious.

- In an effort to win critical acclaim from foreign critics, producers have increasingly made wines with characteristics that appeal to international tastes, such as deep color and rich mouthfeel; many internationally-known varieties have these characteristics.

Ironically, most of these varieties existed in Italy all along.

The Major Grapes

Because growing conditions and local traditions vary so much throughout Italy, grape varieties vary tremendously from one region to the next. The country as a whole grows red varieties more than white varieties, and many of its red grapes are top-notch varieties that make superior wine. A few white varieties do excel in Italy as well, however.

Reds aplenty

We consider 21 red grape varieties to be Italy's major varieties for red wine. Four of these are especially important, either for the quality of wine they produce or for their dissemination throughout the country. We describe these four varieties first, according to their relative importance.

Sangiovese

The indigenous Sangiovese *(san joe VAE sae)* is the most planted red variety in Italy's vineyards. It's the lifeblood of red wine production in the central Italian regions of Tuscany and Umbria, and it also grows in several other regions. It is the major grape of Chianti and Vino Nobile di Montepulciano, and the only variety in Brunello di Montalcino; many critically-acclaimed Super-Tuscan wines also derive largely from Sangiovese. (Chapter 8 describes all these wines.) Common blending partners for Sangiovese include the native Canaiolo *(can eye OH lo)* grape, Cabernet Sauvignon, and Merlot.

Dozens of *clones,* or sub-varieties, of Sangiovese exist, some finer than others. (This variety changes in response to its grape-growing environment, which accounts for its diversity.) One family, of clones responsible for many of the best Sangiovese wines is called Sangiovese Grosso ("large Sangiovese"). Some Tuscan producers call Sangiovese Grosso "Sangioveto," but this is not an official name.

The characteristics of Sangiovese include only a medium intensity of color, high acidity, firm tannin, and aromas and flavors of cherries and herbs. Most wines made from Sangiovese are lean in structure; they're generally medium-bodied, but some are light-bodied or full-bodied, depending on where the grapes grow. The more serious wines based on Sangiovese are capable of developing forest-floor aromas and a seductive smoothness and harmony with age.

Nebbiolo

The Nebbiolo *(nehb be OH loh)* variety is a specialty of the Piedmont region. This native Italian grape makes two of Italy's very greatest red wines, Barolo and Barbaresco, as well as several less exalted wines. (Chapters 4 and 6 discuss many Nebbiolo-based wines.)

Nebbiolo produces full-bodied, characterful wines that are high in acid and have marked tannin, but generally have only medium color intensity. Nebbiolo's aromas and flavors vary according to the vineyard site, but cover a wide spectrum, from fruity (strawberry) to herbal (mint, camphor, and anise) to earthy (mushrooms, white truffles, and tar) to floral; these aromas can be very vivid and pure. The finest Nebbiolo-based wines take many years to develop and can live for decades; many approachable, young-drinking wines from Nebbiolo also exist. Nebbiolo is usually not blended with other varieties; when it is, Barbera and Bonarda are predictable partners.

Barbera

Until Sangiovese dethroned Barbera sometime in the past 20 years, Barbera *(bar BAE rah)* was the most planted red variety in all of Italy. It still grows in many parts of the Italian peninsula, but its finest wines come from Piedmont, Barbera's home turf.

Barbera is a very unusual red variety because it has almost no tannin. It does have deep color and high acidity, as well as spicy and red-fruit aromas and flavors that are vivid in young wines. The combination of high acid, low tannin, and vivid flavor make Barbera wines particularly refreshing. The finest expressions of Barbera are unblended, but many blended wines containing Barbera do exist.

Aglianico

This unsung native variety is the pride of the Campania and Basilicata regions, in Southern Italy, where it makes Taurasi and Aglianico del Vulture *(ahl YAHN ee co del VUL too rae)*, respectively. (Chapter 10 discusses these wines.) Aglianico came to Southern Italy from Greece millennia ago, and today grows as far north as Lazio; in the South, it also grows in Molise, Puglia, and Calabria.

At its best, Aglianico makes dark, powerful red wines of high quality. But its production is relatively small, and in many cases the variety is merely part of a blend with other southern varieties. Nevertheless, it is one of Italy's finest red varieties, and has excellent potential.

Other important red varieties

The following 17 red varieties are also quite important in Italy. We describe them here in alphabetical order:

- ✔ **Cabernet Franc *(cab er nay frahnc):*** This French variety has grown in Italy's northeastern regions for more than a century; today, its use is declining somewhat in favor of Cabernet Sauvignon (with which it is often blended). It's most common today in Friuli-Venezia Giulia (although some of what's called Cabernet Franc there is actually another variety, Carmenère), followed by Veneto and Trentino-Alto Adige. Many wines from these regions that use Cabernet Franc are labeled simply as "Cabernet," a name that covers both Cabernet varieties.

✔ **Cabernet Sauvignon** *(cab er nay soh vee n'yon):* This world-famous variety was originally important mainly in Northeastern Italy, but today it grows all over the country, especially in Tuscany. Some Italian wines based on Cabernet Sauvignon show the dark color, firm tannin, and blackcurrant flavors typical of the variety, but many others are lighter in color, body, and tannin, and have vegetal flavors — all indicative of high crop yields and under-ripe grapes. Cabernet Sauvignon is frequently blended with Sangiovese in Tuscany; many other wines are "Bordeaux blends" combining Merlot and/or Cabernet Franc.

✔ **Cannanou** *(cahn nah NOW):* This Sardinian variety is actually Grenache (as it's known in France) or Garnacha (as it's known in its native Spain). In Sardinia, it's the island's main red variety, making light- and/or full-bodied wines as well as rosés.

✔ **Corvina** *(cor VEE nah):* The Verona area of the Veneto is the only seriously important venue for this native variety; it is the finest of the three varieties used to make Bardolino, Valpolicella, and Amarone. Most Corvina-based wines have light to medium body, high acidity, medium tannin, and flavors of red cherries. It has great potential as a stand-alone variety for fine wine.

✔ **Dolcetto** *(dohl CHET toh):* A variety that's quite important in Piedmont, where it's valued not only for its deep color and spicy, berry character, but also for its early-ripening tendency. (Its name means "little sweet one" and derives from the fact that its grapes ripen early for a red variety.) Dolcetto is lower in acidity than Barbera, but is still quite acidic, with medium tannin; its wines are quite dry.

✔ **Lagrein** *(lah GRYNE):* Technically Lagrein Scuro, or Lagrein Dunkel (dark Lagrein), an historic variety in Alto Adige, where it makes perfumed, medium-bodied reds and light rosés, as well as some rich, dark, characterful red wines. Lesser clones of Lagrein also exist.

✔ **Lambrusco *(lam BREWS coh):*** An ancient, native variety that's critical to the health of the wine economy in Emilia-Romagna, thanks to the success of Lambrusco wines in the U.S. This grape has delicious flavors of red fruits and spice, medium tannin, and fairly high acidity. Chapter 6 names its sub-varieties

✔ **Merlot *(mair loh):*** This variety has long been resident in Northeastern Italy, Tuscany, and Lazio. In Italy, this variety typically makes medium-bodied wines, at best, with medium color intensity and flavors that are vegetal and herbal (symptomatic of overly high crop yields or inappropriately cool climates). Some winemakers are making richer, darker wines; in Tuscany, it's a favorite for blending with Sangiovese because it provides the color and fleshiness that Sangiovese lacks. Merlot is also coming on strong in Umbria.

✔ **Montepulciano *(mon tae pull chee AH noh):*** This variety grows in Central and Southern Italy, principally in the Abruzzo and Marche regions. It produces medium-bodied wines with unusual smoky, red-fruity, and vegetal flavors; these wines range from seriously good to quaffable in quality.

✔ **Negroamaro *(NAE grow ah MAH roh):*** Literally, "black and bitter," a native variety that's widely planted in the South, especially Puglia; it makes flavorful, high-alcohol wines.

✔ **Nero d'Avola *(NAE roh DAHV oh lah):*** This high quality variety — known as Calabrese in its native Calabria — is important mainly in Sicily. It makes deeply colored, age-worthy wines that are full-bodied and moderate in tannin, with heady flavors of ripe fruit and herbs. Nero d'Avola has great potential.

✔ **Pinot Nero *(pee noh NAIR oh):*** This variety, Pinot Noir, is significant throughout northeastern Italy and in Lombardy, in the Northwest, for both still and sparkling wines. Because it's one of the world's major red varieties, winemakers in various other regions, including Piedmont and Tuscany, are trying their hands with it.

✔ **Primitivo *(prim ih TEE voh):*** A southern variety of major importance in Puglia, and grown elsewhere in the South. Genetic testing has determined that one clone, Primitivo di Manduria, is the same variety as Zinfandel, and wines from that clone may now be labeled "Zinfandel." Primitivo makes deeply colored wines with spicy, ripe berry character, full body, and high alcohol.

✔ **Refosco** *(reh FOES coh):* A specialty of the Friuli-Venezia Giulia region, this variety makes velvety-textured, medium- and full-bodied wines with ripe plum flavors — many of which are quite good. Two distinct sub-varieties exist, of which Refosco del Punduncolo Rosso (the "red-stemmed Refosco") is considerably the finer.

✔ **Sagrantino** *(sag rahn TEE noh):* This variety is fairly limited in its production zone, but is responsible for the dark, intense, ageworthy red called Montefalco Sagrantino, from Umbria.

✔ **Schiava** *(skee AH vah):* The most common variety in Alto Adige, where it generally makes light- to medium-bodied, easy-drinking red wines. German-speaking locals call it Vernatsch. Several sub-varieties exist.

✔ **Teroldego** *(teh ROHL dae go):* A major, native variety in the Trentino sub-region, in northern Italy, where it produces fresh-tasting, fruity reds with good color; similar to Lagrein.

Over-achieving whites

We consider 17 white grape varieties to be Italy's major varieties for white or sparkling wine production. Five of them are particularly key varieties, and we describe them here, in their rough order of importance.

Trebbiano

If any single factor is to blame for the lackluster quality of the white wine category in Italy, it is the Trebbiano grape. Trebbiano *(trehb bee AH noh),* known as Ugni Blanc in France, can make characterful white wines when it is grown carefully, but to a population that takes wine as casually as the Italians do, this variety is a cheap ticket to bland, neutral-tasting, light-bodied, crisp wines.

Trebbiano is the most common white variety in Italy (in both senses of the word), grown almost everywhere but particularly prevalent in the central regions. It has several sub-varieties, or clones, of which Trebbiano Toscano is probably the most planted; other clones include Trebbiano di Romagna, Trebbiano d'Abruzzo (which might actually be Bombino Bianco), Trebbiano Giallo, Trebbiano di Soave, and the relatively fine Procanico. In one manifestation or another, it's the backbone of numerous classic Italian white wines, such as Frascati.

The main aroma and flavor descriptor of Trebbiano-based wines is "vinous" — a fancy way of saying that they smell and taste winey. These wines are usually dry and high in acid, but in recent years many producers seem to be making them with some sweetness, which to our taste eliminates their one virtue — their crisp, refreshing, food-friendly style — without improving the wines' quality one iota.

Pinot Grigio

Pinot Grigio *(pee noh GREE joe)* is the Italian name for the French variety Pinot Gris. Like other varieties of French origin, Pinot Gris emigrated to Northeastern Italy more than a century ago; its production has increased since the late 1970's, however, because its wines have found such commercial success.

Because of high crop levels and popular taste in Italy, Pinot Grigio most often makes light-bodied, pale, high-acid wines; some producers make more characterful styles, with concentrated flavors of peach or mineral, but none as rich as Alsace Pinot Gris wines. (Our book, *French Wine For Dummies*, published by Hungry Minds, Inc., describes those wines.) The best Pinot Grigios come from Friuli-Venezia Giulia.

How much Pinot Grigio is in Pinot Grigio?

When an Italian wine carries a grape variety name (some do, and some don't; Chapter 3 explains this), it must contain from 85 to 100 percent of that variety, depending on the circumstances. Italy's default minimum is 85 percent, the general European Union standard. But the regulations of some DOC zones (also explained in Chapter 3) mandate 90, or even 100, percent of the named variety in varietal wines. In Chapters 4 through 11, whenever we mention any of Italy's varietal wines, the required percentage of the named grape is 85 percent, unless we state otherwise.

Verdicchio

Verdicchio *(ver DEEK kee oh)* excels in the Marche region, on the Adriatic coast. It has far more potential for flavor and character than Trebbiano does, making wines with medium body, crisp acidity, and aromas of lemon and sea air. It's used mainly for un-oaked wines that are varietally labeled.

Vernaccia

Two distinct white Italian varieties go by the name Vernaccia *(ver NAHTCH cha)*, one in Tuscany and the other in Sardinia. (There's also a red Vernaccia from Marche!) The Tuscan Vernaccia is the finer of the two whites. Although its wines have the trademark Italian high acidity and light to medium body, the best examples show depth and character, with mineral nuances. Vernaccia usually makes un-oaked wines, but can sometimes age quite nicely in oak barrels.

Tocai Friulano

While Pinot Grigio gets the lion's share of attention, many fans of Friulian wines favor the Tocai Friulano *(toh KYE free oo LAH no)* grape — and this variety is the most widely planted white variety in Friuli. Tocai makes light- to medium-bodied wines with crisp acidity; the best of them have a rich, viscous texture and are more flavorful than the Italian norm.

Some experts believe Tocai to be Sauvignon Vert, a variety that often passes for Sauvignon Blanc in Chile, although Italy's Tocais are quite different from Chile's Sauvignons. Whatever the variety actually is, it will soon go under a different name, yet to be determined: The European Union has required producers to desist from using the name Tocai by 2007, to avoid confusion with Hungary's classic wine zone, Tokaji.

Other important white varieties

The following 12 white varieties are also quite important in Italy. We describe them here in alphabetical order:

- ✔ **Arneis *(ahr NASE):*** This old, Piedmontese variety is newly popular in the wine zones around the city of Alba. It is low in acidity and fairly flavorful, making soft and round wines with notes of melon, almonds, and flowers.

- ✔ **Chardonnay *(shar doh nay):*** In the late 1970s, winemakers in northeastern Italy "discovered" that they had Chardonnay in their vineyards (mis-identified as Pinot

Blanc) and began making Chardonnay wines. In more recent times, Chardonnay has become popular all over Italy, from Piedmont to Sicily, as winemakers try their hand at making world-class white wine with a world-class grape. In general, the Italian versions are leaner and crisper than the Chardonnay norm, and many don't have enough fruit character to sustain their oak aging.

✓ **Cortese** *(cor TAE sae):* Grown in various parts of northern Italy, but a specialty of Piedmont's Gavi zone, Cortese makes crisp, light-bodied wines with citrus and appley flavors; the best have mineral character and even notes of honey.

✓ **Fiano** *(fee AH no):* A perfumed and flavorful variety that's probably the finest white variety of Southern Italy, grown mainly in Campania. Its wines are medium-bodied and capable of aging, developing aromatic richness as they do.

✓ **Garganega** *(gar GAH nae ga):* The main variety of Soave, this is one of Italy's unsung native white grapes that's finally earning respect. Producers such as Pieropan have proved that it's capable of making rich, unctuous wines with character and class.

✓ **Greco** *(GRAE co):* Grown throughout Italy's South, this fine variety makes crisp, fairly aromatic (citrusy, floral) wines that have good weight, viscosity, and character.

✓ **Malvasia** *(mahl vah SEE ah):* This variety grows throughout Italy. Several white sub-varieties exist, including the better Malvasia Toscana, the ancient and flavorful Malvasia Istriana, and the weaker Malvasia di Candia. It's often paired with Trebbiano, to lend wines a bit of richness, but it has the downside of oxidizing easily. Malvasia produces innocuous whites as well as the rich Vin Santo (see Chapter 8). A red Malvasia, called Malvasia Nera, also exists.

✓ **Moscato** *(moh SKAH toh):* The Muscat Blanc à Petits Grains grows all over Italy, making all sorts of wines, from delicate Moscato d'Asti to rich dessert styles; its most famous version is the sparkling wine, Asti. The floral, perfumed notes that Moscato attains in the North are among the most finesseful expressions of this variety anywhere in the world. The golden and red types of Moscato are also used to make certain Italian wines. Another Muscat, Muscat of Alexandria or "Zibibbo," makes some of Southern Italy's dessert wines.

✔ **Pinot Bianco** *(pee noh bee AHN coh):* Known as Pinot Blanc in France, this variety has grown in Northeastern Italy for more than a century. In Alto Adige (see Chapter 7), its wines attain a character and richness unknown from this variety elsewhere in the world.

✔ **Riesling Renano** *(REES ling rea NAH noh):* "Renano" means "Rhine," and this name represents the classic Riesling grape, which grows throughout Northeastern Italy. (Riesling Italico is Welschriesling, a different variety.)

✔ **Sauvignon** *(soh vee n'yahn):* Italians call the Sauvignon Blanc variety only by its first name; it grows throughout the Northeast, where it makes herbal, intensely flavorful wines; some growers are cultivating it in less traditional areas, such as Piedmont and Tuscany, to make internationally-styled wines.

✔ **Vermentino** *(ver men TEE noh):* This variety is at home in Sardinia, Liguria, and coastal Tuscany, where it makes crisp, light- or medium-bodied wines. It has solid potential for fine wines.

Grape mania

Because so many American wines are named after grape varieties, wine drinkers have become accustomed to knowing which grape varieties make up each wine they drink. But it doesn't pay to get obsessed over the grape varieties of Italian wines. Italy simply has too many varieties for anyone to play that game without going crazy in the process. The more you enjoy Italian wines and seek to master them, the more you encounter obscure and unusual grape varieties. That's just the way it is.

Chapter 3

The Language of the Label

. . . .

In This Chapter

▶ Place names, grape names, and fantasy names

▶ DOC and DOCG

▶ IGT and *vino da tavola*

▶ The pedigree-quality relationship

. . . .

*W*e've heard people say that Italian wine labels are the most difficult wine labels of all to understand. And it's true, to some extent. Italy's wine names are unfamiliar to most wine drinkers — and Italy has so many (very long) wine names! Factor in the Italian propensity for getting around official regulations, and you end up with some very confusing labels.

Of course, it's the taste of the wine that counts, not the wine laws, official appellations, and labels. But maybe you share this odd little idiosyncrasy of ours: We like to know what we're drinking. If so, don't skip this chapter. It does more to clarify Italian wine labels and Italian wine names than anything else you can read. (If you're still confused at the end, blame the bureaucrats.)

The Name Game

In *French Wine For Dummies*, published by Hungry Minds, Inc., we talk a lot about *terroir*, a French concept that says the place where grapes grow (the climate, soil, altitude, and so forth) shapes the quality and character of the wine made from those grapes. What does that have to do with Italian wines? Well, France's wine laws — which identify wines according to *terroir*, where their grapes grow — were the model for most other European countries' wine laws. Which means that Italy's wine laws are also based on the concept of *terroir,* even if some Italian winemakers have never heard the word.

Wine laws based on the *terroir* concept split hairs. If you can show that your climate, soil, or other natural condition (including human factors, such as tradition) is different from that of a nearby area, then you presumably make a different type of wine than that other area — and, upon request, the authorities can give you a unique, official name for your type of wine. In Italy, this process has occurred more than 300 times, resulting in more than 300 official wine names. These names are all names of places, because vineyard location is the fundamental issue, but sometimes they include a grape variety name.

The DOC calls

Italy's official wine names are called DOC or DOCG names:

✔ DOC stands for *Denominazione di Origine Controllata (dae no mee naht zee OH nae dee oh REE gee nae con trol LAH tah),* which translates as "controlled (or protected) place name"; the long Italian phrase appears on the wine label (see Figure 3-1).

✔ DOCG stands for *Denominazione di Origine Controllata e Garantita (. . . ae gah rahn TEE tah),* which translates as "controlled and guaranteed place name"; this even longer Italian phrase appears on the labels of DOCG wines.

Every DOC or DOCG wine comes from a specific place that's defined by law, is made from specific grapes stipulated by the law (although sometimes the law gives producers a lot of leeway in their choice of grapes), is aged for a certain length of time, and so forth. In the end, a wine that carries a DOC or DOCG name should taste more or less the way the law says that wine should taste, although the official taste descriptions are loose; for example, they might say that a particular wine should taste "dry, crisp, harmonious, and slightly tannic." Lots of room for interpretation there.

Using a DOC or DOCG name for his or her wine restricts a producer somewhat, but in exchange it gives the wine a pedigree of sorts.

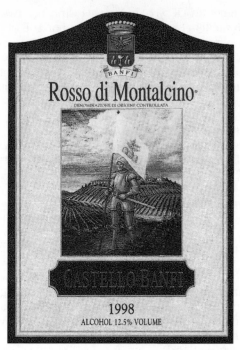

Figure 3-1: The words *Denominazione di Origine Controllata* on the label indicate that this is a DOC wine.

Non-DOC/G wines

Not every producer values that pedigree, however. Some Italians instinctively rebel against anything official, such as wine laws, speed limits, and taxes.

If a producer in a certain DOC/G area wants to make a different kind of wine than what the regulations dictate, he or she does have some options. For one thing, many areas have more than one DOC/G wine because official vineyard areas often overlap; the producer can then make one type of wine instead of the other. Otherwise, he or she can relinquish the official name and call the wine by another name.

Not every Italian wine has to have a DOC or DOCG name, but it does have to carry the name of a place where the grapes grow, because that's the ultimate law. Our hypothetical producer, who renounces a DOC/G name for his wine, has two choices: to state on the label a less precise area than the DOC/G area — for example, a broad, regional name — or to state only the country of origin, namely Italy. Wines with broad geographic designations are called IGT wines, and a wine with no geographic designation other than the country of origin is called a *vino da tavola.*

IGT stands for *Indicazione Geografica Tipica (in dee caht zee OH nae gee oh GRAF ee cah TEE pee cah),* which translates as "typical place name" and appears on the label, in Italian (see Figure 3-2).

Vino da tavola (VEE no dah TAH vo lah) translates as "table wine"; it might appear on the label in Italian or in English.

U.S. regulations define "table wine" as "grape wine having an alcoholic content not in excess of 14 percent by volume." Most DOC/G and IGT wines are table wines, by the U.S. definition, and they might carry the words "Table Wine" in English on their labels. But unlike Italy's *vino da tavola,* their labels also have the Italian words indicating which Italian category they fall into, and the name of the place the grapes were grown (other than just "Italy").

Figure 3-2: The words *Indicazione Geografica Tipica* on the label indicate that this is an IGT wine.

At this moment, 120 broad territories of Italy are official IGT zones. (Yes, even these less formal names are still official.) Wines with IGT names can come from grapes grown anywhere within the broad territory of the zone, such as Toscana or Veneto, and can come from any of a large list of grape varieties approved for that area. The IGT designation, in other words, gives producers more freedom of individual expression than a DOC/G designation does.

But the *vino da tavola* designation deprives producers of certain privileges. They cannot put a vintage year on the wine, for example, and they can't name the grape variety that made the wine.

And there you have it — Italy's four official wine categories: DOC and DOCG for classic wines from the most important and prestigious wine zones; IGT for more innovative wines with less of a pedigree; and *vino da tavola* for everything else.

Because the IGT category is only about ten years old, and some IGT territories are very new, you can still find Italian wines whose labels predate the existence of an available IGT territory. These wines are considered *vini da tavola* — but if they carry a geographic designation smaller than Italy itself, they're the equivalent of IGT wines. Older vintages of Super-Tuscan wines (described in Chapter 8) fall into this category, for example.

One DOC equals one to 50 types of wine

One of the more confusing aspects of Italy's DOC/G wine zones is the scope of wines that each official name encompasses. Some DOC/G names apply to one type of wine only: Rosso di Montalcino — one zone, one wine — is an example. But some DOC/G areas make red *and* white wine, and maybe a rosé, and maybe a sparkling wine, all under the same DOC/G name, with qualifiers such as *Rosso* (red), *Bianco* (white), or *Spumante* (sparkling) added to the name. Some DOC/G areas have subzones that can use their name on the wine, as if they're separate DOC/G names. Other DOC/Gs allow producers to make several different varietal wines — wines named after their sole or dominant grape variety — that all have the same DOC/G name but with a different grape name on the label. The most super-sized of all DOC/Gs is Alto Adige DOC, which covers 51 different types of wine!

Putting faith in the DOC

Knowing the legalese of wine categories helps you determine which category of wine you're buying — but in the end, does it really matter? If you buy a DOC/G wine, do you have a better wine than if you buy an IGT wine or a *vino da tavola?*

We wish that we could answer "Yes." But the DOC/G system isn't really about quality. It's about authenticity. When you buy a DOC/G wine, you're buying the real thing, and it might or might not be as high-quality as another wine with an IGT or even a *vino da tavola* designation. Ultimately, any wine's quality boils down to how carefully the grapes were grown and how talented the winemaker is, not to the political and legal technicalities of wine categories. But with DOC/G wines, at least you know (or can research, in Chapters 4 to 11) which fairly restricted, fairly classic vineyard areas the wines came from, and which grape/s made the wines.

Italy created its wine laws in 1963 — 28 years after France established its AOC wine law system — and recognized the first DOC wines in 1966. But the process of recognizing wine zones as DOCs is ongoing. In recent years, the traffic has gotten particularly heavy, as Italy tries to bring a higher percentage of its wines into the DOC/G category. (In the European Union, having a high percentage of your wine production in the top category earns you bragging rights as a high-quality wine producing nation; Italy has historically had a relatively small percentage of its wines in the top category.) The number of DOC/G wines has increased by about 10 percent in the past four years, to a current total of 316 — assuming *that* number hasn't already changed!

DOCG wines now number 21. These wines are officially the elite of Italy, and some of them are Italy's top wines — such as Barolo, Barbaresco, Brunello di Montalcino, and Chianti Classico. But some of them are elite in title only, not in their quality or renown — such as Albana di Romagna and Ghemme. The number of DOCG wines will increase as producers in DOC zones petition the authorities to elevate their zones to the higher status.

Common Wine Label Words

Besides their official place name, and the name of the producer, most Italian wines carry other names on their labels. The most common are the following:

- ✔ A proprietary name, sometimes a "fantasy name" that a producer creates for a particular wine

- ✔ The name of a grape variety. DOC/G wines can carry a grape name only if their individual regulation permits. (In Chapters 4 to 11, you see that some DOC zones permit a couple of varietally-labeled wines along with a couple of wines that carry no grape indication.) IGT wines may carry a grape name.

- ✔ The name of an individual vineyard where the grapes grew (somewhat common) or an official sub-zone of the DOC/G territory (unusual)

Other words and phrases that may appear on Italian wine labels are the following:

- ✔ *Abboccato:* Semi-dry

- ✔ *Annata:* Vintage

- ✔ *Amabile:* Semi-sweet

- ✔ *Azienda agricola/vinicola/vitivinicola:* Refers to the producer

- ✔ *Bianco:* White

- ✔ *Cantina sociale(often abbreviated as C.S.):* Cooperative winery

- ✔ *Chiaretto:* Rosé

- ✔ *Classico:* Indicates that the grapes came from the original and finest part of the wine's DOC zone

- ✔ *Consorzio:* Voluntary trade association of producers

- ✔ *Dolce:* Sweet

- ✔ *Fattoria:* Estate

- ✔ *Frizzante:* Fizzy, or slightly sparkling

- ✔ *Imbottigliato all'origine:* Estate-bottled

- ✔ *Liquoroso:* A wine fortified with alcohol

- ✔ *Novello:* A young wine, usually red, released early

- ✔ *Passito:* A sweet wine made from dried grapes

- ✔ *Produttore:* Producer

- ✔ *Riserva:* A wine that has aged longer at the winery than a non-riserva version of the same wine; this term implies that the wine is of a higher than average quality, and is therefore worthy of that additional aging.

- ✔ *Rosato:* Rosé

- ✔ *Rosso:* Red

- ✔ *Secco:* Dry

- ✔ *Spumante:* Sparkling

- ✔ *Superiore:* Indicates that a wine has a higher minimum alcohol content than the non-superiore version of the same wine

- ✔ *Tenuta:* Estate

- ✔ *Vendemmia:* Vintage

- ✔ *Vigna or Vigneto:* Vineyard

- ✔ *Vino:* Wine

- ✔ *Vitigno:* Grape variety

Part II
The Wine Regions of Northern Italy

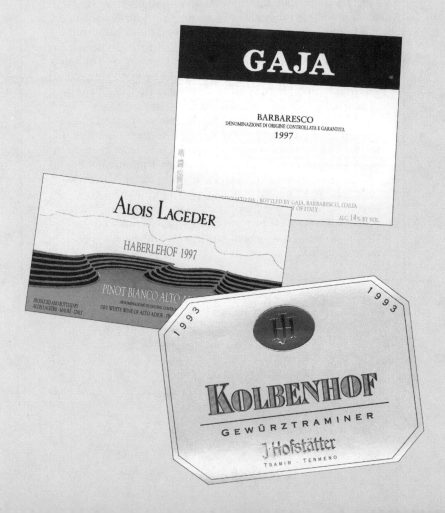

In this part . . .

*N*orthern Italy has enough great and diverse wines for three countries. We begin your journey with Piedmont because, well, we love everything about that region. But then you must visit, at least through their wines, the other two contrasting, off-beat regions of Italy's northwest — Valle d'Aosta, nestled in the snowy Alps, and Liguria, bathing in the sun of the Italian Riviera. A shopping trip to Milan brings you into Lombardy, Italy's wealthiest region, with its eclectic wines. Then on to gastronomic heaven, Emilia-Romagna, where you can enjoy some *dry* Lambrusco with your *pasta a la bolognese*. Next stop: Italy's unique northeast, into the dramatically beautiful, mountainous Alto Adige for a sip of Pinot Bianco — unless hearty Lagrien is your flavor. Follow the Adige River south to Verona, home of Soave and Valpolicella. Finish off with a visit to the multi-lingual Friuli-Venezia Guilia, home of Italy's best white wines. We wish you *buon viaggio!*

Chapter 4

The Wines of Piedmont

In This Chapter

▶ Two red superstars

▶ The re-birth of Barbera

▶ Wining and dining in wine country

▶ Asti, a world-class sparkler

▶ Nebbiolo, north and south

*P*iedmont is remote from the rest of mainland Italy. That fact hit home to us one Sunday morning several years ago when we drove from Tuscany to Piedmont. Having nothing better to do, we decided to count the tunnels as we drove through them on the *autostrada;* we must have encountered at least 30 of them on the way down to Tuscany, we figured. In fact, there are 94 tunnels along that stretch of highway — each tunnel a shortcut through a hill or a mountain that people once had to circumnavigate, the long way, in order to leave or enter Piedmont from the south. How on earth, we wondered, did anyone ever travel regularly to or from Piedmont even two generations ago, before the *autostrada*?!

The remoteness of this part of Italy has helped to preserve local traditions, local cuisine, and local wine styles. And we're not just talking about quaint local color: Some of the wines from northwestern Italy are among Italy's very greatest, period.

The Majesty of Piedmont

We know Piedmont, Italy's northwestern-most region, and its wines better than any other region of Italy, because we've visited there about twice a year for the last 20 years. The region has something majestic about it. (In fact, it was the home of unified Italy's first king, Victor Emmanuel II.) The feeling comes from the people, the place itself, and certainly the wines — especially Barolo and Barbaresco. The food is majestic, too. Piedmontese cuisine ranks among the finest in Italy, if not the world; its specialty is the numerous *antipasto* dishes that precede the pasta and main course.

True to its name, Piedmont — "foot of the mountain" — is surrounded by mountains on three sides. The mighty Alps separate it from France to the west and from Switzerland (and the tiny Aosta Valley region) to the north, while the Apennines separate it from the region of Liguria to the south. Only Piedmont's eastern border, facing Lombardy and Milan, offers easy, mountain-free (and, frankly, visually boring) access.

Piedmont's capital city, Turin, in the center of the region, is one of Italy's largest cities and the home of Fiat. Turin is situated in the Po River Valley, the plains area of Piedmont — not the area to find top vineyards and wineries. Most of Piedmont's best wines come either from the foothills of the Apennines in the south or the foothills of the Alps in the north. Although Piedmont is Italy's second-largest region, good vineyard land is scarce and very expensive: The mountains and the Po Valley occupy most of the region, leaving only 30 percent of the land suitable for hillside vineyards.

The Piedmontese

We find the Piedmontese to be reserved people — quite different from many other Italians. Many Piedmontese seem melancholy, but they have a wonderful, ironic sense of humor. They're friendly, and even warm — when you get to know them — and they're generally self-effacing and humble, even when they ought to be proud of their accomplishments, such as their fine wines. In this part of Italy, next door to France, everyone speaks French, and the older generation speaks a Piedmontese dialect similar to the Occitan dialect in France's Languedoc. They take life seriously, especially their wines: Perhaps nowhere else in Italy is wine regarded with such respect.

Piedmont generally has a continental climate: cold winters and mainly dry, hot summers. The mild autumns, with heavy fog especially in southern Piedmont, are extremely beneficial for late-ripening grape varieties, such as Nebbiolo — Piedmont's finest variety.

The wines of Piedmont

In Italy, only Tuscany rivals Piedmont for the greatness of its red wines. (In the year 2001, the Gambero Rosso Italian Wine Guide, Italy's most prestigious wine rater, gave 64 "Three Glass" awards, its highest rating, to Piedmontese wines — its largest number ever given to one region; Tuscany was second with 55.) Piedmont — specifically the Barolo and Barbaresco districts — was the first region in Italy to recognize the importance of making separate wines from exceptional vineyards, a concept that Burgundy and other regions of France had practiced for some time. Producers such as Vietti and Prunotto began making single-vineyard Barolos and Barbarescos in 1961.

In volume, Piedmont makes more DOC/G wine than any other region in Italy; the region also boasts the highest number of DOC/G wine zones, 50, and the most DOCG wines, seven. In fact, Piedmont is the only region in Italy (so far) that has created a network of DOCs that in effect covers practically all the wines grown there. Upwards of 84 percent of Piedmont's wine production is DOC or DOCG. (See Chapter 3 for more information on the DOC and DOCG designations.)

About 90 percent of Piedmont's wine comes from the southern part of the region. This production roughly falls into the following two areas:

- ✔ The Alba area, in southcentral Piedmont, which includes the Langhe Hills area and the Roero area
- ✔ The Asti/ Alessandria area, in southeast Piedmont, extending south of the Po River to the border with Liguria, and including the Monferrato Hills (see Figure 4-1)

Additionally, wine comes from two separate parts of northern Piedmont, and from a few, scattered wine zones in the pre-Alpine, western part of the region.

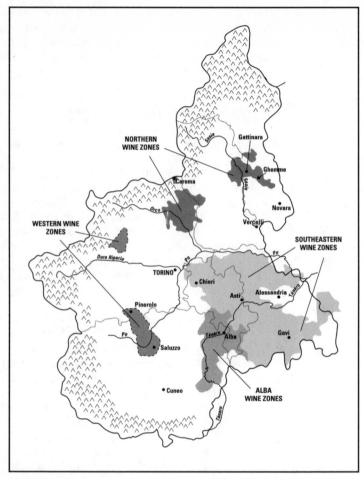

Figure 4-1: Piedmont's wine zones are concentrated in the southeastern quadrant of the region.

The grapes of Piedmont

Piedmont boasts three major red grape varieties and two major white varieties. These varieties are the following:

- **Nebbiolo:** A noble but difficult, late-ripening red variety that nowhere in the world grows as well and makes such superb wine (when conditions are right) as it does in the Langhe *(LAHN gae)* hills around the town of Alba.

- ✔ **Barbera:** A native red Piedmontese variety that until a few decades ago was Italy's most planted red variety; in Piedmont it grows mainly in the Asti and Alba areas, making serious as well as everyday wines.

- ✔ **Dolcetto:** A spicy red variety seldom seen outside Piedmont; it's widely grown in the Alba and southeastern areas of the region.

- ✔ **Moscato:** A world-renown white grape with floral aromas and flavors; a specialty of the Asti area.

- ✔ **Cortese:** A grape that makes delicately-flavored dry white wines; a specialty of the Gavi area.

In addition to these varieties, the vineyards of Piedmont grow numerous other native varieties, such as the white Arneis, Favorita, and Erbaluce and the red Grignolino, Freisa, Malvasia Nera, Pelaverga, Bonarda, Croatina, Vespolina, and several more. Internationally-famous varieties include Chardonnay, Sauvignon Blanc, Cabernet Sauvignon, and Merlot.

Wines of the Alba Area

The Alba wine zone consists of two areas in southcentral Piedmont, the Langhe hills and the Roero, which surround the town of Alba. This fairly small area is Piedmont's major vineyard territory in terms of the quality of the wines produced there. The area encompasses 11 DOC/G zones, including Barolo and Barbaresco, Piedmont's — and Northern Italy's — two greatest red wines.

A prosperous town of about 35,000 inhabitants, Alba is surrounded by hills — the Roero hills to the north and west, and the Langhe hills to the south and east. The Tanaro *(TAH nah ro)* River, which flows from the Apennine Mountains in the south, cuts through the town; it separates the hills of the Roero *(roh AE roh)* from those of the Langhe. Alba's wealth comes from its many industries: clothing, hazelnuts, chocolate and other confections, and, of course, food and wine. Perhaps Alba's greatest gastronomic treat is its white truffles, which grow in the ground on local hillsides, and are harvested in the fall. (In the section, "Visiting the Alba-Asti area in Piedmont," in this chapter, we list the many excellent restaurants in this area, certainly among the finest in Italy.) And then there's the wine.

Barolo

A well-made Barolo from a good vintage is one of the greatest red wines in the world. It's powerful and full-bodied, with all sorts of intriguing aromas and flavors — ripe strawberries, tar, mint and/or eucalyptus, licorice, camphor, tobacco, chocolate, roses, spices, vanilla, and white truffles — and it only gets better with age. Often referred to as "the king of wines," Barolo is austere and tannic in its youth, and it usually requires many years of aging before it is ready to drink — and even then, decanting and aerating the wine help soften it. Barolo's longevity is foreshadowed by its production regulations: The wine must age a minimum of three years before release (five for *riservas*). Along with Italy's other two big "B" wines — Barbaresco and Brunello di Montalcino — Barolo was among the first Italian wines granted DOCG status in 1980.

Barolo's vineyard district is in the Langhe hills, just a few miles southwest of the town of Alba. Barolo is also the name of one of the 11 communities that grow the wine (five of which are really important).

Barolo must be made entirely from Nebbiolo. This is its blessing and its curse. The blessing is that the Nebbiolo variety expresses itself brilliantly in the Barolo and Barbaresco zones of the Langhe hills. The marly clay soil is alkaline enough to tame the fiercely high acidity of Nebbiolo. In most years, there's enough warmth from the sun and just enough rain; most importantly, the mild, foggy autumns provide enough time for the notoriously late-ripening Nebbiolo to slowly complete its growth. (The grape's name probably comes from the Italian word for "fog," *nebbia*.) The Tanaro River, which flows through the Barolo and the Barbaresco areas, tempers the summer heat and fosters the mild and misty autumns. Nebbiolo normally ripens in late October in the Langhe hills areas, long after other varieties have been picked; it has ripened as late as mid-November.

The curse of Nebbiolo is that weather conditions don't always allow it to ripen sufficiently — in which case Nebbiolo's tannin and acidity can be too great, making harsh wine. Fortunately, global warming or good fortune in recent years have brought many excellent vintages for both Barolo and Barbaresco: 1989, 1990, 1996, 1997, and 1998 are all outstanding. In general, Barolo has never been better than in the last 20 years.

The key to our Piedmontese passion

Barolo has been one of our very favorite wines for a long time. We loved it even before we took our first trip to Piedmont, in the autumn of 1975 — but that journey cemented our love affair with Barolo, and with Piedmont. Discovering how complex the Barolo area is, how delicious its food, and how warm its people, made a permanent imprint on us. Now, we consider some families there among our dearest friends, and each year, we can't wait to return and renew our Piedmontese connection. Barolo, the great wine, got us there in the first place. And it keeps us coming back.

The intricacies of a tiny DOCG zone

The Barolo wine zone is not large compared to other famous wine areas. Physically, it extends a little over seven miles southwest of Alba, and is about five miles wide, at its widest point. (Actually, it seems a _lot_ larger, when you travel up and down the steep Langhe hillsides, visiting Barolo producers.) The entire annual production of Barolo amounts to only a little over a half million cases annually, a small amount compared to Burgundy, and a tiny fraction of the amount of Bordeaux produced annually. Production is small not only because the zone is tiny, but also because the Nebbiolo grape is _extremely_ choosy as to where it grows well — generally only on hillsides facing south or southeast.

A now-ingrained custom in Barolo (and in Barbaresco) is to make wines from specific vineyards which have demonstrated individual merit. Many producers make three or four different Barolo wines from separate vineyards. (Some producers combine the grapes of several vineyards and name the wine for the commune, or community, where those vineyards are situated, if their production of each vineyard is small. And some producers also make a Barolo that's blended from grapes grown in different parts of the zone.)

Basically, five communities produce most (87 percent) of Barolo, and most of the best Barolo. These communities are the following:

- ✔ La Morra
- ✔ Barolo

✔ Serralunga d'Alba

✔ Castiglione Falletto

✔ Monforte d'Alba

(The six other communities, which produce small amounts of Barolo, are Verduno, Novello, Diano d'Alba, Grinzane Cavour, Roddi, and Cherasco.)

Not counting the producers' individual imprints, two different types of Barolo exist, according to the location of the vineyards:

✔ The Barolo wines of the Serralunga (eastern) Valley — which includes the communities of Serralunga d'Alba, Castiglione Falletto, and Monforte d'Alba — tend to be more austere, powerful, and long-lived; they are more tannic and more full-bodied than other Barolos, generally have more extract (solid grape matter) and alcohol, and require long aging — 12 to 15 years — to develop and mature.

✔ The Barolo wines of the Central (western) Valley — basically the largest community, La Morra, which accounts for about one-third of all Barolo wine, and part of the community of Barolo — often have more perfumed aromas, such as white truffles; they are typically more elegant and have a velvety texture, are less full-bodied, and are less tannic than the Barolos of the Serralunga Valley. They are usually readier to drink sooner — often within eight to ten years of their vintage date.

Vineyards in the commune of Barolo itself, which extend into both valleys, make both styles of Barolo wine — depending on their location and, to some extent, the wine producer.

Slight differences in soil account for the two different types of Barolo. The soil in the Central Valley has more clay, magnesium oxide, and manganese; the soil in the Serralunga Valley has more sand, limestone, iron, phosphorus, and potassium.

Bear in mind that a winemaker's own style can override the style of his or her vineyard area to some extent. For example, Giuseppe Rinaldi makes some Barolo from the Brunate vineyard in La Morra. But his very traditional style of winemaking is such that his Barolo wines resemble those from the Serralunga Valley more than the typical, softer La Morra Barolo. Conversely, Paolo Scavino's "Bric del Fiasc" Barolo from Castiglione Falletto is much less tannic and more approachable than traditionally-made Barolos from Castiglione Falletto, such as those of Giuseppe Mascarello.

Barolo, the wine, and its different styles

We cannot discuss Barolo without mentioning stylistic differences related to winemaking technique, although the winemaking style and the vineyard style are invariably intertwined. About ten to 15 years ago, two positions clearly existed regarding Barolo winemaking:

- **Traditionally-styled Barolo:** These Barolos were produced with long maceration, or soaking, of the skins in the juice (20 days or more) during and after fermentation, a practice which brings lots of tannin to the wine; the wine was then given long aging in large, old oak barrels; absolutely no new, small French oak barrels (known as *barriques*) were used. These traditionally-made Barolos tend to be very tannic, austere, and full-bodied, and they normally require 15 or more years to develop. Leading proponents of traditional Barolo, then and now, are the producers Giacomo Conterno, Bartolo Mascarello, Giuseppe Mascarello, Giuseppe Rinaldi, Francesco Rinaldi, and Bruno Giacosa.

- **Modern-styled Barolo:** Championed by the late Renato Ratti, and continued by Angelo Gaja and Elio Altare, among others, modern-styled Barolo represents an attempt to make Barolo ready sooner, and more palatable to wine drinkers who find traditional Barolo too austere. The fermentation period was shorter (often a week or less), wood aging was shorter, and in many cases *barriques* were used for at least part of the aging period. These new-styled Barolos mature faster (between six and ten years), and are less tannic and austere; also, the wines generally don't last as long as traditionally-styled Barolos. In addition to Gaja (who now makes Nebbiolo Langhe rather than Barolo) and Altare, other new-style Barolo winemakers include Paolo Scavino, Domenico Clerico, Luciano Sandrone, and Roberto Voerzio.

Having described these differences, we hasten to add that the producers of Barolo have *not* divided themselves into two camps which bitterly contest the proper techniques for making Barolo. Nowadays, even the most traditional winemakers, such as the great Giovanni Conterno (of Giacomo Conterno), have made some concessions to modern times and, for example, are aging their wines in wood for shorter periods (ten years or more *was* a bit long). Many winemakers have found a middle ground between both poles, and have combined the best aspects of each way of thinking.

Changes that have occurred in the vineyards over the last 20 years — such as more severe pruning and greater ripeness in the grapes — have changed the nature of the wines in any case, regardless of winemaking. Today, Barolo is better than ever, and no clear-cut division of styles exists. (But if you really pinned us down, we'd have to admit that we love the producers who have kept a firm hand with tradition.)

Recommended Barolo producers

Barolo is similar to red Burgundy in that you have to search for the best producers if you really want a true representation of these fine wines. Both types of wine have some things in common, in fact: Both grape varieties, Nebbiolo and Pinot Noir, are difficult to work with, and both wines are noted for their exquisite aromas. When choosing a Barolo or Barbaresco, we suggest the following:

- ✔ Select the producer first, based on his reputation.

- ✔ Consider the relative excellence of the vintage.

- ✔ Look for the name of a well-known single vineyard on the label.

- ✔ Check the name of the commune, such as La Morra or Castiglione Falletto (in the case of Barolo); it gives you an indication of the style of the wine — as we discuss earlier.

We list Barolo producers in two classes, alphabetically, and the communes where most, or all, of their vineyards are located. The producers in Class One are our very favorite producers; but all of the producers in Class Two are excellent producers, as well. Their wines start at $35 to $40 retail, and can go to well over $100 for single-vineyard wines.

Class One

Giacomo Conterno (Serralunga d'Alba)

Gaja (Serralunga d'Alba; La Morra) — through the 1995 vintage

Bruno Giacosa (Serralunga d'Alba; Castiglione Falletto)

Bartolo Mascarello (Barolo)

Giuseppe Mascarello (Castiglione Falletto; Monforte d'Alba)

Giuseppe Rinaldi (Barolo; La Morra)

Luciano Sandrone (Barolo)

Paolo Scavino (Castiglione Falletto)

Vietti (Castiglione Falletto)

Class Two

Elio Altare (La Morra)

Giacomo Borgogno (Barolo)

Brovia (Castiglione Falletto)

Tenuta Carretta (Barolo)

Cavalotto (Castiglione Falletto)

Ceretto, also known as Bricco Rocche (Castiglione Falletto)

Michele Chiarlo (La Morra)

Clerico (Monforte d'Alba)

Elvio Cogno (Novello)

Podere Colla (Monforte d'Alba)

Aldo Conterno (Monforte d'Alba)

Conterno-Fantino (Monforte d'Alba)

Cordero di Montezemolo (La Morra)

Corino (La Morra)

Luigi Einaudi (Barolo)

Fontanafredda (Serralunga d'Alba)

Elio Grasso (Monforte d'Alba)

Silvio Grasso (La Morra)

Manzone (Monforte d'Alba)

Marcarini (La Morra)

Marchesi di Barolo (Barolo)

Oddero (Serralunga d'Alba)

Parusso (Monforte d'Alba)

Pio Cesare (Serralunga d'Alba)

E. Pira & Figli (Barolo)

Luigi Pira (Serralunga d'Alba)

Prunotto (Monforte d'Alba)

Renato Ratti (La Morra)

Francesco Rinaldi (Barolo)

Rocche Costamagna (La Morra)

Rocche dei Manzoni (Monforte d'Alba)

Seghesio (Barolo)

Gianni Voerzio (La Morra)

Roberto Voerzio (La Morra)

Barbaresco

The other great red wine of the Langhe hills, Barbaresco *(bahr bah RES co),* also a DOCG wine, is very similar to Barolo, with most of its bigger brother's virtues, and few of its faults. The reasons for the similarities between Barolo and Barbaresco are that they're both made entirely from Nebbiolo, they share similar soils and climate (because they are within ten miles of each other), and many producers make both wines, using similar production methods.

Barbaresco is a sturdy, austere, powerful wine, generally only slightly less full-bodied than Barolo: Its minimum alcohol content is slightly less (12.5 percent, compared to 13 percent for Barolo), and its minimum aging at the winery (two years minimum, four for *riservas*) is one year less than Barolo's.

The Barbaresco zone is a few miles northeast of the town of Alba, and about a 20-minute drive from the Barolo zone. It's a slightly smaller area than Barolo, covering only three communities: Barbaresco itself, Neive, and Treiso. All three villages are high in the Langhe hills. The Tanaro River cuts through the northwestern part of the Barbaresco zone, and the zone's closeness to the flatter Tanaro Valley helps make the Barbaresco area slightly warmer and dryer than the Barolo zone. As a result, the Nebbiolo grape ripens earlier here than in the Barolo area, and generally has less tannin.

The aromas and flavors of Barbaresco wines are very much the same as those of Barolo (see the section, "Barolo," earlier in this chapter). But Barbaresco is more elegant, typically less austere, and more accessible in its youth. For this reason, it is generally a better choice in restaurants, especially when most of the available wines are from recent vintages. As with any generalization, however, exceptions exist. The very traditional producer Bruno Giacosa, for example, makes powerful, tannic Barbarescos from the Neive area that require many years of aging before they are ready to drink — just like Giacosa's Barolos.

Barbaresco's annual production is only about 2.5 million bottles, which is 35 percent of Barolo's production — one reason that top producers, such as Bruno Giacosa, Angelo Gaja, Ceretto, and Marchesi di Gresy, have no trouble selling their limited supply of rather expensive Barbarescos. (Barbaresco prices are about the same as Barolo, from $35 to well over $100 a bottle.)

Because Barbaresco has fewer producers than Barolo, in a smaller, more consistent territory, it's a more consistently reliable wine, generally speaking. About 200 producers make Barolo, quite a few of whom are not very good. On the other hand, we seldom come across a poor Barbaresco producer. Barbaresco has attained international status in the last 20 years thanks to one dynamic, charismatic producer, Angelo Gaja (*GUY yah*). The reputation of Gaja's wines, and the messianic nature of the man himself, who globetrots the world delivering his message, has brought attention not only to Barbaresco and Piedmont, but also to all Italian wines (see the sidebar in this chapter, "Angelo Gaja, man on a mission").

Vineyard and winemaking styles in the Barbaresco zone

The soils of the vineyards around the three villages where the grapes for Barbaresco grow are more uniform than those of the Barolo communities; consequently, you don't see such striking differences among Barbaresco wines as you do among Barolos. But some differences do exist among Barbarescos according to their vineyard area (remember that winemaking style can camouflage the characteristics of the vineyard area, however):

- ✔ The community of Barbaresco itself produces about 45 percent of Barbaresco wine. Many of the best vineyards are here, as well as many of the largest, most renowned wineries (although no Barbaresco winery is very large), such as Angelo Gaja, Ceretto's Bricco Asili, Produttori del Barbaresco (perhaps the most respected wine cooperative in the world), and Marchesi di Gresy, owner of the entire, renowned Martinenga vineyard. In general, the wines of the Barbaresco area tend to be a bit lighter in color and lighter-bodied than those of Neive, but they are known for their perfumed aromas and their structure.

- ✔ The community of Neive, on the next hill east of Barbaresco, produces the most full-bodied, tannic Barbarescos in the region. Neive accounts for almost 31 percent of Barbaresco, and is the home of the great Bruno Giacosa, as well as Fratelli Cigliuti and the historic Castello di Neive.

- ✔ Treiso d'Alba (or simply, Treiso), south of Barbaresco, is the least-known of the three areas; some of the Barbaresco zone's highest hills are here. Treiso produces about 20 percent of the zone's wine; its Barbarescos tend to be lighter-bodied than the others, and they are known for their finesse and their elegance.

Angelo Gaja: man on a mission

One of the two people who have done the most to improve the image of Italian wine in the last 25 years (along with Tuscany's Marchese Piero Antinori) is Piedmont's Angelo Gaja, a fourth generation winemaker whose family emigrated from Spain into Piedmont about 300 years ago. No one outside of Italy had ever heard of Gaja Barbaresco — or Barbaresco itself — when Angelo took over the reins from his father in the 1960s. He changed everything: the vineyards, the winemaking style, the bottles, the labels, and even the corks (Gaja's corks have become famous: the longest corks possible, and of the highest quality).

Gaja brought many winemaking innovations to Piedmont, including shorter fermentation times and the use of *barriques* — even for his Nebbiolo wines. In the vineyards, he reduced crop size to improve ripeness and quality. The resulting wines always have intense concentration, are cleanly made and well-balanced, and are never overly tannic. And they also age remarkably well. Always an iconoclast, Gaja was also the first to make Chardonnay and Cabernet Sauvignon in the region. Many of his Piedmontese colleagues scoffed at these innovations, but the wines earned good reviews.

Gaja traces his family's quest for excellence to his grandmother, who was one of the first winemakers to focus on quality rather than quantity for Barbaresco. As a result of her efforts, Gaja's Barbarescos always had the best reputation among the wines of the region. But it wasn't until Angelo took over that Gaja Barbarescos started gaining an international reputation. As Gaja's reputation grew, so did the status of other Barbarescos, Barolos, and now even other Piedmont wines, such as Barbera. Other wine producers emulated him, improving the quality of their wines and charging high prices.

In 1988, Angelo bought a vineyard in Serralunga d'Alba, in the Barolo area, and shortly later bought part of the renowned Cerequio vineyard in La Morra. Ever restless, he has purchased a winery in Montalcino (see Chapter 8) and has built a winery in the Bolgheri region, both in Tuscany. And oh, yes, he's renovating an old building in Barbaresco, which will become a much-needed hotel in that sleepy little village. Angelo Gaja is a leader. Yes, his wines are pricey, but he puts his money to good use — to constantly raise the winemaking bar, and to improve his home town.

Differences among winemaking styles are also not quite so pronounced in Barbaresco. Certainly Angelo Gaja is a leader in the newer style of Barbaresco, along with Moccagatta and other producers. Their wines tend to be less austere and tannic, drinkable sooner, and have somewhat brighter fruity flavors. These wines usually have had some aging in *barriques*. The traditional style of Barbaresco, as exemplified by Bruno Giacosa and Produttori del Barbaresco, tends to be powerful, full-bodied, and tannic; these wines require ten years or more of aging before they are ready to drink. Many producers make Barbaresco combining elements of both styles.

In general, Barbaresco tends to be drinkable sooner than Barolo, but many exceptions exist. Both Bruno Giacosa's and Angelo Gaja's single-vineyard wines (Gaja's, as of the 1996 vintage, are actually called Nebbiolo Langhe DOC rather than Barbaresco) easily last for 20 or more years in good vintages (see our Vintage Chart in Appendix B).

Recommended Barbaresco producers

We list our favorite Barbaresco producers in two classes, alphabetically within each class, and name the communes where most, or all, of their vineyards are located. Many Barolo producers also make good Barbarescos; if a producer's primary wine is Barolo, we list that producer only under "Recommended Barolo producers," (see the section earlier in this chapter). Barolo producers whose Barbarescos are of greater or equal importance — such as Gaja, Bruno Giacosa, and Ceretto — appear on both lists. The producers in Class One are our very favorite producers — but all of the producers in Class Two are good producers, as well:

Class One
Ceretto, also known as Bricco Asili (Barbaresco)
Fratelli Cigliuti (Neive)
Angelo Gaja (Barbaresco)
Bruno Giacosa (Neive)
Marchesi di Gresy (Barbaresco)

Class Two
Luigi Bianco (Barbaresco)
Ca' Romé (Barbaresco)
Castello di Neive (Neive)
Giuseppe Cortese (Barbaresco)
De Forville (Barbaresco)
Moccagatta (Barbaresco)

Fiorenzo Nada (Treiso)
Sorì Paitin, also known as Secondo Pasquero-Elia (Neive)
Parroco di Neive (Neive)
Pelissero (Treiso)
I Vignaioli Elvio Pertinace (Treiso)
Produttori del Barbaresco (Barbaresco)
Roagna, also know as I Paglieri (Barbaresco)
Albino Rocca (Barbaresco)
Bruno Rocca (Barbaresco)
La Spinetta (Neive)
La Spinona (Barbaresco)

Barbera, Dolcetto, and Nebbiolo of Alba

The town of Alba gives its name to three red varietal wines, each made entirely from its named grape: Nebbiolo d'Alba *(nehb bee OH loh DAHL bah)*, Barbera d'Alba *(bar BAE rah DAHL bah)*, and Dolcetto d'Alba *(dohl CHET toh DAHL bah)*.

Of these three, Barbera d'Alba is generally the finest and most serious wine — despite the fact that Nebbiolo is the most serious of the three grape varieties. In fact, Barbera in the Alba zone is about as good as Barbera gets — except for parts of the Asti zone, where it can be at least as good, but subtly different. (See the section "Barbera d'Asti" later in this chapter.)

Barbera is a strange variety. It has lots of pigmentation, and very high acidity, but almost no tannin in its skins and seeds; its wines are therefore dark in color but crisp and refreshing, rather like white wines, instead of being firm and mouth-drying like most reds — but its berry-cherry and spicy flavors are red wine all the way. When you taste most Barbera d'Albas, you find a red wine that's more mouthwatering and refreshing than most other reds; it goes amazingly well with food.

In many parts of Italy, Barbera wines are only average in quality because the farmers grow too large a crop, or because the climate doesn't let the grapes ripen optimally. But in the Alba area, the growers respect Barbera, and the grapes return the favor by making rich, flavorful wines with intense fruity and spicy flavors.

When the grapes are especially good, some winemakers age some of their Barbera d'Alba for a short time in small barrels of French oak, which gives the wine some of the tannin the grapes themselves lack, and brings the wine closer in style to other red wines. (Angelo Gaja pioneered this style when he made a 1971 single-vineyard Barbera d'Alba called Vignarey and aged it in previously-used French oak barrels; by 1978, he was using new *barriques* for the wine.) Both styles of Barbera d'Alba can be excellent if the winemaker is good; the oaked styles generally cost more — about $22 to $45 rather than $12 to $20 for the un-oaked wines.

The Barbera d'Alba territory is a fairly large area that encompasses the Langhe hills as well as the Roero; this area includes the production zone for both Barolo and Barbaresco. Many of the best wines come from vineyards within Barolo territory, which are some of the best vineyards of the entire area. For example, what we consider the finest Barbera d'Alba of all comes from a vineyard called Scarrone, which grew Nebbiolo grapes to make Barolo when the Vietti winery purchased it in the late 1960s; five years later, winemaker Alfredo Currado replanted the vineyard with Barbera (a risky decision, considering the lower prestige of that grape) because he found Nebbiolo difficult to ripen there — not due to any natural factors but because a medieval fortress atop the hill shaded the vines and slowed ripening. Sure enough, Barbera, an earlier-ripening variety, rose to new heights of quality in the superior Barolo terrain.

Although Barbera grows elsewhere in Piedmont, it's particularly close to the hearts of the Albese, the people of the Alba area (which is ironic considering that these people can claim the great Barolo and Barbaresco as their very own). Barbera, along with Dolcetto, is the wine they drink most often, and it's one of the wines that parents lay down for their newborn children to enjoy at maturity.

Barbera d'Alba is enjoyable both young and with age, up to about 15 years, to our taste — although as it ages beyond about eight years, it loses its spicy vibrancy and becomes a more normalized red wine. Simple, inexpensive Barbera is our favorite wine with pizza, but the best examples are really too good for such casual food. Barbera is terrific with pasta with tomato sauce, spicy foods, bitter greens, and hearty dishes.

Our favorite producers of Barbera d'Alba, listed alphabetically, are the following:

Elio Altare	Bartolo Mascarello
Elvio Cogno	Giuseppe Mascarello
Aldo Conterno	Moccagatta
Giacomo Conterno	Prunotto
Gaja	Giuseppi Rinaldi
Manzone	Paolo Scavino
Marcarini	Vietti

Dolcetto d'Alba

Dolcetto d'Alba comes from vineyards in the Langhe hills but not the Roero area. It's made entirely from Dolcetto, which ripens earlier than other red varieties of the area. Dolcetto d'Alba is also earlier maturing as a wine than Barbera or Nebbiolo, and in meals is usually served before Barbera — to accompany the five or six (or eight) antipasto courses of a typical Piedmontese meal.

Dolcetto has lower acidity than Barbera, but it's still acidic, as any self-respecting Italian wine should be; its acid suits it well to food. It's more tannic than Barbera — a dry, medium-bodied, rich-textured wine with aromas and flavors of black pepper and ripe berry fruit.

Dolcetto is the featured variety in a total of seven Piedmontese DOC zones. The Alba zone, whose Dolcettos are the easiest to find in the U.S., is one of the top two areas in terms of the quality of the wines, along with Dogliani (described later in this chapter). Good as it is, though, Dolcetto d'Alba has improved even more in the past 15 years, thanks to modern vineyard practices and more advanced winemaking. This winemaking does not involve aging in expensive French oak barrels, however, because Dolcetto is a relatively inexpensive wine to drink young, not a serious wine for aging. Most Dolcettos taste like ripe Dolcetto fruit rather than having smoky, toasty nuances of oak.

We love to drink Dolcetto with some of the same kind of foods as Barbera — pizza, somewhat spicy dishes, earthy vegetarian foods — but it's also terrific with casual meals such as chef salads, cold cuts, sandwiches, or turkey burgers. Dolcetto d'Alba costs about $12 to $20 per bottle, and is best when it's no more than three years old, in our opinion. Many Barolo producers also make Dolcetto d'Alba; our favorite producers, alphabetically, are Elio Altare, Clerico, Elvio Cogno (a specialty), Giacomo Conterno, Conterno-Fantino, Marcarini, Ratti, Sandrone, and Vietti.

Nebbiolo d'Alba

To our way of thinking, Nebbiolo d'Alba runs a distant third among the three Alba varietal wines. Not that it's not a perfectly fine, well-made wine most of the time; we just prefer to experience Nebbiolo in its most dramatic, highest-quality expression — as Barolo and Barbaresco. Nebbiolo d'Alba lacks the intensity and flair of those wines, and instead is just a good, medium-bodied, firm red wine with delicate flavors of tar, red fruits, and herbs.

The grapes for Nebbiolo d'Alba grow in certain parts of the Langhe hills and in the entire Roero. Although many Barolo and Barbaresco producers make Nebbiolo d'Alba, their wine is never a de-classified Barolo or Barbaresco, because the Nebbiolo d'Alba vineyard area doesn't overlap with those of the two great DOCG wines. Some Barolo and Barbaresco producers source their grapes for Nebbiolo d'Alba from vineyards across the river, in the Roero.

Nebbiolo d'Alba is a relatively light style of Nebbiolo for drinking young; the wine must age only one year before release. Its best drinkability period is three to seven years from the vintage, in our opinion. Also to its advantage, it's relatively inexpensive — generally about $15 to $18 a bottle. One Barolo producer who makes a specialty of producing fine Nebbiolo d'Alba is Tenuta Carretta. DOC regulations permit the production of a sweet, sparkling Nebbiolo d'Alba, but in our travels through the area, we've never encountered it.

Roero and Roero Arneis

The Roero *(roh EH roh)* is an area north of the city of Alba, across the Tanaro River from the Barolo and Barbaresco zones. It's a hilly area, but the hills are lower than on the other side of the river; the soils are also lighter, for the most part, than in the Barolo and Barbaresco zones, with a high percentage of sand, although parts of the Roero have a richer, calcareous clay soil similar to that found in the hills south of the river.

The Roero territory has several overlapping or partially overlapping DOC zones, including parts of the Barbera d'Alba and Nebbiolo d'Alba zones; growers here have traditionally cultivated both Nebbiolo and Barbera for these two wines. Part of the Langhe DOC zone (described in the next section) falls into part of the Roero, too. But the real excitement in the Roero these days is wines made with the DOC Roero, a relatively new appellation (created in 1985).

Roero Rosso is a red wine that's almost entirely Nebbiolo; a token 2 to 5 percent of the local white Arneis *(ahr NASE)* variety may also be used. What's different about it compared to

Barolo and Barbaresco, in theory, is that it's a lighter wine — but in practice the difference is the avant garde attitude with which many producers approach the wine. Free of any accountability to tradition, they readily employ modern wine-making methods designed to produce concentrated wines with intense fruity character framed by the taste and structure of French oak. Producers whose vineyards are in the part of Roero with the richest soils, such as the northern area around Canale, have the best resources for making such wines; lighter Roero wines also exist.

The following producers, listed alphabetically, are on the vanguard of high-quality Roero Rosso: Cascina Ca' Rossa, Tenuta Carretta, Cascina Chicco, Cornarea, Matteo Correggia, Deltetto, Funtanin, Filippo Gallino, Malvirà, Monchiero Carbone, and Angelo Negro e Figli.

The Roero DOC also covers a white wine called Roero Arneis, made entirely from the Arneis variety. This local white variety was well on its way to extinction before Alfredo Currado of Vietti, a leading winemaker in the Barolo zone, salvaged it 30 years ago. He discovered it in 1967, and decided to vinify a small batch as an experiment. The grape was so uncommon — just a few vines here and there, interspersed among the Nebbiolo or Barbera, to distract birds from the more valuable grapes — that to obtain one ton of grapes, he had to buy the production of 46 growers. In 1970, he sold his first Arneis and received enthusiastic reviews from Italian wine critic Luigi Veronelli. Today, Arneis is a beloved part of Alba's wine culture.

Roero Arneis is a medium-bodied white with pronounced aromas and flavors that suggest fresh grass, flowers, and ripe, white fruits; it's usually dry, although some producers make it slightly off-dry, and it sometimes has a refreshing prickle of CO_2 in its rich texture. Arneis is best enjoyed young, within three years of the harvest. Our favorite producers are Ceretto, Matteo Correggia, Deltetto, Funtanin, Bruno Giacosa, Malvirà, and Vietti.

Other DOC wines of Alba

Depending on exactly where their vineyards are situated, producers in the Alba area have another five DOC designations at their disposal. Three of these apply to wines made entirely from Dolcetto:

✔ **Dolcetto delle Langhe Monregalesi** *(dohl CHET toh del lae LAHN gae mahn rae gah LAE see):* From a territory that spans both sides of the Tanaro River upstream (south) from the Barolo district — where the river runs north-south; somewhat lighter than Dolcetto d'Alba.

✔ **Dolcetto di Diano d'Alba** *(dohl CHET toh dee dee AH no DAHL bah):* Also called just "Diano d'Alba," this is a smaller area, specifically the hilly part of the commune of Diano d'Alba, which nestles between the Barolo and Barbaresco zones.

✔ **Dolcetto di Dogliani** *((dohl CHET toh dee doh L'YAH nee):* This zone begins about where the Dolcetto d'Alba, Nebbiolo d'Alba, and Barbera d'Alba zones end, to their south, and takes its name from the small town of Dogliani. Some of the Dolcetto wines here are very good, more concentrated than those of the Alba zone and needing a bit more time to develop. Because this is a traditional Dolcetto area, that grape earns the best vineyard sites — one theory as to why it can be more intense than Alba Dolcettos. Seek out the Dolcetto of Luigi Einaudi and the brilliant wines of Quinto Chionetti.

A new DOC wine, since 1995, is **Verduno Pelaverga** *(ver DOO no pel ah VER gah),* made primarily from the local red Pelaverga grape mainly in the community of Verduno, one of the fringe areas of the Barolo zone west of Alba. This wine is medium-bodied and vibrant with red fruits and spicy flavors. Pelaverga is a nice change of pace (and, according to local legend, an aphrodisiac), but you wouldn't want to have nothing else to drink for a whole week — as once happened to us quite by mistake when we visited the Piedmont Alps!

The final additional DOC zone of the Alba area — called simply **Langhe** DOC — is the largest of all. It covers approximately the territory of all the DOC/G zones we've discussed so far in this chapter, and extends eastward into the Asti DOCG area (which we describe later in this chapter). The Langhe DOC came into existence in the 1990s, basically as a catch-all category for wines that producers were categorizing as *vino da tavola.* These include wines whose grapes (or blends) did not conform to the various other DOC/G regulations of the area — as well as wines of the other DOC/G zones that producers wished to declassify (for example, to make a Nebbiolo in the Barolo zone with less than the three years of aging required for Barolo).

Six varietal wines fall under the Langhe DOC (each one deriving 100 percent from its named grape): Nebbiolo, Dolcetto, Freisa, Favorita, Arneis, and Chardonnay. The Langhe name also applies two very important non-varietal wines, a Rosso and a Bianco.

Langhe Nebbiolo can be declassified Barolo, Barbaresco, Nebbiolo d'Alba, or Roero Rosso, or Nebbiolo grown in other parts of the zone. Langhe Freisa comes from the local red Freisa *(FRAE sah)* variety, which makes an exceptionally lively, vibrant red wine with high acid and high tannin, often vinified in a *frizzante,* slightly sweet style that's popular locally. Some producers now successfully make Freisa as a dry, oak-aged wine. Three Langhe Freisas that we enjoy are Giacomo Conterno's, G. Mascarello's Vigna Toetto, and Varaldo's. Langhe Favorita comes From the local white Favorita variety, which makes dry, crisp wines with delicate flavors that are slightly floral or citrusy.

Langhe Rosso and Langhe Bianco are wide-open designations in terms of the varieties permitted: Each may be made from any one or more locally-grown grape varieties of the appropriate color.

The Langhe Rosso designation is particularly noteworthy for stunning, modern wines that are non-traditional blends of Nebbiolo, Barbera, and/or Cabernet Sauvignon. These wines include Altare's Vigna Arborina, Clerico's Arte, Conterno-Fantino's Monprà, and Rocche dei Manzoni's Vigna Big.

Visiting the Alba-Asti area

The region around Alba and Asti, where most of the great Piedmont wines are made, is one of the finest restaurant areas in Italy, if not the world. If you happen to visit between October and December, you'll assure yourself ample shavings of the special treat of this region — pungent white truffles — on your pasta, soups, meat courses, and anything else you desire (we especially recommend them with egg dishes). But any time of the year, the restaurants perform their magic for you. (Bear in mind that it does get rather hot in this area during July and August.) To accompany your Barolo or Barbaresco, we recommend beef braised in wine, roast pork, rabbit (all local specialties), game, game birds, and aged hard cheeses.

All of the restaurants we mention here are relatively inexpensive to moderate in price compared to their equivalents in major European cities, and the wines are downright bargains! The following is a survey of some of the leading restaurant-inns in the area:

- ✔ **Da Guido** (Costiglione d'Asti, Tel. 0141 966012): Probably the most renowned restaurant in Piedmont, and one of the best in Italy; superb food and service; astounding wine list, for both Italian and French wine; located between Alba and Asti

- ✔ **Da Cesare** (Albaretto della Torre, Tel. 0173 520141): The chef-artist, Cesare Giaccone, rivals Da Guido with his brilliant, typically Piedmontese cuisine; a local favorite; located in a high hill town in the Alta Langhe (the high hills), south of Alba

- ✔ **La Pergola** (Vezza d'Alba, Tel. 0173 65178): This fine restaurant northwest of Alba offers the largest, most complete Piedmontese wine list in the world (ten pages of Barolo alone!)

- ✔ **Ristorante La Contea** (Neive, Tel. 0173 67126): Very typical Piedmontese fare; a great prelude to the region; Tonino Verro is host, his wife Claudia, the excellent chef; has a few rooms

- ✔ **Giardino da Felicin** (Monteforte d'Alba, Tel. 0173 78225): Restaurant-inn in the heart of Barolo country; host-owner Giorgio Rocca speaks English and acts as your guide to the wine region, if you are fortunate enough to get a room (in busy season, it's booked a year in advance)

- ✔ **Hotel Belvedere** (La Morra, Tel. 0173 50190): Traditional and very fine restaurant in Barolo country, with a better chance of getting rooms than in Giardino da Felicin; also fabulous views

- ✔ **Il Cascianalenuovo** (Isola d'Asti, Tel. 0141 958166): A hotel with a swimming pool and tennis court; very fine restaurant with an excellent wine list; northeast of Barbaresco

- ✔ **Gener Neuv** (Asti, Tel. 0141 57270): Asti's leading restaurant; fine wine list

- ✔ **Vincafe** (Alba, Tel. 0173 364603): Best wine bar in Alba; 240 wines on the list, 70 wines open by the glass every day; local cheeses; lunch available; in the heart of town

✔ **Ristorante Enoclub** (Alba, Tel. 0173 33994): Good, casual restaurant in downtown Alba; very good wine list

✔ **Tornavento** (Treiso, Tel. 0173 638333): Beautiful country restaurant-inn in Barbaresco country; some rooms available

✔ **Le Torri** (Castiglione Falletto, Tel. 0173 62930): Fairly new hotel-restaurant in the center of this old hill town; some rooms have a fine view of Barolo country

✔ **Locanda nel Borgo Antico** (Barolo, Tel. 0173 56355): Fine restaurant in the town of Barolo

✔ **Trattoria Marsupino** (Briaglia, Tel. 0174 563888): Excellent country restaurant about 12 miles south of the town of Dogliani; a few rooms

✔ **La Carmagnole** (Carmagnola, Tel. 011 9712673): A private home converted into a small, charming restaurant; excellent food; proprietor treats you like a guest in his home; the town is off the *autostrada* on the road north to Turin

✔ **Al Rododendro** (Boves, Tel. 0171 387822): Even though Boves is a bit distant — about an hour's drive south of Alba — we must include this restaurant because it's one of Italy's finest, on the level of Da Guido; outstanding food, wine, and service; rooms available; chef-owner, Mary Lombardi

The Wines of Southeastern Piedmont

The Alba wine zone is small in comparison to the wine-producing areas of southeastern Piedmont (see Figure 4-1). These areas make more wine than any other part of the region. The reason is logical: They have a greater concentration of hilly land for grape growing than other parts of the region do.

The Alba wine zones, for example, lie within the province of Cuneo, a large province occupying the southwestern quarter of Piedmont — most of which is either too mountainous for vineyards, or so flat that it's better suited to growing kiwis and maize. (The Po River rises in the Alps of southwestern

Piedmont, and the Po Valley — which stretches all the way across northern Italy — begins in the Cuneo area.) But the provinces of Asti, east and north of the Alba area, and Alessandria, east of Asti, are mainly hilly. This is the area of the Monferrato Hills, which extend from the Po River south to the Apennines. The name Monferrato appears as part of many wine names, as does Asti, the province — but oddly enough, not Alessandria.

Nebbiolo recedes in importance in Asti and Alessandria, and Barbera comes strongly to the foreground — along with a minor red variety called Grignolino *(gree n'yoh LEE no)*, the red Malvasia, the white Cortese *(cor TAE sae)* grape, and, above all, Moscato.

Asti DOCG

Asti is a famous name around the world, even to those who have never visited that city. The reason is the DOCG wine called Asti, Italy's flagship sparkling wine and one of the most unique sparkling wines in the world. Asti is made entirely from the Moscato grape — the Muscat à Petits Grains type, the best Muscat variety of all. It's a sweet (Oh no! The dreaded "S" word!), absolutely delicious bubbly with rich floral, peachy flavors and lots of acidity to balance its sweetness.

On our first-ever trip to Piedmont, the harvest was in progress at the Cinzano winery, and we stole a taste of ripe Moscato grapes being delivered to the winery by a local farmer. To our amazement, the grapes tasted *exactly* like Asti Spumante (as the wine was then called); we had never experienced such a close correlation between grapes and their wine — and we still haven't. That was when we realized what integrity Asti has as a wine. We always loved it, but from that point on, we respected it as well.

The vineyard area for Asti is quite large, extending beyond the province of Asti itself into limited parts of the Alba area to the west and the Alessandria province to the east. Asti is made using a particular process whereby the juice begins fermenting, then stops, then begins again, several times. This process makes a low alcohol wine (only about 8 percent) that retains the grapes' fresh flavors.

And freshness is what Asti is all about. Once the wine is about two or three years old, it starts to taste richer and somewhat heavy — still tasty, but no longer at its best. To complicate the matter, however, Asti doesn't carry a vintage date, so you don't know *how* old a particular bottle really is. Our suggestion is to purchase Asti from a store that sells a lot of it, and to purchase a brand that sells well, because the turnover assures freshness. Our favorite brands are Fontanafredda, Martini & Rossi, and Cinzano, but freshness is even more important than which brand you choose. And make sure the wine is genuine Asti; imitations do exist!

A companion wine to Asti — made from the same grapes in the same vineyard areas and covered under the same DOCG — is Moscato d'Asti *(mo SCAH toh DAHS tee)*. This wine is quite similar to Asti except that it's just *frizzante* — lightly bubbly, or fizzy — rather than sparkling, and its flavors are more delicate than Asti's. It's also even lower in alcohol — generally from 5 to 7.5 percent (in some states, that's technically too low to be wine!). Freshness is even more crucial for Moscato d'Asti than it is for Asti, but fortunately the wines are vintage dated. Buy the youngest vintage possible, and never buy any vintage that's more than two years old.

The ultimate Barbera d'Asti

If you'd like to experience what just might be the pinnacle of quality in Barbera d'Asti, look for a wine called Quorum (and look hard; its production is quite limited.) Quorum is a Barbera d'Asti produced by an association called Hastae — the Roman name for the city of Asti — which was formed by five local wineries and one distillery; the wineries all own vineyards in the Asti zone and individually make some of the finest Barbera d'Asti wines of all. These producers — Braida (the winery of the late Giacomo Bologna), Michele Chiarlo, Coppo, Prunotto, and Vietti — each give an equal amount of their best Barbera grapes to the joint effort, and consulting enologist Riccardo Cotarella makes the wine. (Distilleria Berta, the sixth member of Hastae, makes a fine grappa from the remains of the grapes.) All proceeds from the sale of this wine go to promote the culture, food, and the wine of the Asti area, and to support the study of the Barbera grape. The 1998 vintage of Quorum sells for $72 to $80 per bottle retail, where available.

Moscato d'Asti has a real following among some wine lovers in the U.S. In New York, for example, we see it offered by-the-glass as a dessert wine (with *biscotti,* almond cookies that aren't very sweet) in some restaurants. But you don't have to relegate this wine to after-dinner just because it's sweet. Frankly, it's so delicate and crisp that its sweetness is a non-issue for us: We just drink it whenever we want a light, delicious, refreshing wine. We particularly love it with brunch — and the wine's low alcohol is a welcome bonus at that time of day. It's particularly refreshing on a lazy summer afternoon.

Moscato d'Asti is actually more expensive than Asti, the sparkling version. Asti generally runs from $10 to $12 at retail, while Moscato d'Asti tends to cost about $12 to $15. Our favorite Moscato d'Asti is Cascinetta, made by Vietti; La Spinetta is a well-regarded brand, but the wine is slightly less delicate. Other good brands are Ceretto's Santo Stefano, Piero Gatti, Dante Rivetti, and Paolo Saracco.

Barbera d'Asti

The Barbera grape is thought to have originated around Asti, in the Monferrato Hills; the province of Asti (like the Alba wine area) has grown Barbera for over 200 years. The DOC production zone for Barbera d'Asti is large, covering most of the Asti province and extending into Alessandria somewhat.

Barbera d'Asti wines are typically lighter and leaner than Barbera d'Alba — or at least the majority of them are. The Asti zone is a larger area than Alba's Barbera zone, and it includes some parts where the grape makes racy wines with tart fruit flavors and very pronounced acidity. But some parts of the zone grow superior grapes from old vines that make the finest Barbera wines anywhere: rich, dark, ripe, and spicy Barberas.

Actually, the Asti zone was not just the birthplace of Barbera but also the site of its re-birth, in the early 1980s. A popular local restaurateur and winemaker, the late Giacomo Bologna, aged a single-vineyard Barbera wine in French oak barrels and produced such a lovely wine — smooth and soft, Barbera's tart acidity all tamed down — that wine critics and wine lovers who had shunned Barbera began to believe in the variety. Bologna's first vintage of Bricco dell'Uccellone, the 1982, sold for more than $20 in the U.S. — an unheard of price for humble Barbera then.

Today, *barrique* aging is common among Barbera producers — both in the Asti and Alba zones — whose grapes have the substance to sustain the impact of oak (its tannin and the toasty flavors that it gives the wine), and who want to make a truly serious wine from Barbera. (Many such producers also make somewhat lighter Barberas for everyday enjoyment.)

Barbera d'Asti ranges in price from about $10 for the lightest wines to about $45 for the richer, *barrique*-aged wines. Our favorite producers of Barbera d'Asti, listed alphabetically, are the following:

Cascina La Barbatella	Prunotto
Bava	Scarpa
Boffa	Scrimaglio
Braida	Tenuta La Tenaglia
Michele Chiarlo	Trinchero
Coppo	Vietti
Franco Martinetti	

Other varietal wines

Much of the wine production of Asti and Alessandria is varietally-labeled wine, mainly red but also white. With the exception of Barbera d'Asti, most of these wines aren't particularly outstanding in quality, or of significant commercial importance in the U.S. — although some good wines, even some gems, are among them.

Dolcetto

The Dolcetto variety is widely dispersed in southeastern Piedmont. In addition to the five DOC Dolcetto wines produced in the Alba area, another three (all 100 percent varietal) come from the provinces of Asti and Alessandria:

- ✔ **Dolcetto d'Asti** *(dohl CHET toh DAHS tee):* A fairly light Dolcetto from vineyards in the southern part of the Asti province

- ✔ **Dolcetto d'Acqui** *(dohl CHET toh DAH kwee):* The Acqui zone lies in the province of Alessandria and takes its name from the town of Acqui Terme, known for its mineral baths. The wine is noted for its floral perfume.

✔ **Dolcetto di Ovada** *(dohl CHET toh dee oh VAH dah):* The Ovada zone is in the very south of Piedmont, just west of the Gavi zone. Dolcetto is ingrained here, on hills with poor soils that are exposed to something of a maritime influence from the nearby Liguria region and its seacoast. This Dolcetto is fuller-bodied and more tannic than other Dolcettos, and ages nicely.

Freisa

The unusual and ancient Piedmontese variety called Freisa is a local specialty in two additional zones besides Langhe DOC, discussed earlier in this chapter. These two other wines are the following:

✔ **Freisa d'Asti** *(FRAE sah DAHS tee):* A dry or sweetish red wine from a zone that covers practically the whole province of Asti. Coppo makes an excellent dry Freisa d'Asti called Mondaccione, which, unusually enough, ages in small oak barrels.

✔ **Freisa di Chieri** *(FRAE sah dee key AE ree):* The Chieri area is actually in the province of Torino, in the western Monferrato hills, east of the city of Turin. This wine can be dry or sweetish, and the sweeter style is labeled *amabile*. Production is small.

Grignolino

If Freisa is mainly a local specialty, Grignolino is even more so; it holds little interest for wine lovers outside of Piedmont. This native variety makes rather pale, fairly light-bodied but tannic red wines with delicate flavors of tart red fruits and what the official regulations describe as a "pleasantly bitterish aftertaste." Actually, Grignolino can be refreshing in the heat of summer, and it goes well with many antipasto dishes, but Piedmont has so many fine wines that we tend not to bother with Grignolino. Two DOC Grignolinos are the following:

✔ **Grignolino d'Asti** *(gree n'yoh LEE no DAHS tee):* Mainly from Grignolino with a small amount of Freisa, its production zone is an area roughly centered around the city of Asti.

✔ **Grignolino del Monferrato Casalese** *(gree n'yoh LEE no del mahn fer RAH toh cah sah LAE sae):* A small amount of Freisa is optional in this wine, produced in the northern Alessandria province in the hills south of the Po River, east of the town of Casale Monferrato — a classic Grignolino area.

Malvasia

In any discussion of Italian wines, most references to the Malvasia grape mean the white Malvasia. But, like the Muscat grape, Malvasia also exists in red form, called Malvasia Nera in Italy. In Piedmont, this red grape makes two of its most unusual wines:

✔ **Malvasia di Casorzo d'Asti** *(mahl vah SEE ah dee cah SORt zoh DAHS tee):* This wine grows in a small zone mainly in Asti province; it's a spritzy, sweet, pale red with fragrant, fruity aroma and flavor; a sparkling version is scarce.

✔ **Malvasia di Castelnuovo Don Bosco** *(cahs tel N'WOH voh don BOS coh):* From a Malvasia Nera variant, sometimes with a bit of Freisa, this is a sweet, spicy, *frizzante* (or *spumante*) red, from a small zone in northern Asti province.

Brachetto, Cortese, and Ruché

These three varieties are all Piedmont specialties. Cortese is the most famous because it's the variety that makes Gavi, Piedmont's renowned still white wine (described in the next section). But Brachetto is the variety whose star seems to be on the rise, because its wine is now DOCG. The three varietal wines from these grapes are the following:

✔ **Brachetto d'Acqui** *(bra KET toh DAH kwee):* Sometimes called just Acqui, this wine derives entirely from the Brachetto variety. It's a sweet red that's most often seen as a sparkling wine, with pronounced fruity and floral flavors that might remind you of Moscato or even Lambrusco. Really quite delicious. Banfi (of Montalcino fame) produces a Brachetto d'Acqui in its Piedmont winery that sells in the U.S. for $22 to $24.

- **Cortese di Alto Monferrato** *(cor TAE sae dee AHL toh mahn fer RAH toh):* A dry, delicate white from Cortese grapes grown in a fairly large zone of the Alto Monferrato (high Monferrato hills), in the southern Asti and Alessandria provinces, overlapping several other DOC zones.

- **Ruché di Castagnole Monferrato** *(roo KAE dee cahs tah N'YOH lae mahn fer RAH toh):* A dry or slightly sweet, medium-bodied red with pronounced aromas, made mainly from the local Ruché variety in a fairly small zone northeast of the city of Asti.

Gavi DOCG

The Gavi district is in southernmost Alessandria province, close to Liguria. This area has been a wine production zone for more than 1,000 years, but that wine was traditionally red, from Barbera and Dolcetto grapes, usually blended. The local white grape, Cortese, was grown to make a base wine for sparkling wines — for which it was ideal, because of its high acidity and its subtle flavors. In the post-World War II period, however, one local grower, La Scolca, commercialized Cortese as a still wine, with great success. Today, the Gavi zone is one of the proudest wine zones in Italy, and its still white wine, Gavi (or Cortese di Gavi) DOCG is considered among Italy's best whites.

But Gavi is not an easy wine to appreciate. The high acidity of the Cortese grape — with not a lot of alcohol to counterbalance it — makes the wine crisp and austere rather than soft; also, Cortese's flavors are subtle rather than pronounced. It's easy to write Gavi off as just another crisp, white Italian wine.

When Gavi is made by a good producer, however, it has delicate but complex aromas of ripe apple, grapefruit, honey, flowers, or minerals, and it can develop for a few years. In ripe vintages such as 1997 or 2000, it can be particularly fine. Gavi is generally an un-oaked white, but some producers are aging their Gavis partially in oak, and that style can also be good, although the wines tend to taste heavier and less fresh. Wines labeled Gavi di Gavi come from vineyards around the town of Gavi itself — which is considered by locals as a sort of "classico" area — as opposed to other areas of the DOCG zone.

Gavi costs from $12 to $18 a bottle for the basic wines, with premium wines such as La Scolca's Black Label running about $35. Our recommended Gavi producers, listed alphabetically, are the following: Nicola Bergaglio, Broglia "La Meirana," Castellari Bergaglio, La Chiara, La Giustiniana, La Scolca, La Toledana, Morgassi Superiore, and Villa Sparina.

Other wines of Piedmont's southeast

A new but significant DOC designation of southeastern Piedmont is **Monferrato** *(mahn fer RAH toh),* a large area extending throughout most of the combined Asti and Alessandria provinces. Like Langhe DOC, this appellation is a catch-all DOC for wines that otherwise would fall between the DOC/G cracks. Its most flexible wines are Monferrato Bianco and Monferrato Rosso, each made from one or more locally-grown varieties. Like Langhe Rosso, Monferrato Rosso is a useful "home" for serious wines that are orphaned by the requirements of other DOC zones; La Spinetta's Pin and Martinetti's Sul Bric are two fine examples.

Monferrato DOC also features a Dolcetto and a Freisa; Monferrato Casalese Cortese, mainly Cortese grapes, grown in a sub-zone around Casale Monferrato, in the south; and Chiaretto (also called Ciaret), a rosé or light red wine that derives primarily from any or all of nine red varieties (Barbera, Bonarda, Cabernet Franc, Cabernet Sauvignon, Dolcetto, Freisa, Grignolino, Pinot Nero, and Nebbiolo).

The maze of DOCs in southeastern Piedmont includes another six wines, which are the following:

- ✔ **Albugnano** *(ahl boo N'YAH no):* A dry or semi-dry red or rosé mainly from Nebbiolo (85 percent), with Freisa, and/or Barbera, and/or Bonarda; in the northern part of Asti province.

- ✔ **Barbera del Monferrato:** Piedmont's third original zone for Barbera, along with the Alba and Asti zones. This large area lies partly in the province of Asti and partly in Alessandria, but most of the wines come from Alessandria.

✓ **Loazzolo** *(loh ahtz ZOH lo):* A sweet, still wine from the Moscato variety, in a small part of the Asti province that is possibly Piedmont's smallest DOC zone. The grapes are dried, and in some cases affected by noble rot; the resulting wine is rich, high in alcohol (15.5 percent), and delicious. Borgo Maragliano and Forteto della Luja are two good producers.

✓ **Gabiano** *(gah bee AH no):* A dry, medium-bodied red from Barbera, Freisa, and Grignolino varieties, grown in a small part of northern Alessandria province with distinct, clayey soils.

✓ **Rubino di Cantavenna** *(roo BEE no dee cahn tah VAIN nah):* A dry red wine made mainly from Barbera, with Grignolino or Freisa, from the first hills of Alessandria rising above the Po Valley — roughly the same area as Gabiano.

✓ **Colli Tortonesi** *(COH lee tor toh NAE see):* The Tortona Hills are in the very east of Southern Piedmont, north of Gavi and bordering Lombardy. This DOC covers a Dolcetto and a Barbera, each at least 85 percent from that variety, and a Cortese deriving entirely from that variety; it also covers a Bianco, Rosso, and Chiaretto (rosé) made from locally-grown grapes.

Northern Piedmont

Even though Northern Piedmont accounts for only 10 percent of the region's wines, it's the only other area in the world, besides the Langhe region in southern Piedmont and the Valtellina region in northern Lombardy (described in Chapter 6), where the Nebbiolo grape variety makes good red wines. The Nebbiolo wines of Northern Piedmont — such as Carema, Gattinara, and Ghemme — resemble Barolo and Barbaresco mainly in their similarity of aromas; their structures are quite different. The cooler temperatures and, in the case of Carema, higher altitudes, of Northern Piedmont make for lighter-bodied, less tannic, and often more acidic Nebbiolo wines than the Barolo and Barbaresco wines of the Langhe region.

One advantage that these less tannic northern Nebbiolo wines have is that they're readier to drink sooner. We wouldn't dream of ordering a five or six-year old Barolo or Barbaresco in a restaurant, but we wouldn't hesitate to order a Gattinara. And in most cases, the Nebbiolo wines of Northern Piedmont are about half the price.

Carema and Caluso

The Carema DOC zone is in northwest Piedmont, around the village of Carema; it's the last Piedmontese village before the border with the Valle d'Aosta region (see Figure 4-1). The stunningly dramatic Carema *(cah RAE ma)* vineyards perch on the very steep, eastern slopes of the Alps at altitudes of over 1,000 to nearly 2,000 feet.

The thin, acidic soil of Carema combined with the elevation of the vineyards yields light- to medium-bodied, elegant wines made entirely from Nebbiolo. The high acidity of Carema helps to guarantee rather long-lasting wines. We have encountered Carema wines from good vintages, such as 1971, 1974, 1978, and 1982, that needed 20 years to fully mature. Unfortunately, the difficult task of making a living in Carema's vineyards — plus the availability of jobs in the city of Ivrea *(eve RAE ah)*, about seven miles south of Carema — has led to a serious decline in Carema's production; fewer than 10,000 cases per year are made. Part of the challenge for producers is that DOC regulations require that Carema be aged for four years before it can be sold — a hardship for small producers in need of ready cash.

 Only two producers have Carema available for sale outside the area: Luigi Ferrando and Produttori Nebbiolo di Carema. Fortunately, both of these producers do an excellent job with this increasingly difficult-to-find wine. Look for Luigi Ferrando's black-label Carema Riservas; they are especially fine. His 1995 and 1996 vintages, both very good, are still available (in New York, at Rosenthal Wine Merchant, Tel. 212-249-6650). If you're ever passing through the area, stop at Ferrando's excellent wine shop in Ivrea; you'll find older vintages of his Caremas there. The Cantina dei Produttori Nebbiolo di Carema is a very fine cooperative whose Carema, especially its best wine, Carema Carema, is usually top-notch. Because Carema can be too lean and acidic in lesser vintages, we suggest buying Carema only in good vintages (see Piedmont in the Vintage Chart, Appendix B).

Erbaluce di Caluso *(ehr bah LOO chae dee cah LOO so),* or simply Caluso, is a fairly large vineyard area in the hills of a glacial basin south and east of the city of Ivrea; Caluso is one of the 32 communities within the zone. Erbaluce is a white grape variety used locally for centuries; in the Middle Ages, it made golden or amber dessert wines from semi-dried grapes, called Caluso Passito. Today, the *passito* style and the fortified sweet wine called Caluso Passito Liquoroso are becoming rarities. As a dry white wine, Erbaluce di Caluso is crisp, with pronounced acidity that can be too severe in the hands of a mediocre producer; a sparkling style also exists. Like Carema, Caluso wines are now difficult to find. We recommend the following producers, listed alphabetically: Vittorio Boratto, Colombaio di Candia, Luigi Ferrando, and Orsolani.

A third DOC zone of this area is **Canavese** *(cah nah vae sae),* the largest of the three. It encompasses the Caluso zone and features five types of wine: a Nebbiolo and a Barbera; Canavese Bianco, entirely Erbaluce; Canavese Rosso (in normal or *novello* styles), made at least 60 percent from Nebbiolo, Barbera, Bonarda, Freisa, and Neretto, singly or together; and a rosato, from the same grapes.

Vercelli and Novara hills wines

The Vercelli and Novara provinces occupy the whole northernmost part of Piedmont (see Figure 4-1). Their alpine hillsides sit in a favorable microclimate right between the Po River basin to the south and the Alps and Lake Maggiore to the north. The Sesia River flows south from the Alps, separating the two provinces. Three red-only wine zones, including Gattinara *(gah tee NAH rah),* are in Vercelli, to the west; four red wine zones, including Ghemme *(GAE mae),* are in Novara, the eastern province. (All seven zones are east of Carema, at about the same latitude, but considerably lower in altitude, as Carema is in the Alps, not just the foothills.) Two other DOC zones for red and white wine have recently been designated, one in each province, bringing the total number of wine zones in this area to nine.

The seven totally-red wine zones all feature Nebbiolo — called "Spanna" in these two northern provinces; you sometimes see Spanna as part of the name of wines from these parts. Gattinara is clearly the standout wine of the area, followed by Ghemme.

None of these seven wine zones could be called dynamic, however. Production has fallen due to a combination of circumstances: a general decline in wine quality, a decline in the wines' status, less demand and lower prices, and a migration of farmers to the cities. Only about 80,000 cases of wine are produced annually from the seven zones, about half of which is Gattinara.

Nevertheless, a well-made Gattinara, Ghemme, or any other of the Nebbiolo-based DOC wines from Northern Piedmont is a more accessible wine than Barolo or Barbaresco, at about half the price. (Choose a wine from our recommended producers later in this section.) The fact that these wines are lighter in body and color than Barolo or Barbaresco doesn't mean that they're short-lived; their tannin and pronounced acidity allow these wines — particularly Gattinara and Ghemme — to continue developing and maturing for 20 years or more, especially in good vintages (see Piedmont vintages in the Vintage Chart in Appendix B).

Gattinara

Gattinara, a DOCG wine, is the most renowned wine of Northern Piedmont. Its vineyard area is the hillside north of the community of Gattinara. The wine must be at least 86 percent Nebbiolo, with Bonarda and Vespolina permitted, and it must age for at least three years, or four years for *riservas*. Like other Nebbiolo wines, Gattinara's color turns garnet with age, and the wine develops a penetrating bouquet of violets and tar, characteristic of the finest Piedmontese Nebbiolos. Antoniolo, Nervi, and Travaglini are three leading producers of Gattinara; all of these producers' Gattinaras are widely distributed in the U.S.

Ghemme

Ghemme, from a vineyard area across the Sesia River from Gattinara, around the town of Ghemme, is often mentioned in the same breath as Gattinara and is also a DOCG wine. It's quite similar to Gattinara, and as long-lasting — if not even longer-lasting — but Ghemme is generally less fine than Gattinara, perhaps because less Nebbiolo is required in its blend. Ghemme must be 65 to 85 percent Nebbiolo, with 10 to 30 percent of the local Vespolina, and up to 15 percent Bonarda Novarese. The minimum aging requirement for Ghemme is four years. Antichi Vigneti di Cantalupo is the leading Ghemme producer.

Other wines of the Novara-Vercelli hills

The remaining seven DOC wines also come from the hills of the Vercelli and Novara provinces:

- ✔ **Lessona** *(lehs SOH nah):* The Lessona DOC zone is in the hillsides around the community of Lessona, west of Gattinara. Like all Nebbiolo-based wines, the austere Lessona needs time to develop its violet aromas, but is generally ready to drink before Gattinara or Ghemme. Nebbiolo constitutes at least 75 percent of Lessona, and Vespolina and Bonarda are optional. One producer, Sella, dominates the zone; Sella makes two single-vineyard Lessona wines as well as a standard Lessona.

- ✔ **Bramaterra** *(bra ma TER rah):* We enjoyed our first Bramaterra in the excellent restaurant-inn north of Gattinara, Al Sorriso (in the village of Sorriso, in the Novara province). The Bramaterra zone encompasses seven communities between Gattinara and Lessona; Bramaterra is the name of the area. The wine is 50 to 70 percent Nebbiolo and 20 to 30 percent Croatina, with up to 20 percent Bonarda and/or Vespolina. Bramaterra is drinkable sooner than either Gattinara or Lessona. Its two leading producers are Sella and Luigi Perazzi.

- ✔ **Boca** *(BOH cah):* The Boca area is the northernmost of the seven Nebbiolo zones. Boca is 45 to 70 percent Nebbiolo and 20 to 40 percent Vespolina, with up to 20 percent Bonarda; minimum aging is three years. Antonio Vallana, known for his Spanna (Nebbiolo) wines, is a leading producer of Boca.

- ✔ **Sizzano** *(sitz ZAH no):* The Sizzano zone is south of the town of Ghemme. The wine derives 40 to 60 percent from Nebbiolo and 15 to 40 percent from Vespolina, with up to 25 percent Bonarda. Having less Nebbiolo in the blend, Sizzano is lighter-bodied and drinkable sooner than Ghemme, Gattinara, and Lessona. Giuseppe Bianchi is the leading producer.

- ✔ **Fara** *(FAH rah):* This is the southernmost DOC area of the seven Nebbiolo zones, and the lightest-bodied of the seven wines, as it contains only 30 to 50 percent Nebbiolo in its blend, along with 10 to 30 percent Vespolina, with up to 40 percent Bonarda Novarese. The well-known wine house, Dessilani, is the leading producer of Fara, making two Fara wines — one called Caramino and the other Lochera.

✔ **Colline Novaresi** *(co LEE nae no vah RAE see):* This large zone encompasses 26 communities throughout Novara province. It makes five varietal wines — Spanna (Nebbiolo), Bonarda, Barbera, Vespolina, and Croatina — as well as a blended dry red called Colline Novaresi Rosso (at least 30 percent Nebbiolo, up to 40 percent Bonarda, and up to 30 percent Vespolina and/or Croatina) and a dry white called Colline Novaresi Bianco, made entirely from Erbaluce. Cantalupo and Dessilani are two fine Colline Novaresi producers. The wines are good values, retailing for as low as $10.

✔ **Coste della Sesia** *(COSE tae del lah SAE see ah):* The newest DOC in Northern Piedmont, and similar to Colline Novaresi, but in the Vercelli province, where it covers 18 communities. Four varietal wines may use this DOC name: Spanna (Nebbiolo), Bonarda, Vespolina, and Croatina. Another three wines include Coste della Sesia Rosso (a dry, blended red made at least 50 percent from Nebbiolo or Bonarda or Vespolina or Croatina, with the optional addition of other red varieties; a *Novello* is also made); Coste della Sesia Rosato (a dry rosé from same varieties as the Rosso); and Coste della Sesia Bianco (a dry white, 100 percent Erbaluce). Two producers are Antoniolo and Nervi.

Recommended Novara-Vercelli wine producers

We name our recommended northeastern Piedmont producers alphabetically, with their specialties:

Antichi Vigneti di Cantalupo: Ghemme; Colline Novaresi

Antoniolo: Gattinara; Coste della Sesia Nebbiolo

Giuseppe Bianchi: Sizzano; Ghemme

Le Colline: Gattinara (Monsecco); Ghemme

Dessilani: Fara; Gattinara; Ghemme; Colline Novaresi Spanna

Umberto Fiore: Gattinara

Nervi: Gattinara; Coste della Sesia Spanna

Luigi Perazzi: Bramaterra

Sella: Lessona; Bramaterra

Travaglini: Gattinara

Antonio Vallana: Boca; Spanna

Villa Era: Spanna

Other Piedmont Wines

Three DOC zones of Piedmont are off the beaten track. One is in the province of Cuneo — but in the foothills of the Alps, in the west of the region, about an hour's drive from Alba. The other two are also in the Alpine foothills, but farther north, mainly in the Torino province:

- **Colline Saluzzesi** *(co LEE nae sah lootz ZAE see):* This area, straddling the Po River in the western part of Cuneo province, is named after the town of Saluzzo, the last size-able town before the roads climb toward the mountain resorts. This area makes a varietally-labeled Pelaverga (the supposed aphrodisiac) that may be dry or sweetish, and a Quagliano, a pale, full-bodied, but sweetish red from a local variety of the same name, that can be still or sparkling. There's also a Colline Saluzzesi Rosso that's at least 60 percent Pelaverga and/or Barbera.

- **Pinerolese** *(pee neh ro LAE sae):* This area north of the Colline Saluzzesi zone overlaps it somewhat. Its wines are all red, except for a rosé, and they include five varietal wines (Barbera, Bonarda, Freisa, Dolcetto, and Doux d'Henry). There's also a Pinerolese Rosso (made at least 50 percent from Barbera, Bonarda, Nebbiolo, and Neretto, singly or together), a Rosato (from the same varieties as the Rosso), and Pineroloese Ramie *(RAH mee ae),* a red from a two-village sub-zone that's blended from 30 percent Avana, at least 20 percent Neretto, and at least 15 percent Averengo, with up to 35 percent of other local grapes permitted.

- **Valsusa** *(vahl SOO sah):* A new DOC zone (1997) in the area known as the Susa Valley, in Torino province. It produces only a red wine made at least 60 percent from Barbera, Dolcetto, Neretta, or Avana, together or alone— a dry, moderately tannic red; also *Novello.*

The final DOC of Piedmont is, literally, **Piemonte.** From its name, you'd think that this appellation would cover the entire region, but in fact it applies specifically to vineyards only in Asti, Alessandria, and Cuneo (which, anyway, are most of Piedmont's vineyards). It's a multi-purpose designation, providing a fall-back DOC for producers making Barbera, Grignolino, Brachetto, Cortese, Moscato, or Chardonnay in other parts of the three provinces — if their wines somehow don't precisely fit the DOC requirements for their zone, or if they choose not to use their local DOC for whatever reason. The following types of wines may be Piemonte DOC:

- ✔ A *spumante* made from Chardonnay, Pinot Bianco, Pinot Grigio, and Pinot Nero, in any combination or singly; and varietally-labeled Spumante wines from any of these grapes other than Chardonnay

- ✔ Five varietal wines: Cortese, Chardonnay, Barbera, Bonarda, and Grignolino

- ✔ A varietally-labeled Brachetto from a limited sub-zone, and from the same area, a still or *frizzante* Moscato or a Moscato *passito*, from dried grapes

Chapter 5

Other Northwest Regions

In This Chapter

▶ The French accent of Valle d'Aosta

▶ Where to eat in the Alps

▶ Liguria's charming vacation wines

▶ Pigato, Rossese, and other obscure grapes

*L*iguria, the region bordering Piedmont to the south, and Valle d'Aosta, the region bordering Piedmont to the north, are only about as distant from each other as Baltimore is from New York City — as the crow flies. But the two regions couldn't be more different: Valle d'Aosta is thoroughly alpine, and Liguria is the Italian Riviera. (In fact, not being a crow, you'd need the better part of a day to travel from one region to the other, crossing the Alps into Piedmont and crossing the Apennines into Liguria.) Besides being different from each other, these two regions are different from every other part of Italy, too. As are their wines.

The wines of Liguria and Valle d'Aosta aren't the greatest in Italy, nor are they particularly easy to find in foreign markets, but they perfectly depict one of the fascinating aspects of Italy and its wines: the incredible local color.

Alpine Valle d'Aosta

When we visit Piedmont, we like to land in Geneva, Switzerland, just so that we can drive through the Alps of southeast France, into Italy, and through the dramatically beautiful Valle d'Aosta, surrounded by mountains. Valle d'Aosta *(VAH lae dah OHS tah),* or Aosta Valley, home of the famed ski resort town, Courmayeur, sits in the extreme north-west corner of Italy (see Figure 1-1). It is entirely in the Alps; France and Switzerland are to its north, France is to its west, and Piedmont is directly south and east.

Valle d'Aosta is Italy's smallest region, in size, population, and the amount of wine produced. About 119,000 hardy souls live in this cold, alpine outpost, part of which is covered with snow for at least half of every year. If you travel there, don't forget your mittens — but it also helps if you know a bit of French or Italian. French is as widely spoken here as Italian, but very little English is heard.

The town of Aosta, the capital of the region, is in the region's very center. It's also the heart of the region's winegrowing; vineyard areas are located east and west of town, along the Dora Baltea River, which flows down from Mont Blanc, the Alps' highest peak (see Figure 5-1).

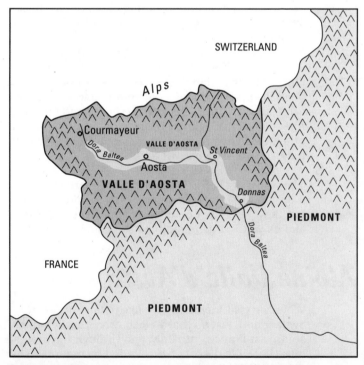

Figure 5-1: Valle d'Aosta wine zones follow the Dora Baltea River.

But Valle d'Aosta's vineyards yield only about 330,000 cases of wine annually — fewer cases than one large Champagne house, such as Lanson or Pommery, produces each year. And the region's total annual DOC wine production is *really* miniscule, amounting to 36,000 cases. It has only one DOC, Valle d'Aosta/Vallée d'Aoste — written in both Italian and French, as many locals call French their first language.

Red wines from cool climes

Burton Anderson, in his epic tome on Italian wines, *The Wine Atlas of Italy,* refers to the grape growers who work the steep terraces carved into the Alps in the Valle d'Aosta, and says, "There are few places in Italy or anywhere else where viticulture could be so aptly described as heroic." Tractors are useless on the precipitous slopes; work must be done on foot, with only a few brave mules, perhaps, to help.

We were surprised when we first discovered that 75 percent of the wine in the region is red, because red wine grapes need summer heat to ripen. But when we came to realize that the climate in Aosta's Central Valley, where many of the vineyards are, is dry and hot in the summer, red wine production made sense. Despite the climate, however, many of the red wines are relatively light-bodied and high in acidity.

The soil is primarily sandy on the high slopes, and a blend of alluvial sand, clay, and gravel in the valley. The climate is strictly continental — intensely cold in the winter, and really hot in July and August — at least in the valley. But summer ends in early September; only early-maturing red grape varieties, such as Pinot Noir, Gamay, Petit Rouge (the best and most reliable native red variety), and Dolcetto, can regularly produce decent red wines here. In the southeastern part of Aosta Valley, just at the Piedmont border, is a vineyard area, Donnas, where Nebbiolo grows. Donnas wines are quite light in body, bearing only a vague resemblance to the sturdy Barolo and Barbaresco wines of Southern Piedmont.

The region's most interesting wine for us is white; it's called Blanc de Morgex et de la Salle (or simply, Blanc de Morgex). This vineyard area, in the northwest (mainly French speaking) part of the region, south of Courmayeur, is the highest vineyard in Europe, climbing as high as 3,937 feet! Blanc de Morgex, an indigenous variety, makes a very light, lively wine, with aromas of mountain grasses. It's ideal as an apéritif in the summer — but practically all of its small production stays in Valle d'Aosta.

Regional and varietal wines

The Valle d'Aosta DOC wine zone extends for about 50 miles, from just south of Courmayeur in the northwest to Donnas in the southeast; it follows the path of the Dora Baltea River, which created the Aosta Valley. The vineyards are along this valley, mainly on the eastern side, and in smaller valleys near the river. The single Valle d'Aosta DOC designation encompasses 22 wines, which differ according to their grape varieties or vineyard location — both of which can appear on the label. The three vineyard areas are the following:

- **Valdigne** *(vahl DEEN yae):* The upper valley, in northwest Valle d'Aosta

- **Valle Centrale** *(VAH lae chen TRAH lae):* The central valley, east and west of Aosta

- **Bassa Valle** *(BAH sah VAH lae):* The lower valley, in southeast Valle d'Aosta

On the high slopes of the Valdigne, around the community of Morgex, the white variety Blanc de Morgex thrives, making the wine called **Blanc de Morgex et de la Salle.** This might be one of the only varieties that can grow nearly 4,000 feet above sea level! Besides its still (non-sparkling) wine, there's also a sparkling wine, in *extra-brut*, *brut*, and *demi-sec* versions. The phyllloxera louse, which devastated Europe's vineyards in the late 19th century, never made it this high up to the Morgex vineyards, and so the vines are that rare exception in Europe — planted on ungrafted rootstocks.

The Central Valley (Valle Centrale) has four vineyard subzones, and produces most of the region's wines:

- **Enfer d'Arvier** *(on fer DAR vee ae)* is a relatively fullbodied, rustic red wine with a slightly bitter finish; it's produced around the village of Arvier, west of Aosta, and made mainly from Petit Rouge, blended with Dolcetto, Pinot Noir, Gamay, and two native red varieties, Vien de Nus and Neyret.

✔ **Torrette** *(tor rett)* is a dry red wine that's lighter-bodied and more finesseful than the red Enfer d'Arvier. The Torrette sub-zone is east of Arvier. Made from 70 percent Petit Rouge, with Pinot Noir and/or Gamay and/or Dolcetto and/or three native red varieties: Fumin, Vien de Nus, and Neyret.

✔ **Nus** *(noos)* is a village and the name of three wines, a Rosso or Rouge, made from at least 50 percent Vien de Nus, with at least 40 percent Petit Rouge and/or Pinot Noir; a very aromatic dry white called Malvoisie, which is the local name for the Pinot Gris variety; and a Malvoisie *passito*. The Nus sub-zone is a fairly large vineyard area that runs east of Aosta.

✔ **Chambave** *(shahm BAHV)* is a village just east of Nus; the sub-zone also includes the communities of St. Vincent, and Châtillon. Chambave has three DOC wines: a Rosso or Rouge, made from at least 60 percent Petit Rouge, with Dolcetto and/or Gamay and/or Pinot Noir; a delicate, dry, aromatic Moscato Bianco; and a sweet, golden Moscato *passito*.

The Lower Valley (Bassa Valle) has two wines:

✔ **Arnad-Montjovet** *(ahr nahd mahn jho vae)* is a dry red, medium-bodied wine that's at least 70 percent Nebbiolo, with Dolcetto and/or Vien de Nus and/or Pinot Noir and/or Neyret and/or Freisa. The vineyards are south and east of the Chambave area.

✔ **Donnas** (or Donnaz) is a red DOC wine that's at least 85 percent Nebbiolo, with Freisa and/or Vien du Nuys and/or Neyrat; the vineyards are in the extreme southeast part of Valle d'Aosta.

Typical of all Nebbiolo-based wines, both Arnad-Montjovet and Donnas are quite austere when young, and need a few years to soften. Neither one reaches the quality of Carema, the 100 percent-Nebbiolo wine that comes from just south of Donnas, in Piedmont.

Other Valle d'Aosta DOC wines include nine varietal wines that must contain at least 90 percent of their named variety: Müller-Thurgau, Gamay, Pinot Noir/Nero (made either as a red or white wine), Pinot Grigio/Gris, Petite Arvine (a white Swiss variety), Chardonnay, Premetta (a native red variety), Fumin (a purplish-red variety), and Petit Rouge. Valle d'Aosta Bianco (or Blanc), Rosso (or Rouge), and Rosato (or Rosé) may contain any locally-grown varieties of the proper color.

The best-known producer in the Valle d'Aosta region, and the one whose wines you see most frequently abroad, is Ezio Voyat. Located in Chambave, Voyat makes all the Chambave DOC wines plus a number of fine table wines *(vini da tavola)*, including an excellent dry Moscato called La Gazzella, a Moscato Passito called Le Muraglie, and a dry red called Rosso Le Muraglie. The most renowned winery making Blanc de Morgex is Maison Alberto Vevey, whose winery is in Morgex, with vineyards in Morgex and La Salle. (Valle d'Aosta has no IGT designations; its non-DOC wines are all *vini da tavola*.)

Two great Alpine rest stops

In the course of our journeys through Valle d'Aosta, we've discovered two wonderful restaurants. One is La Maison de Filippo, in the tiny mountain village of Entrèves, a hamlet of Courmayeur. Entrèves sits just off the main road, about a mile south of the (France to Italy) Mont Blanc Tunnel. The restaurant's setting is storybook beautiful; the building is nestled into the mountains, with a gorgeous view of the town church and the Alps behind it. The food is hearty mountain Italian, family style; you should be hungry, because you'll be passed about a dozen "first plates" (which you can choose to eat or not) before your main course. The wines are strictly local, not memorable, but interesting. During warm weather,

you can dine outdoors; if it's cold, roaring fireplaces warm the inside. La Maison de Filippo is a very typical, casual Italian Alps restaurant. Great place for lunch!

Our other favorite, La Clusaz, is both a restaurant and an inn. It's in the commune of Gignod, on the main road which heads towards the Grand Saint Bernard Pass into Switzerland, north of Aosta. La Clusaz is more formal, at least in the evening; the food is excellent, and the wine list is truly superb, with great wines — served in fine glassware — from all the major regions of Italy. The place boasts a roaring fireplace, and rooms are available.

Other prominent producers in Valle d'Aosta are the following: La Cave du Vin Blanc de Morgex et de La Salle, Antoine Charrére et Fils, Les Crêtes, La Crotta di Vegneron, Fratelli Grosjean, and Renato Anselmet.

Liguria: The Riviera

Liguria offers something for everyone. Its capital, Genoa, is one of Italy's great, historic cities, home of Christopher Columbus; in the Middle Ages, when the waterways were all-important, the two great seaport city-states and rivals — Genoa and Venice — ruled the world. Liguria also boasts the dramatic beauty of the precipitous Apennine Mountains, where you find terraced vineyards clinging to the slopes in the region called Cinque Terre (meaning "five lands"), and descending in a sheer drop into the sea. After you trek through the mountain paths in Cinque Terre, you can cool off at any number of fine beaches that dot the Ligurian Riviera.

Liguria is a small, narrow region (18th of 20 in size) in the southernmost part of northwest Italy. It hugs the coast of Italy from the French Riviera in the west to Tuscany in the south. Piedmont is to the north, and the Ligurian Sea (part of the Mediterranean) borders Liguria to the south (see Figure 1-1).

So much of Liguria is mountainous or urban that not much land is left for vineyards; the region produces only about one and a half million cases of wine annually — less than half of one percent of Italy's annual total. And yet wine has been made here for over 2,500 years, initially by the Greeks and/or the Etruscans (the early inhabitants of Tuscany), and later by the Liguri tribe, who settled here. The Romans particularly prized the wines of Cinque Terre — an area made up of five villages on the cliffs of eastern Liguria.

Liguria and Valle d'Aosta *do* have many things in common: Both areas are mountainous, neither area makes much wine (and certainly not any "important" wine), and in both areas, cultivation of the vines must be done by hand. (In Liguria's Cinque Terre, a monorail transports grapes to a road below.)

One significant difference in the two areas is the type of wine produced: Only about 12 percent of Liguria's wines are DOC, and 80 percent of this is white, whereas most of Valle d'Aosta's wines are red. Perhaps the needs of the inhabitants play a role: In alpine Valle d'Aosta, people need the warming effects of red wine to get through the winter; in the mild, sunny climate of Liguria, chilled white wines are in order while relaxing by the sea.

Liguria's vineyards and wines

Liguria has a Mediterranean climate: fairly hot, dry summers, with mild winters. Being on the seacoast, it receives more than its share of autumn rains, jeopardizing late-maturing grape varieties. The soil is poor and stony throughout the region, but grapevines and olive trees thrive (many connoisseurs regard Ligurian olive oil as the best in Italy). The sunny summers favor the vineyards on the coastal flank of the mountains; Liguria's interior is too cool and damp for grapevines. Liguria has six DOC zones, which fall into two general areas (see Figure 5-2):

 ✔ **The western Riviera (west of Genoa, near the French Riviera):** This area, the "Riviera di Ponente," includes the DOCs Rossese di Dolceacqua and Riviera Ligure di Ponente.

 ✔ **The eastern Riviera (east of Genoa, nearer to Tuscany):** This area, the "Riviera di Levante," includes the DOCs Cinqueterre, Colli di Lune, Colline di Levanto, and Golfo del Tigullio.

The region's IGT designations are Colline Savonesi and Val Polcevera.

Liguria's two traditional vineyard areas, which became its first two DOCs, are Cinqueterre *(CHEEN kwae TER rae),* an area of five fishing villages along the cliffs of the easternmost coastline, which are collectively known as Cinque Terre; and Rossese di Dolceaqua *(rohs SAE sae dee dohl chae AH kwah),* or simply Dolceaqua, the western area next to France.

Dolceacqua

Rossese di Dolceacqua is a red wine from the Rossese grape grown around the medieval town of Dolceacqua, in western Liguria. Vineyards in 13 villages extend from the coast near the city of Ventimiglia into the foothills of the Ligurian Alps. Rossese is Liguria's best known red wine, and Dolceacqua is the finest version of it. At its best, Dolceacqua is an aromatic, full-flavored, soft wine with good depth — but it's best young.

Riviera Ligure di Ponente

The large Riviera Ligure di Ponente *(ree vee AE rah lee GOO rae dee po NEN tae)* DOC area extends from the French border to just west of Genoa, overlapping Dolceacqua. Two whites and two reds are made here; the whites — Pigato and Vermentino, both varietal wines — have the most renown. The indigenous Pigato grape makes a rather full-bodied, dry, fruity white wine, with a slightly almondy flavor and a touch of bitterness on the finish — similar to Gavi from Piedmont, but weightier and, frankly, better. Vermentino is similar to Pigato, but a bit lighter and more delicate. Both whites can accompany the Ligurian specialty, *pasta al pesto*.

Ormeasco, a variant of Dolcetto, grows in the western part of the zone. The red wine made from this variety is dry and medium-bodied, with a slightly bitter finish. A dry rosé version of this wine, with its own DOC name, Ormeasco Sciac-trà, also exists. Riviera Ligure di Ponente Rossese is a lighter-bodied wine than the Rossese of Dolceacqua. Pigato, Vermentino, and Rossese wines with the names Albenga, Finale, or Riviera dei Fiore come from grapes grown exclusively in those sub-zones.

Cinqueterre

This limited zone is made up of steep, terraced hillsides overlooking the sea around the town of La Spezia and five villages that gave Cinque Terre its name: Monterosso, Vernazza, Corniglia, Manarola, and Riomaggiore. The light-bodied, neutral-tasting Cinqueterre white is at least 60 percent Bosco, with Albarola and/or Vermentino. Quality-oriented producers tend to use a full 40 percent Vermentino, clearly the best variety of the three — but because tourists buy Cinqueterre on its name alone, little incentive exists to improve this rather vapid, overrated wine. A rich, high-alcohol (17 percent), tawny-colored dessert wine, called Sciacchetrà *(shahk keh TRA)*, made from the same grape varieties as Cinqueterre, but semi-dried, is much finer. At any rate, the Cinque Terre vineyards are so difficult to work that production is declining.

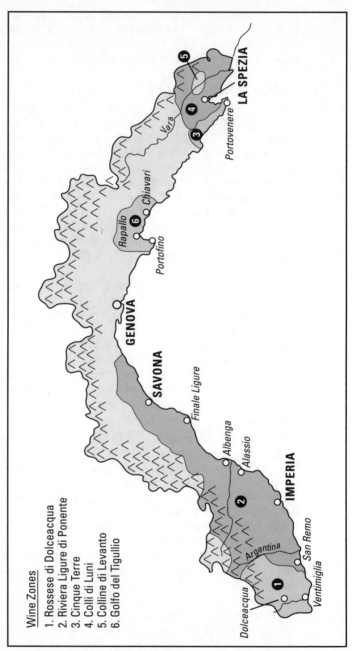

Figure 5-2: Liguria's wine zones are east and west of Genoa.

Seeing Cinque Terre

If you're in this beautiful part of the world, take the local train from La Spezia to Riomaggiore, the eastern-most of the *cinque terre,* and hike along the footpaths that link the five villages. In this way, you capture the true majesty of Cinque Terre, one of the most dramatically beautiful areas in the world. When you reach the last village, Monterosso, you can either take the train or start hiking back. The train stops at each of the five villages.

Colli di Luni

The Colli di Luni *(CO lee dee LOO nee)* DOC area, in the hills of eastern Liguria, extends slightly into Tuscany. The Tuscan influence is evident, as the area's red wines use Sangiovese and its whites Trebbiano, the two most common Tuscan varieties. The three Colli di Luni wines are a Rosso (60 to 70 percent Sangiovese), a Bianco (at least 35 percent Vermentino, with 25 to 40 percent Trebbiano Toscano), and a Vermentino. The whites, especially the Vermentino, are considerably better than the dry white wine of Cinque Terre.

Colline di Levanto

Colline di Levanto *(co LEE nae dee leh VAHN toh)* is actually surrounded by the larger Colli di Luni zone. Colline di Levanto Bianco is at least 40 percent Vermentino, with at least 20 percent Albarola. The Rosso is at least 40 percent Sangiovese and at least 20 percent Ciliegiolo.

Golfo del Tigullio

Liguria's newest DOC wine, Golfo del Tigullio *(GOHL foh del tee GOO lee oh)* is from a zone on the coast, about 15 miles east of Genoa; this area includes the Italian Riviera's most renowned resort town, Portofino. DOC wines include Golfo del Tigullio Rosso (mainly Dolcetto) and three varietal wines: two whites, Vermentino and the now rare Bianchetta Genovese; and the red Ciliegiolo. Enoteca Bisson, known for its Vermentino, is the area's leading producer.

Ligurian wine producers

Unfortunately, the combination of small wine production and heavy tourist traffic means that very little Ligurian wine makes its way out of the region — but we have seen Pigato and Vermentino in New York restaurants (including a Ligurian restaurant called Cinque Terre). Here are our recommended Ligurian wine producers, alphabetically:

Anfossi
Maria Donata Bianchi
Enoteca Bisson
Bruna
Giobatta Mandino Cane
Colle dei Bardellini
La Colombiera
Cooperativa Agricola di
   Cinqueterre
Walter De Battè
Cascina du Fèipu

Forlini e Cappellini
Tenuta Giunchio
Octaviano Lambruschi
Lupi
Terre Bianche
Cascina delle Terre Rosse
Il Torchio
La Vecchia Cantina
Claudio Vio

Chapter 6

North-Central Italy

In This Chapter

▶ Affordable Nebbiolo wines

▶ Not one, but two, major sparkling wine regions!

▶ Lakeside delights

▶ Lambrusco and sausage

▶ Fizzy whites and reds galore

*L*ombardy, a large, scenic region, is more famous as the home of Milan — fashion capital of the world and the business-industrial center of Italy — than as a wine-producing region. It's also renowned as a tourist mecca, thanks to the fabulously beautiful Lake Como and Lake Garda, plus the majestic Alps that cover Lombardy's northern third. But Lombardy is also the home of most of Italy's best sparkling wines and interesting reds made from Piedmont's famed Nebbiolo variety.

Emilia-Romagna is really two regions joined at the hip. The Emilia sub-region is often called the gastronomic capital of Italy; it's the home of Bologna, Modena (renowned for balsamic vinegar, among other gastronomic delicacies), Parma, and the Reggiano district (is there a better cheese than Parmegiano Reggiano?). Emilia is also the home of one of Italy's most famous wines — Lambrusco.

Lombardy Has It All

In many ways, Lombardy is the most fortunate region in Italy — and a pretty darn good place to live. It has everything going for it. The mighty Po River, Italy's largest, which forms most of the region's southern border, has created a vast fertile plain for cultivating rice and wheat. Lombardy's beautiful lakes spread across the center of the region, from one end to the other, crowned by the Alps in the north. Thriving cities such as Milan, Bergamo, and Brescia, provide a high quality of life for their residents, including great wine and food.

Lombardy is directly south of Switzerland, east of Piedmont, north of Emilia-Romagna, and west of Veneto and Trentino-Alto Adige (see Figure 1-1). It is the fourth largest region in Italy, and the most-highly populated. It's also the wealthiest.

Because of the incredibly varied climate and terrain of the region, Lombardy produces diverse wines. But "cool" is the operative climatic descriptor for all of Lombardy's wine areas.

The region's far northern wine zone is the Valtellina — which makes one of Lombardy's two DOCG wines. Here, the Nebbiolo grape has found a second home. The wines certainly don't resemble the more muscular Nebbiolo wines — Barolo and Barbaresco — of warmer, Southern Piedmont, but they're interesting, nevertheless, and a lot less expensive than their famous Piedmont cousins.

The most renowned wines of Lombardy are its sparkling wines. In fact, two distinct wine zones exist: Oltrepó Pavese in the region's southwest corner, and Franciacorta (the region's other DOCG wine), in the hills west of Brescia, around breezy Lake Iseo (in central Lombardy; see Figure 6-1). Most of Italy's best sparklers are made in Franciacorta. Several wine zones are scattered throughout the rest of Lombardy, producing light-to medium-bodied red, rosé, and white wines, many of which are consumed on the Riviera of Lake Garda. The most famous Lake Garda wine is a white wine called Lugana.

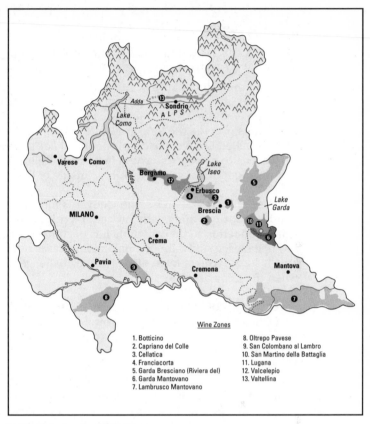

Figure 6-1: Lombardy's wine zones.

Wine Zones

1. Botticino
2. Capriano del Colle
3. Cellatica
4. Franciacorta
5. Garda Bresciano (Riviera del)
6. Garda Mantovano
7. Lambrusco Mantovano

8. Oltrepo Pavese
9. San Colombano al Lambro
10. San Martino della Battaglia
11. Lugana
12. Valcelepio
13. Valtellina

The Valtellina: Nebbiolo's most austere face

In the northernmost part of Lombardy, just east of Lake Como, the Adda River and its valley cut through the steep slopes of the Alps, from west to east. This isolated alpine terrain is one of the unlikeliest places in the world to find vineyards — but they indeed are here. To see them clinging to the high mountainsides, some at 2,500 feet altitude, is an awe-inspiring sight — and has been, since the 5th century. If you ever visit this area, continue east, if you're an adventurer, and drive into Switzerland on incredibly steep roads through the Stelvio Pass (we did it, *once*). Much of the wine from this part of Lombardy, in fact, *is* consumed by the Swiss.

Along a dramatic 30-mile stretch called the Valtellina *(vahl tel LEE nah)*, Nebbiolo grapevines flourish in south-facing vineyards on the sunny banks of the Adda River. The steep Alps on both sides protect the valley from harsh, cold weather, and also trap heat; the stony soil retains this heat at night. These conditions provide the long growing season that Nebbiolo (locally called Chiavennasca, pronounced *key ah ven NAHS cah)* needs to ripen properly. In fact, the Valtellina is the only major production zone of Nebbiolo outside of Piedmont.

Because of their steepness, the vineyards must be tended by hand, a laborious and costly procedure; this is one reason that wine production in the Valtellina has declined over the past few decades, to only about a half-million cases annually. The sturdy local farmers must also face the challenge of landslides when the rains are heavy.

Several types of Valtellina wine exist, differentiated primarily according to where the grapes grow. Simpler wines, labeled Valtellina DOC, come from grapes (mainly Nebbiolo) grown anywhere in the Valtellina district, while wines with the better Valtellina Superiore DOCG designation (about one-third of Valtellina's wines) come from riper grapes grown in a smaller area that includes four specific sub-zones. Valtellina Superiore wines must age a minimum of two years, and those aged four years are called Valtellina Superiore Riserva. Almost all of them are light- to medium-bodied reds.

The Valtellina Superiore sub-districts

The four Valtellina Superiore sub-zones, from west to east, are Sassella, Grumello, Inferno, and Valgella. Wines made from grapes grown in one of these four areas carry the name of the area on their labels.

Of these four wines, Sassella is generally the finest and the longest lasting (although Valtellina wines — with one exception noted later — usually won't age well beyond seven or eight years), followed by Grumello, then Inferno, with Valgella definitely the lightest wine of the four. The Valgella sub-zone is the largest of the four, and produces the most wine, although it's generally not *riserva*-grade. The Inferno area — one of

Italy's most colorful wine names — is quite rocky, and is the warmest area in the Adda Valley (hence its name!).

Sturdy Sfursat

Just as Valpolicella has its stronger brother, Amarone (see Chapter 7), Valtellina has its Sfursat *(s'foor sat)*, also known as Sforzato. Like Amarone, Sfursat is made with semi-dried, extra-ripe grapes. The resulting wine is high in alcohol (14.5 percent minimum), sturdy, full-bodied, and concentrated. Sfursat can easily last up to 20 years or more, and is great with cheeses such as Parmesan or Asiago, beef dishes, and stews. Sfursat needs about four hours of aeration in a decanter to soften.

Enjoying Valtellina wines

With the exception of Sfursat, Valtellina wines are light red in color (typical of Nebbiolo), and they turn garnet with about six years of aging. They have pronounced Nebbiolo aromas (tar, violets, and strawberries), and are very dry, even austere, with high acidity and tannin. Unlike Piedmont's major Nebbiolo wines, Barolo and Barbaresco (see Chapter 5), Valtellina wines are delicate and elegant, and are best in their youth. They go well with pasta dishes, risotto, and light meat dishes, such as chicken.

Wine drinkers in the U.S. see only two Valtellina producers on a consistent basis: Nino Negri, whose wines retail for $15 to $18 (excellent Sfursats for $30 to $40), and Rainoldi, whose wines are in the $8 to $15 range. Negri's 1997 Sfursat 5 Stelle, about $40, is Valtellina's current superstar.

Oltrepó Pavese: Sparkling wines and more

Pavia is a town and a province in southwest Lombardy, directly south of Milan. That part of the province south of the River Po is known as Oltrepó Pavese *(ohl trae POH pah VAE sae)*, meaning "Pavia across the Po" (see Figure 6-1). More than half of Lombardy's wine — and two-thirds of its DOC wine — is produced here, where the plains of the Po Valley give way to the foothills of the Apennine Mountains to their south. Oltrepó Pavese (once a part of Piedmont, its neighbor to the west) provides Milan with much of its everyday wines, mainly red, and provides all of Italy with sparkling wines.

The Piedmontese connection

Oltrepó Pavese is a prime source for Pinot Nero, especially light-bodied, acidic Pinot Nero that's good for sparkling wines. Many sparkling wine producers in Piedmont — such as Martini & Rossi, Fontanafredda and Gancia — buy Pinot Nero and other varieties of grapes and juice from this district. (Sparkling wines are often made from grapes brought in from a different region.) The great Piedmontese red wine producer, Bruno Giacosa, buys his Pinot Nero in Oltrepó Pavese, and he makes clearly one of Italy's best sparkling wines — simply called Bruno Giacosa Brut (100 percent Pino Nero) — which we order in Italian restaurants every time we see it.

The wines of Oltrepó Pavese

The Oltrepó Pavese area produces white, rosé, red, and sparkling wines. The main type of red is a blended wine simply called "Oltrepó Pavese Rosso," from Barbera, Croatina, Uva Rara (a typical local trio), Vespolina, and Pinot Nero grapes; aged two years, it becomes *riserva*. The same varieties make a rosé as well as two reds from specific zones within the district; these reds are Buttafuoco *(boo tah FWOH coh,* meaning "fire-thrower") and Sangue di Guida *(SAHN gwae dee JEW dah,* meaning "Judas' blood"). Buttafuoco is dry or *frizzante,* and Sangue di Guida is usually made in a *frizzante,* slightly sweet style.

Other Oltrepó Pavese reds can also be varietal wines, from Barbera, Croatina (under its local name, Bonarda), or Cabernet Sauvignon. Barbera is Oltrepó's leading red variety, and a best-selling wine; it can be lightly sparkling *(frizzante),* as the Bonarda often is. When made as a *frizzante,* Bonarda — less acidic than Barbera — goes well with sausages and other fatty meats.

Nine varietal Oltrepó Pavese white wines are Welschriesling (labeled as Riesling Italico), Riesling (labeled Riesling Renano), Cortese, Moscato, Malvasia, Pinot Grigio, Chardonnay, Sauvignon, and Pinot Nero (vinified as a white wine). Most of them come in both still and fizzy styles, and several can be sparkling. Moscato has two additional variations: Moscato *liquoroso,* a dry or sweet fortified style; and Moscato *passito,* a sweet style from dried grapes.

The best white or rosé sparkling wines with the Oltrepó Pavese designation carry the words *metodo classico* (classic, or Champagne, method) and derive mainly from Pinot Nero, with up to 30 percent Pinot Bianco, Chardonnay, and/or Pinot Grigio.

Nearby — but on the Milan side of the Po River — a DOC zone called **San Colombano** *(sahn coh lohm BAH noh),* makes only one type of wine, a dry red mainly from Croatina, Barbera, and Uva Rara.

A few leading Oltrepó Pavese producers

Historically, the Frecciarossa estate (which makes the wine with the red arrow on its label), has been the most famous Oltrepó Pavese wine estate; after a down period, it has now returned to form, thanks to the work of renowned enologist Franco Bernabei. Other top producers from the area include Lino Maga, La Muiraghina, Tenuta Mazzolino, and Doria for still wines; Fontanachiara for sparkling wine; and Anteo and Monsupello for both sparkling and still wines.

Franciacorta: Sparklers with style

Just northwest of the city of Brescia lies the greatest sparkling wine zone of Italy, and one of the best anywhere outside of Champagne — Franciacorta *(frahn cha COR tah).* It's the home of Italy's largest *méthode champenoise* sparkling wine house, Guido Berlucci, (see *Wine For Dummies* or *Champagne For Dummies,* both published by Hungry Minds, Inc., for an explanation of *méthode champenoise*) as well as the two most prestigious sparkling wine houses in Italy, Ca' del Bosco and Bellavista.

Unlike Oltrepó Pavese, where Pinot Nero is the primary variety for sparkling wines, Chardonnay and Pinot Bianco are the main grapes of Franciacorta sparklers, with a maximum of 15 percent Pinot Nero. A rosé style, however, requires a *minimum* of 15 percent Pinot Nero in its blend. A *crémant* style (a gentler wine, with lower CO_2 pressure) may contain no Pinot Nero. This last style is a specialty of Franciacorta; the wines carry the trademarked name, *Satèn.* Some of the district's very best sparklers, such as Ca'del Bosco's *Satèn,* are this style.

Franciacorta non-vintage wines must age 18 months in the bottle (vintage-dated wines, 30 months) — an unusually strict requirement that speaks to the seriousness of the producers. Vintage-dated wines must be only 85 percent from the vintage indicated, however, and *brut* (dry) wines may contain up to 20 grams per liter of sugar, compared to only 15 for *brut* Champagnes.

Then and now in Franciacorta

Conditions are ideal for grape growing in the Franciacorta zone, thanks to the area's stony, well-drained soil, and to nearby Lake Iseo, which has a moderating effect on the climate. Local growers have produced red and white still wines for centuries. But Franciacorta has emerged as a major wine zone only in the last 40 years, since a young enologist named Franco Ziliani convinced the Berlucchi estate to plant Pinot Nero and make *méthode champenoise* sparkling wines.

Bellucchi released its first 3,000 bottles of *champenoise* sparkling wines in the early 1960s; by 1975, Berlucchi Cuvée Imperiale had become Italy's best-selling *champenoise* sparkling wine; by 1990 Berlucchi was producing 5 million bottles of sparkling wine a year — about one-third of Italy's total. To sustain this large volume, however, the company has had to source about 75 percent of its grapes outside Franciacorta.

Now, the producers of Franciacorta are firmly committed to sparkling wine. In 1995, when Franciacorta was elevated to DOCG status, they "spun off" their still wine production into a separate DOC appellation, **Terre di Franciacorta.** These white wines are made from the same varieties as the sparkling wine — Chardonnay, Pinot Blanc, and Pinot Noir — together or singly, but not varietally labeled. A creative formula for Terre di Franciacorta Rosso allows plenty of stylistic freedom to individual producers: a minimum of 25 percent Cabernet Franc and Cabernet Sauvignon, with a minimum of 10 percent each of Barbera, Nebbiolo, and Merlot. Time will tell which variation of this formula ultimately works best.

Other Franciacorta estates

Although many of Italy's sparkling wines are made by very large companies from purchased grapes or wine, small private estates (that make wine from their own grapes) are the standard in Franciacorta. We recommend eight producers, all leaders in the area, for sparkling wines (mentioning their best still wines, too). Seven of them have vineyards in the Monte di Erbusco area in western Franciacorta, around the villages of Erbusco, Adro, and Capriolo, which seems to have the best microclimate for grapes destined for sparkling wine. We believe that many of their wines vie with Champagne as some of the world's best sparkling wines. In alphabetical order they are the following:

- ✔ **Bellavista:** This beautiful estate, which is now also home of the Michelin three-star Gualtiero Marchesi Restaurant and inn, is clearly one of the area's two quality leaders (along with Ca' del Bosco), and its prices reflect that status. Its least expensive sparkler, the Cuvée Brut NV, is a relative bargain at about $27 retail; the Vintage Grand Cuvée goes for $40; and the excellent, top-of-the-line Riserva Vittorio Moretti will cost you $90. Bellavista also makes a fine Chardonnay, a Cabernet Sauvignon-Merlot blend called Solesine, and a Pinot Nero called Casotte — all in the $40 to $45 price range.

- ✔ **Ca' del Bosco:** Mauizio Zanella, who founded this estate about 30 years ago, is Lombardy's most respected wine producer. His winery is state-of-the-art, and all of his wines, both still and sparkling, are superb. The basic Brut NV goes for $40, the Vintage Brut Zero is in the $52 to $55 range, the classic Vintage Satèn is $60, and the premium Cuvée Annamaria Clementi Vintage Brut is $65 to $70. Ca' del Bosco's Chardonnays and its Bordeaux-style red, Maurizio Zanella, are all first-rate.

- ✔ **Cavalleri:** Giovanni Cavalleri is making very good sparkling *bruts* as well as some of the best Chardonnays in the district. His Brut NV retails for $27 to $30, the Satèn is $32 to $35, and his Vintage Brut and Rosé are about $40.

- ✔ **Cornaleto:** A small but very good producer, not only for his Franciacorta, but also for a fine Rosso, made primarily from Cabernet Franc.

- ✔ **Enrico Gatti:** Another small winery with impressive Franciacorta, a still Bianco (mainly Chardonnay), and Rosso.

- ✔ **Monte Rossa:** This estate is the leader in the Corte Franca area, east of Erbusco and closer to Brescia. The soils here are more fertile than in the Erbusco area, and so Monte Rossa's *bruts* are rather full-bodied; the Satèn is a standout.

✔ **Ricci Curbastro:** A small, quality estate whose fine Satèn Brut retails for $45 to $50; its Rosso, Vigna Santella, is $30.

✔ **Uberti:** A small family winery making fine sparkling *bruts* and white wines, and a good Cabernet called Rosso dei Frati Priori.

Lake Garda's vineyards

Lake Garda is a great tourist attraction from spring through fall. On the eastern, or Veneto, side of the lake is the charming village of Sirmione and the famous wine village of Bardolino. On the western shores are four Lombardy wine districts.

Riviera del Garda Bresciano

Along the western shores of the lake lies the Riviera del Garda Bresciano zone (also known as Garda Bresciano; its extension in the Veneto region is Garda Orientale). This area makes delicious wines to quaff while sitting around Lake Garda — or any surrogate lake — in the summer. One of our favorite types of summer wines is Chiaretto *(kee ah REHT toh);* this term applies to several dry Italian deep-colored rosé wines. Here it's made mainly from the local Gropello grape, with Sangiovese, Barbera, and Marzemino (another local grape), and sometimes other varieties. This rosé is fresh, completely dry, and low in alcohol, with a slight bitterness in the finish. It's best when it's young and cool.

The Rosso from Riviera del Garda Bresciano *(riv ee AIR ah del GAR dah breh she AH noh)* is very similar to the Chiaretto, but darker and with a little more body. Gropello is a straight varietal wine, full-bodied, rich, and tannic. The local Bianco derives from Riesling or Welschriesling, together or singly.

Three Riviera del Garda producers to look for are Cascina La Pertica, Comincioli, and Costaripa. As you can imagine, the best places to find these wines are hotels and restaurants around Lake Garda. A good excuse to visit this lovely area!

Lugana

Lugana is a white wine area along the south shores of Lake Garda, a small part of which extends eastward into the Veneto region. Lugana is made from a particular sub-variety of Trebbiano called Trebbiano di Lugana. It's a dry, medium-bodied wine with good fruitiness and somewhat rich texture that can actually age for a few years — unlike other Trebbiano-based wines. It's perfect with lake fish.

The two finest producers are Visconti and the Ca'dei Frati estate. Ca' dei Frati's Lugana retails for $14 to $15, and its single-vineyard Lugana Brolettino is about $17 to $18 — a great value.

Other Garda DOCs

San Martino della Battaglia *(sahn mar TEE no del lah baht TAH l'yah)* is a white wine mainly from Lombardy but, like Lugana, its territory encroaches into Veneto. It derives from the Tocai Friulano variety — unusual for Lombardy — and is a dry wine of decent quality; a *liquoroso* style also exists.

Colli Morenici Mantovani del Garda *(COH lee more ae NEE chee mahn toh VAH nee del GAR dah),* also called Garda Colli Mantovani, is a Bianco blended from Trebbiano and Garganega, as well as a Rosso and Rosato from Molinara (a variety from nearby Veneto) and Merlot.

Other Lombardy DOC wines

Lombardy produces several other DOC wines whose names you might see in wine shops, sooner or later. Here we list these wines and the province they come from, and describe them briefly:

- ✔ **Valcalepio** *(vahl cah LAE pee oh);* Bergamo: Rosso blended from Merlot and Cabernet Sauvignon; Bianco from Pinot Bianco and Pinot Grigio; also Moscato Passito, a sweet red wine from dried Moscato Rosso grapes

- ✔ **Cellatica** *(chel LAH tee cah);* Brescia: Dry, light red made mainly from Schiava and Barbera

- ✔ **Botticino** *(boht tee CHEE noh);* Brescia: Dry red; same grapes as Cellatica

- ✔ **Capriano del Colle** *(cah pree AH noh del COH lae);* Brescia: Dry, lively red made mainly from Sangiovese and Marzemino; also a dry white from Trebbiano

- ✔ **Lambrusco Mantovano** *(lam BREW skoh mah toh VAH noh);* Mantova: Dry or semi-dry red

Emilia-Romagna: One Region, Really Two

Italians who live in this region tell you they're from Emilia or Romagna — never both. Emilia, the larger, western part of the region, identifies with northern Italy and Milan. Romagna, the southeastern third, looks towards Tuscany and Central Italy; it even shares two of Tuscany's main grape varieties, Sangiovese and Trebbiano. In Emilia, Lambrusco is the reigning king.

Emilia and Romagna *do* have some things in common:

- ✔ The Apennine Mountains (the spine of Italy, which starts in Southern Piedmont and Liguria in the northwest and ends in Southern Italy) occupy much of the region's southern flank.

- ✔ The plains of the Po Valley account for half the region's area.

- ✔ Cooperatives, such as Emilia's gigantic Riunite, dominate both halves of the region, accounting for 70 percent of Emilia-Romagna's wine production, and contributing to the region's rank as Italy's fourth largest wine producer.

The plain between Piacenza, in the northwest corner of Emilia, and Bologna in the east is known as the Val Padana. This area grows over two-thirds of Emilia's wines — much of it Lambrusco, a bubbly dry or sweet red from the Lambrusco grape variety. In the Apennine foothills south of Piacenza, Parma, and Bologna are some vineyard areas such as Colli Piacentini, Colli di Parma, and Colli Bolognesi, for more serious wines (see Figure 6-2).

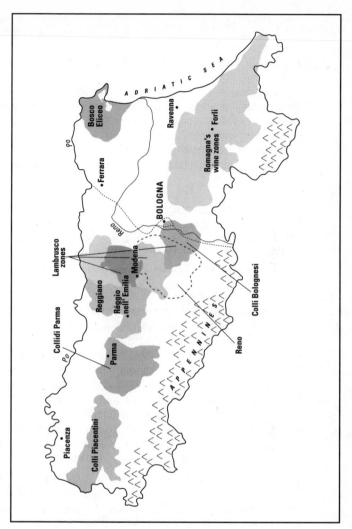

Figure 6-2: The dual region of Emilia-Romagna.

Emilia's beloved Lambrusco

During the 1970s and early 1980s, Lambrusco *(lam BREWS coh)* was *the* biggest-selling imported wine in the U.S. — from any country. Almost all of it was semi-sweet and slightly sparkling. As wine drinkers turned to dryer wines, Lambrusco sales decreased (although this inexpensive, easy-to-drink style of Lambrusco still has a following). And yet Lambrusco can be a more "serious" wine. The term is relative, of course: Any wine with Lambrusco's foamy pink froth and appealing berry flavors can't really fit in with the world's serious reds. But Emilians love their Lambrusco. The wine's bubbles and the high acidity of the dry style help cut through the rich local cuisine, built around salami, sausages, pasta, prosciutto, cheese, cream, and butter. (One of the most satisfying food and wine pairings we've ever experienced was a dry, bubbly Lambrusco with *cotechino con lenticchie,* fresh pork sausage served with lentils.)

Quite a lot of Lambrusco is DOC-level, from four zones in the provinces of Reggio Emilia *(RAE joe ae ME lee ah)* and Modena *(MOH deh nah).* The names of three of these zones are also, confusingly, the names of clones of the Lambrusco grape variety. These four types of Lambrusco are the following:

✔ **Lambrusco Reggiano** *(rej gee AH noh):* This is the largest zone for production and exports. Most of the Lambrusco grapes from the plains around the town of Reggio nell'Emilia are turned into light-bodied wines, *frizzante,* and semi-sweet. This area is the seat of the huge cooperative, Cantine Riunite, whose wines have been so successful in the U.S. In higher vineyards toward the south of the province, small producers, such as Venturini & Baldini, Medici, and Moro, make fuller-bodied, dry, deep-colored Lambrusco. Four different clones of Lambrusco can be used in Lambrusco Reggiano, along with up to 15 percent Ancellotta (a dark grape used for color).

✔ **Lambrusco di Sorbara** *(dee sor BAH rah):* The most highly regarded Lambrusco subvariety, or clone, Lambrusco di Sorbara, grows in the plains north of Modena, around the village of Sorbara, as does Lambrusco Salamino di Santa Croce. Lambrusco di Sorbara wine may contain only these two types of grapes, and the Sorbara clone must be at least 60 percent of the wine. The wine ranges from ruby to purple in color, and has fragrant, grapey aromas and flavors reminiscent of violets; like all Lambruscos, it can be dry or semi-sweet. Fine producers such as Cavacchioli (with its Vigna del Cristo) and Francesco Bellei make fresh, fruity, flamboyant Lambruscos — dry (for domestic sales) and semi-sweet (mainly for the export market).

✔ **Lambrusco Salamino di Santa Croce** *(sah lah MEE noh dee SAHN tah CROH chae)*: This wine comes from vineyards around the village of Santa Croce, about 7 miles west of Sorbara. Wines with this name contain at least 90 percent of the Salamino clone, which is similar to the Sorbara subvariety, but usually makes wines that are a bit lighter in color and body. The *frizzante* wines are dry or semi-sweet.

✔ **Lambrusco Grasparossa di Castelvetro** *(grahs pah ROHS sah di cas tel VAE troh):* The smallest of the four Lambrusco DOC zones, 10 miles south of Modena, in the foothills of the Apennines, near the village of Castelvetro. Here, small producers, such as Vittorio Graziano, Villa Barbieri, and Enzo Manicardi, *do* make serious Lambrusco — deep purple-red, dry, and full-bodied. You might have to visit Modena or Bologna to find a bottle, though. Wines are at least 85 percent from the Grasparossa clone. They also come in semi-sweet styles.

Most of the Lambrusco shipped to the U.S. carries the designation IGT Emilia. These wines, with brand names such as Riunite and Giacobazzi, sell for $5 per 750 ml bottle. Dry Lambruscos, many of which *are* DOC, and some of which are *spumante,* are a small category — difficult to find outside of Emilia.

Another DOC wine from the Emilian plains is **Montuni del Reno,** a dry or semi-sweet white, still or fizzy, from the local Montù variety.

The hillside wines of Emilia

Four DOC zones in the Apennine foothills of Emilia grow numerous grape varieties, but most wines are made in the style Emilians seem to prefer: *frizzante* and *amabile* (semi-sweet). Perhaps nowhere else in the world can you find a sweet, sparkling Cabernet Sauvignon or Merlot!

Colli Piacentini

Like Oltrepó Pavese to its west, Colli Piacentini *(COH lee pee ah chen TEE nee),* was once a part of Piedmont. All its vineyards are in the hills south of Piacenza; the zone's name, in fact, translates as "Hills of Piacenza." Most of the wines that head to Bologna or Milan, whether white or red, are slightly bubbly and slightly sweet. But some estates are now making dry, still wines for export.

Colli Piacentini is the most renowned wine district in Emilia — and no wonder, because it's a vast district making 17 different wines. These include varietally labeled reds (Barbera, Croatina — called Bonarda here — Cabernet Sauvignon, and Pinot Nero) and varietal whites (Chardonnay, Malvasia, Ortrugo, Pinot Grigio, and Sauvignon), all at least 85 percent from the named grape, except Ortrugo, at 90 percent. The white or rosé Colli Piacentini Pinot Spumante is mainly Pinot Nero, with Chardonnay. Two different Vin Santo wines (from dried grapes) also exist. A *novello*, wraps up the repertoire; it's a still or spritzy young red mainly from Pinot Nero, Barbera, or Croatina, singly or together.

Four more Colli Piacentini wines come from sub-zones within the district, and carry the name of the zone where the grapes grow:

- **Gutturnio** *(goot TOUR nee oh):* Red wine made 55 to 70 percent from Barbera, with the rest, Croatina; comes in dry and semi-dry styles; *frizzante* or still; *riserva* is an aged, still type.

- **Trebbianino Val Trebbia** *(treb bee ah NEE no vahl TREB bee ah):* Dry or semi-dry white made from the local Ortrugo, the aromatic Malvasia di Candia, Moscato Bianco, Trebbiano Romagnolo, Sauvignon, and others; *frizzante* or *spumante.*

- **Valnure** *(vahl NOO rae):* White wine, similar in composition to Trebbianino, except with more Malvasia and no Moscato.

- **Monterosso Val d'Arta** *(mohn tae ROHS so vahl DAR tah):* Similar to Trebbianino, except with less emphasis on Ortrugo, and more Sauvignon required in its blend.

Four wine estates are noteworthy in Colli Piacentini. At La Stoppa, charming owner Elena Pantaleoni has a fine, elegant, dry Cabernet Sauvignon called Stoppa, a good Pino Nero named Alfeo, a Barbera-Croatina blend called Macchiona (all about $23 to $25) and a Barbera. La Tosa makes a very good Gutturnio called Vignamorello ($28 to $30), a great Cabernet Sauvignon, Luna Selvatica ($37 to $39), and fine Sauvignon

Blanc ($20 to $22). The experimental estate of Vigevani makes
not only standard DOC reds and whites, but also many non-
DOC wines, and dry sparkling wines. Finally, Fugazza boasts an
excellent Gutturnio.

Colli di Parma

The Colli di Parma DOC zone occupies hillsides south of
Parma. With their world-renowned *prosciutto* ham, Parma
locals prefer Malvasia, their elegant, fragrant white wine. It's
made dry *(secco)* or semi-sweet *(amabile);* the dry wine can
be still, fizzy, or sparkling, while the sweet style is only fizzy or
sparkling. The aromatic Malvasia di Candia variety is the backbone of this wine, with up to 15 percent Moscato. Colli di
Parma Sauvignon is a dry white entirely from Sauvignon Blanc,
in still, *frizzante* or sparkling styles. Colli di Parma Rosso is a
dry red mainly from Barbera (60 to 75 percent), with Croatina
and/or Bonarda Piemontese; it can be still or *frizzante*.

Three notable estates in Colli di Parma zone are Calzetti —
which makes two fine *frizzante* wines, a Malvasia named
Conventino and a Sauvignon, as well as a fine Colli di Parma
Rosso; Lamoretti, known for its excellent Malvasia, fine Rosso
and Sauvignon; and Monte del Vigne — producing good Rosso,
and an interesting non-DOC, oak-aged red called Nabucco,
made from Barbera and Merlot.

Colli Bolognesi

The Colli Bolognesi *(COHL lee boh lon YAY see)* district lies
southwest of Bologna. Producers in this area may make nearly
50 different wines, varying according to grape variety and
vineyard location, all under the umbrella of the Colli Bolognesi
name. The majority of these wines are varietally labeled
whites and reds from the following grapes: Barbera, Cabernet
Sauvignon, Merlot, Sauvignon, Pinot Bianco, Welschriesling,
Pignoletto (a fragrant local white variety making dry, semi-dry,
frizzante, or sparkling wines), and Chardonnay (still or
sparkling). These wines derive 85 to 100 percent from the
named variety, depending on which part of the district is
named on the label. Seven sub-zones may use their name on
the label: Colline di Riosto, Colline Marconiane, Zola Predosa,
Monte San Pietro, Colline di Oliveto, Terre di Montebudello,
and Serravalle. A blended white wine, Colli Bolognesi Bianco,
derives mainly from Albana.

Three leading Colli Bolognesi estates are

- **Terre Rosse:** The late Enrico Vallania introduced dry premium wines in Colli Bolognesi at his Terre Rosse estate;
look for his family's Cuvée Enrico Vallania Rosso
(Cabernet Sauvignon) and the late-harvest Welschriesling
named Elisabetta Vallania.

- **Tenuta Bonzara:** A quality leader for Cabernet and
Merlot, not just for Emilia, but for Italy; rich Cabernet
Sauvignon Bonzarone ($28 to $30), good-value Merlot
Rosso del Poggio ($14 to $15), and premium Merlot Rocca
di Bonacciara ($28 to $30).

- **Vallona:** Great Cabernet Sauvignons and Chardonnays;
also, fine Pignoletto.

Colli di Scandiano and di Canossa

Yet another set of DOC wines from Emilia's hills carry the Colli
di Scandiano and di Canossa appellation *(COH lee dee scan
dee AH no / dee cah NO sah).* This area makes nine varietal
wines and three blended wines. The blends include a Bianco,
mainly from Sauvignon with Malvasia, Trebbiano, Pinot
Bianco, or Pinot Grigio, in dry, semi-dry, semi-sweet, sweet,
still or fizzy styles; Bianco *spumante,* a dry sparkling wine from
the same grapes; and *passito*, a sweet white that's at least 90
percent from dried Sauvignon grapes. Varietal wines include
Pinot (a white wine from Pinot Bianco or Pinot Nero, alone or
together, and still, *frizzante,* or sparkling), Sauvignon (dry, and
still or *frizzante),* Chardonnay (dry, and still, *frizzante,* or
sparkling), Malvasia (all styles), Lambrusco Grasparossa,
Lambrusco Montericco (a red or rosé wine), Cabernet
Sauvignon, Marzemino (a red variety, made in all sweetness
styles and still or *frizzante)* and Malbo Gentile (also red, made
in all sweetness styles — dry through sweet).

The wines of Romagna

All of Romagna's better wines come from its southern part,
southeast of Bologna, in the hillsides it shares with Tuscany,
its neighbor to the south. Romagna also shares Tuscany's (and
Italy's) most planted red grape variety, Sangiovese, although
Romagna has its own clone.

One of Romagna's rather obscure DOC wines, Albana, became the first DOCG white wine in Italy in 1987. People questioned the choice, but Romagnans defend their wine. **Albana di Romagna** comes in dry, semi-dry, sweet, and *passito* (sweet, from dried grapes) styles, all produced from the thick-skinned Albana variety. The best style is slightly sweet, with soft aromas and flavors sometimes suggestive of peaches; it must be consumed when it is young. Albana also makes a DOC sparkling wine under the name **Romagna Albana *Spumante*.**

Romagna has eight other DOC wines:

- ✔ **Sangiovese di Romagna:** Dry red from the Romagna clone of Sangiovese; this clone isn't as highly regarded as Tuscany's, but in the hands of a few of Romagna's best producers, its wines can rival Tuscany's.

- ✔ **Trebbiano di Romagna:** Romagna's everyday dry white (also *frizzante* or sparkling) from the Romagnolo clone of Trebbiano.

- ✔ **Cagnina di Romagna** *(cah N'YEE nah):* A somewhat tannic, purple, full-bodied red mainly from Refosco grapes; grows in the Forli province and around Ravenna, near the Adriatic Sea.

- ✔ **Pagadebit di Romagna:** One of Italy's colorful wine names, Pagadebit means "pays the bills," an allusion to cash-poor growers who used this once easy-to-sell wine to stay out of debt; it's a dry or semi-dry white wine from the Bombino Bianco variety, native to Apulia.

- ✔ **Bosco Eliceo** *(BOS co eh lee CHAE oh):* A blended, light-bodied white from Trebbiano Romagnolo, Sauvignon, and Malvasia; also a varietal Sauvignon, Merlot, and Fortana (a local red variety, tannic but grapey); the two whites can be dry or semi-dry, still or *frizzante*.

- ✔ **Colli di Rimini** *(COH lee dee REE mee nee):* A blended, dry white (mainly Trebbiano Romagnolo); blended red (mainly Sangiovese); Cabernet Sauvignon; Biancame (a local white); and Rébola, a white mainly from Pignoletto, which may be dry, semi-sweet, sweet or *passito*.

- ✔ **Colli di Imola** *(COH lee dee EE mo la)* and **Colli di Faenza** *(fa EN za):* These two newly-recognized DOC areas encompass hillsides around the towns of Imola and Faenza.

Romagna's leading wine producers, alphabetically, are the following:

- **Castelluccio:** Very good Sangiovese di Romagna

- **Umberto Cesari:** Huge winery producing cleanly made, widely-available wines; Albana and Sangiovese retail for $7 to $8; Laurento Chardonnay is about $15.

- **Fattoria Paradiso:** Owner Mario Pezzi has been a leader in the revival of Romagna, rediscovering the neglected Refosco and Bombino Bianco varieties, and making a robust red from another neglected grape, Barbarossa. Paradiso has a fine single-vineyard Sangiovese di Romagna Vigna delle Lepri, and a Barbarossa, both about $25.

- **Fattoria Zerbina:** Another standout winery; enologist Vittorio Fiore consults. Two noteworthy wines are the Marzieno Ravenna Rosso (Sangiovese-Cabernet Sauvignon blend) and the Albana di Romagna Passito called Scacco Matto, a honeyed, almondy beauty which might be *the* best Albana.

- **Stefano Ferrucci:** Fine producer of Sangiovese di Romagna and Albana di Romagna.

- **Tenuta La Palazza:** Two fine reds, a Cabernet Sauvignon (Magnificat) and Sangiovese di Romagna, plus a top Chardonnay.

- **Tre Monti:** Good wines at reasonable prices; Colli d'Imola Cabernet Sauvignon Turico (about $16) and Colli d'Imola Boldo (Sangiovese-Cabernet blend, $18 to $20).

A classic restaurant in Romagna

The town of Imola *(EE moh lah)*, 30 miles east of Bologna on Autostrada A14, is the location of one of Italy's great, classic restaurants, San Domenico (with a branch also in New York City). Ask to see the restaurant's outstanding wine cellar.

Chapter 7

Northeastern Italy

● ●

In This Chapter

▶ An Italian region that speaks German

▶ Verona's big three

▶ Prosecco: Italy's affordable sparkler

▶ Friuli: Italy's best white wines?

● ●

*I*n the strange, or let's say, "different," country of Italy,
Northeastern Italy is the most different part of all. In one
region — Alto Adige — you hear and see more German than
Italian. In another, the eastern part of Friuli-Venezia Giulia,
Italian competes with Serbo-Croatian and German as the
native language.

Another way in which Northeastern Italy is different: In all of
the rest of Italy, red wine dominates; the cool Northeast, with
its Austrian and Slovenian influences, is the most important
part of Italy for white wine, however. Northeastern Italy is also
particularly scenic, thanks to the splendor of the Dolomite
Alps, for example, and the incomparable canals of Venice.

This chapter covers three regions: Trentino-Alto Adige,
Veneto, and Friuli-Venezia Giulia.

Trentino-Alto Adige: One Region, Two Cultures

This strikingly beautiful dual region, Italy's northernmost area,
is entirely located in that branch of the eastern Alps known as
the Dolomites. Austria forms its northern border, Friuli-Venezia
Guilia is east, Veneto is south, and Lombardy is west; a small

northwestern part borders Switzerland. Trentino, named after the regional capital, Trento, is the southern part of the region; the northern part is Alto Adige. Figure 7-1 depicts this dual region.

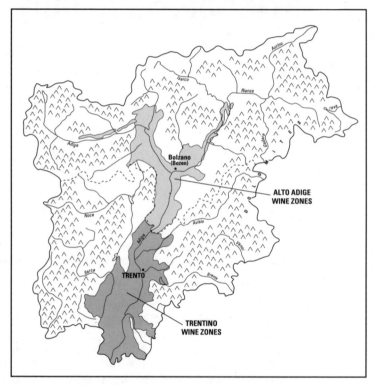

Figure 7-1: Trentino-Alto Adige is really two distinct sub-regions.

The Adige *(AH dee jhae)* River, Italy's second largest, descends from an alpine lake high in the Dolomites, near the Austrian border, and travels south through the center of Trentino-Alto Adige, creating the Valdadige *(vahl DAH dee jhae)* — the Adige Valley, where most of the region's inhabitants live. But this valley is one of the few things that Alto Adige and Trentino have in common. The natives of Alto Adige and Trentino have two distinct cultures, and two distinct wine zones.

Alto Adige, also known as the South Tyrol, encompasses the Bolzano province of the Trentino-Alto Adige region. It was part of Austria until World War I; in 1919, Austria ceded the South

Tyrol (in German, *Südtirol,* pronounced *SOOD tee ROHL*) to Italy, but most of the German-speaking Austrians stayed. Today, German remains the primary language, with Italian the second language. All street signs are in two languages. The capital city is Bolzano, or Bozen — take your choice of languages.

Alto Adige is quite mountainous. In the northernmost part, the mountains are very steep, but they gradually become somewhat lower and less steep towards the south. Many of the grapevines grow on south or east-facing slopes, on the western hillsides. Only 15 percent of the land is cultivable. The climate is continental, with rather hot summers and cold winters. (The city of Bolzano, in the valley's basin, is one of Italy's hottest places in July.) The hillsides are very cool at night during the growing season; the day-night temperature contrast heightens the aromas and flavors in Alto Adige wines.

Trentino, in contrast, is typically Italian; the only German spoken might be by visiting South Tyroleans. The mountains of Alto Adige exist here as well, but much of Trentino's wine comes from grapes grown in fertile, lowland areas. The region also has some fine wine estates with hillside vineyards, and one of Italy's best sparkling wine houses — Ferrari.

Despite their widely disparate cultures, Alto Adige and Trentino *do* have some similarities that apply to their wines: both sub-regions are dominated by wine cooperatives (in Trentino, co-ops account for 75 percent of wine production, in Alto Adige, over 60 percent); both areas grow both native and international grape varieties; and both sub-regions used to make considerably more red wine than they do now. Today, thanks to the increased popularity of Pinot Grigio and Chardonnay, white wines account for about 40 percent of the region's wine production — and this percentage is growing. Altogether, this region produces the equivalent of 11.7 million cases of wine annually.

Eighty-one percent of Trentino-Alto Adige's wine is DOC — which was the highest percentage in Italy until Piedmont surpassed it recently. But the region has the potential to make higher quality wine than it does now. The crop levels in both sub-regions — except at the finest estates — are among the highest in Italy (an average of about 5 tons per acre region-wide), which compromises the quality and intensity of the wines. Wineries find it too easy to sell their wines to hordes of tourists from Austria, Germany, and Switzerland, and the larger cooperatives, especially those in Trentino, have too ready a market for their mass-produced Pinot Grigios and Chardonnays abroad. The region's non-DOC wines have four IGT designations: Vigneti delle Dolomiti, Mitterberg, Mitterberg tra Cauria and Telor, and Vallagarina delle Venezie.

The wines of Alto Adige

White wine production seems to be the future of Alto Adige, but the most popular grape variety by far is a red one. It's a variety that few people outside the region — except German-speaking tourists from the North — have ever heard of, Schiava *(skee AH vah),* more commonly known in the South Tyrol by its German name, Vernatsch *(vehr NAHTSH).* This high-yielding variety presently accounts for over 60 percent of Alto Adige's wines; it's the basis of locally popular, light-bodied red wines. And yet some of the world's finest Pinot Bianco, Sauvignon, Pinot Grigio, Müller-Thurgau, and Gewürztraminer wines also come from Alto Adige today.

Italy's monster DOC

Recent changes in DOC regulations have resulted in one general appellation — Alto Adige, or Südtiroler — which now encompasses most of the DOC wines in Alto Adige, including six sub-zones that formerly were separate DOCs. The general Alto Adige DOC is an umbrella appellation, covering 51 wines: 31 whites, 16 reds, three rosés, and one sparkling wine.

The Tre Venezie

During the Middle Ages, the Republic of Venice was one of the world's commercial and military super-powers. Part of its empire included the three regions of present-day Northeastern Italy. Their common Venetian heritage explains why these regions are known as the Tre Venezie *(trae veh NEHT zee ae),* the "Three Venices." Today, many wines from these regions carry the IGT designation, "delle Venezie," harkening back to the days of Venice's glory. (Chapter 3 explains IGT designations.)

The basic Alto Adige wines — apart from the wines of the six sub-zones — are varietal wines, each deriving 85 to 95 percent from the named variety. The whites are Moscato Giallo, Pinot Bianco, Pinot Grigio, Chardonnay, Sauvignon, Riesling (Riesling Renano), Welschriesling (Riesling Italico), Müller-Thurgau (sometimes labeled Riesling X Sylvaner), Sylvaner, and Gewürztraminer (Traminer Aromatico). The red varietals are Lagrein, Moscato Rosa, Merlot, Cabernet (Sauvignon and/or Franc), Pinot Nero, Malvasia, Schiava, and Schiava Grigia. Additionally, producers may make a Cabernet-Merlot blend and a Cabernet-Lagrein blend. The rosés include Lagrein Rosato, Merlot Rosato, and Pinot Nero Rosato. Alto Adige *Spumante* is a dry sparkler from at least 70 percent Chardonnay and/or Pinot Bianco.

This general Alto Adige DOC appellation covers Alto Adige's finest white wines, such as those of the house of Alois Lageder, clearly a leader in the area, with its single-vineyard Pinot Bianco Haberlehof, its Pinot Grigio Benefizium (both $16 to $18), and its Chardonnay Löwengang ($27 to $30), among other wines. The best reds carrying this appellation are those from the native Lagrein grape, from Cabernet Sauvignon, Cabernet Franc, Merlot, and Pinot Nero. (For us, the red Lagrein *(lah GRYNE)* wines, dark-colored, sturdy, and full-bodied, are among the great, underrated red wines of the world.)

The six sub-zone wines of the Alto Adige DOC come from vineyards in the northern and central part of the larger appellation. We describe these wines here, listing the German names as well as the Italian:

- ✔ **Santa Maddalener (St. Magdalener):** Hillside vineyards north of Bolzano grow Santa Maddalener *(SAHN tah mah dahl LAE ner),* Alto Adige's most beloved Schiava-based wine (with Lagrein and/or Pinot Grigio optional); a bit deeper in color, fuller, and fruitier than the other popular Schiava-based wine, Lago di Caldaro.

- ✔ **Meranese di Collina (Meraner Hügel):** The historic Meranese di Collina *(mer ah NAE sae dee coh LEE nah)* vineyards around the town of Merano, about 20 miles northwest of Bolzano, are the home of the region's fullest and most aromatic Schiava wine, made entirely from that grape; the vineyards are high on the hillsides.

✔ **Terlano (Terlaner):** The Terlano *(ter LAH noh)* area extends many miles north and south of Terlano, a town six miles west of Bolzano; the area is best known for its Sauvignon Blanc, Pinot Bianco, and Chardonnay. Lageder's fine Sauvignon "Lehenhof" ($17 to $18) comes from here. Other Terlano wines are Riesling, Riesling Italico, Müller-Thurgau, Sylvaner, and Terlano Bianco (a dry white or *spumante* mostly from Pinot Bianco).

✔ **Colli di Bolzano (Bozner Leiten):** Colli di Bolzano *(COH lee dee bol ZAH noh)* is the hillsides area around Bolzano; light-bodied, spritzy, Schiava-based wine.

✔ **Valle Isarco (Eisacktaler):** High up in the Alps, along the Isarco River, about 30 miles northeast of Bolzano, is Valle Isarco *(VAH lae ee SAHR coh),* a fine area for mainly Germanic varieties: Sylvaner, Müller-Thurgau, Gewürztraminer, Pinot Grigio (also known by its Germanic name, Ruländer), Kerner, and Veltliner. This zone's one red wine is called Klausner Leitacher *(KLOUWZ nehr LYE tack er),* made from at least 60 percent Schiava, with Blauer Portugieser (an Austrian variety) and/or Lagrein. Perhaps the best winery in this zone, and the northernmost winery in Italy, is the Abbazia di Novacella, an authentic, working Augustinian abbey. Its wines retail in the $15 to $20 price range.

✔ **Valle Venosta (Vinschgau):** Alto Adige's most isolated vineyard area, in the extreme northwest, near the Swiss and Austrian borders; Valle Venosta *(VAH lay veh NOHs tah)* is best known for its Rieslings, but also makes Chardonnay, Pinot Bianco, Pinot Grigio, Müller-Thurgau, Kerner, and Gewürztraminer, as well as Pinot Nero and Schiava.

Other than Alto Adige/Südtiroler, the sub-region's only other DOC is **Lago di Caldaro** *(LAH go dee cahl DAH roh)* or Caldaro (or Kalterer, or Kaltersee — its German names). This very large vineyard area in the southern part of Alto Adige takes its name from Lake Caldaro, about 10 miles south of Bolzano. The region's oldest DOC area, it makes a pale, highly quaffable red wine from the Schiava grape, with Lagrein and/or Pinot Grigio optional.

A great winemaker

In the early 1980s, we tasted a white wine which proved to be one of the most memorable wines we've ever had. It was a 1961 Pinot Bianco, made by an Italian winemaker called Giorgio Grai (pronounced *gry* as in "cry," which this wine almost prompted us to do). We both rated it "20" out of 20. Later, we learned that the late Andre Tchelitscheff, California's legendary enologist, had the same reaction to this wine. We made it our business to meet Grai, which proved to be more difficult than we imagined. A former chef and race car driver, Giorgio is a busy and elusive man who consults for wineries throughout Italy. We finally tracked him down in a bar he owns in Bolzano (where he resides), and had a memorable visit. He now exports a line of wines under the Giorgio Grai label. But like the man, they are hard to find.

Alto Adige producers

Alois Lageder, mentioned earlier, is a leader in the area. The J. Hofstätter estate, Lageder's only real winemaking rival locally, makes two of the finest wines in Italy, the country's best Pinot Nero, called Villa Barthenau Sant'Urbano ($50 to $55), and a Gewürztraminer "Kolbenhof" ($24 to $25) from vineyards near Termeno (Tramin, in German), the birthplace of the Traminer grape variety and its variant, Gewürztraminer. Hofstätter also makes an excellent Lagrein (about $45). Another fine house, Castel Schwanburg, makes a Cabernet blend that's one of the best wines of its kind in Alto Adige.

J. Tiefenbrunner is another Alto Adige winery of note. Tiefenbrunner produces what has to be the world's best Müller-Thurgau (admittedly, not a great white variety), called Feldmarschall, from one of the world's highest vineyards, nearly 3,000 feet in altitude. The wine retails for about $27 to $30, and is an excellent value. Also in Alto Adige, look for the wines of Josef Brigl, Kettmeir, Peter Zemmer, Josef Niedermayr, Hirshprunn, Hans Rottensteiner, Baron von Widmann, Franz Haas, and Elana Walch. In addition, the excellent cooperative, San Michele Appiano, with wines under the Castel San Valentino label, makes fine white wines.

The wines of Trentino

For a long time, the only winery in Trentino internationally known for its quality wines was Ferrari, one of Italy's finest sparkling wine houses, founded in 1902. Growers were content to sell their grapes to the huge cooperatives, such as Cavit in Trento and the MezzaCorona co-op in Mezzocorona. As in Veneto to the south, growers had planted mainly on the fertile valley floor; in the hands of the co-ops, the large crops from these vineyards made a huge amount of rather ordinary, inexpensive wine.

But a number of wine estates and small wine houses have emerged, and are helping to change Trentino's image. Also, a truly superb cooperative, La Vis (in the town of Lavis, north of Trento) is raising the bar for co-ops with its excellent wines. Now Trentino is known not only for mass-produced Chardonnays and Pinot Grigios, but also for some fine red wines made from its local variety, Teroldego (*teh ROHL dae go;* very similar to Alto Adige's Lagrein), and from Cabernet Sauvignon and Merlot — as well as some good-quality white wines.

Sparklers with quality and value

The top sparkling wines of Ca'del Bosco and Bellavista in Lombardy's Franciacorta zone might be finer (and are more expensive!), but *no* winery in Italy has a better, all-around line of sparklers for the price than the Ferrari house, in Trento. Ferrari is one of Italy's largest sparkling wine houses, with an annual production of three million bottles. Its entire line, beginning with its Brut Non-Vintage ($16 to $18) and Brut Rosé NV ($19 to $20), to its 1994 and 1995 Vintage Perlé Brut ($20 to $22), to its top-of-the-line 1990 and 1991 Giulio Ferrari Riserva Brut ($34 to $38), offers excellent value. The Giulio Ferrari Riserva, in particular, one of Italy's best sparkling wines, is a true steal at that price.

Another "Real Deal" in sparkling wines is Rotari Brut, made by Mezza-Corona, offering excellent quality for its $12 to $15 price. It has a bright orange label (borrowed, perhaps, from a famous Champagne with the initials VC?).

Trentino has six DOC zones. Trentino DOC *(tren TEE noh)* is an umbrella appellation that applies to wines made in 72 communities in Trento province. It covers 24 types of wine: 11 white wines, 10 reds, a rosé, a late-harvest white, and a Vin Santo.

Trentino DOC whites include a blended white — Trentino Bianco, made 80 percent from Chardonnay and/or Pinot Bianco — and ten varietally-labeled whites: Chardonnay, Pinot Bianco, Sauvignon, Pinot Grigio, Moscato Giallo, Müller-Thurgau, Riesling, Welschriesling, Gewürztraminer, and Nosiola. The reds include Trentino Rosso — a blend of Cabernet Franc and/or Cabernet Sauvignon with Merlot — and nine varietally-labeled wines: Cabernet Franc, Cabernet Sauvignon, Cabernet, Lagrein, Pinot Nero, Merlot, Moscato Rosa, Rebo, and Marzemino.

Many of the best wines of the Trentino province carry the Trentino DOC, and some of Trentino's best producers — Foradori, Pojer & Sandri, Roberto Zeni, Conti Martini, Guerrieri Gonzaga, Gaierhof, La Vis, Maso Poli, Baroni a Prato, and the Instituto Agrario Provinciale — use this appellation for their white varieties and Pinot Nero. Zeni makes an intriguing Pinot Grigio rosé wine called Cru Fontane ($20 to $22), which is excellent with antipasto.

Trentino's five other DOC zones include the following:

- ✔ **Trento DOC:** A geographically large DOC, but it applies only to sparkling wines, either white or rosé, from Chardonnay, Pinot Bianco, Pinot Nero, and Pinot Meunier, together or singly.

- ✔ **Teroldego Rotaliano** *(teh ROHL dae go roh tah lee AH noh):* Campo Rotaliano, a plain around the town of Mezzolombardo, surrounded by the Dolomites, is the home of this wine; Teroldego, Trentino's best red variety, is the grape. At its best, sturdy Teroldego makes dark, robust, spicy, tannic red wines, most of which need several years to develop; a basic red, a *superiore* version (which includes a *riserva* for wines aged at least two years), and a rosé style exist under this DOC. Perhaps the best wines come from Foradori, with its basic 1998 Teroldego Rotaliano ($16 to $18) and its more serious 1997 Sgarzon (more than $50); Foradori's red wine called Granato ($45 to $48) is an excellent non-DOC blend based on the Teroldego grape. Other good Teroldego Rotaliano producers include Conti Martini, Cantina Cooperativa Rotaliana, Barone de Cles, and Roberto Zeni.

✔ **Sorni** *(SOR nee):* The Sorni zone is a small area named for a hamlet outside of Lavis in northern Trentino. It produces just two wines, a white and a red. Sorni Bianco consists of Nosiola, Müller-Thurgau, Silvaner, Pinot Bianco, Pinot Grigio, and Chardonnay, together or singly; Sorni Rosso comes from Teroldego, Schiava, and Lagrein, together or singly. The La Vis co-op and Maso Poli are two leading producers.

✔ **Casteller** *(cah STEL ler):* This narrow, hilly zone along the Adige River, north and south of Trento, produces light red, quaffable, dry or semi-sweet wines, which are mainly consumed locally; the wines are based on Schiava and a local (raggedy-leaved) type of Lambrusco, blended with Teroldego, Lagrein, and/or Merlot.

✔ **Valdadige** *(vahl DAH dee jhae)* or **Etschtaler:** This interregional DOC covers vineyards in Alto Adige, Trentino, and the Veneto, all in the Adige Valley — but most of the vineyards are in Trentino. Its seven types of wine, all basically inexpensive styles, include three blended wines: Valdadige Rosso (dry or semi-sweet red blend of Schiava, local Lambrusco, Merlot, Pinot Nero, Lagrein, Teroldego, and Negrara; Bianco (dry or semi-sweet white blended from up to nine varieties); and Rosato (dry or semi-sweet rosé from the same grapes as Rosso). The varietal wines are Pinot Grigio, Pinot Bianco, Chardonnay, and Schiava.

Two other Trentino wineries are noteworthy. The fine Tenuta San Leonardo estate (also known as Guerrieri Gonzaga, the family's name), just north of the Veneto, produces the finest Cabernet Sauvignon in Trentino; the 1997 San Leonardo Cabernet retails in the $45 to $48 range; the estate's 1997 Merlot ($16 to $18) is also quite good. In addition, look for wines from the huge Concilio winery; its basic range of very decent wines sell for $10, and its Reserve Collection go for $15.

Veneto: Verona to Venice

The Veneto is the largest and most populous of the three regions in northeastern Italy. Friuli-Venezia Guilia and the

Adriatic Sea are to its east, Emilia-Romagna is south (across the Po River), and Trentino-Alto Adige lies west and north; part of Austria also shares its northern border. The Alps cover the northern third of Veneto; the region's wines come from the southwestern and east-central zones — both hillsides and plains. (See Figure 7-2.) Climate ranges from mild in the coastal area, influenced by the Adriatic, to hot in the central plains, and mild to cool in the Verona area.

Veneto is Italy's third-largest wine producer, after Apulia and Sicily, with a volume of more than 77 million cases of wine a year. Twenty-nine percent of that production is DOC wine, a quantity that makes Veneto one of the largest producers of DOC wines; two-thirds of these wines come from the province of Verona, and are mainly the prolific Veronese trio of Soave, Bardolino, and Valpolicella, plus the up-and-coming Bianco di Custoza. Much of the rest of Veneto's large production is Pinot Grigio. Some of these are labeled with the "Veneto" IGT, or with one of the region's eight other IGTs.

The Veneto has always been a market-savvy region. In the 1950s, along with Tuscany's Chianti zone, it led the way in exporting Italian wines to the rest of the world; by the 1970s, Soave *(so AH vae)*, a dry white wine whose sales were spear-headed by the Bolla winery, had even surpassed Chianti as Italy's largest-selling DOC wine in the U.S. But nowadays, Pinot Grigio leads Italy's white wine exports.

Veneto wine production features many traditional local vari-eties, grown for centuries in the Verona province — such as the red Corvina and the white Garganega — as well as Merlot and both Cabernets, also grown for a long time, and popular white varieties, such as Chardonnay, Pinot Grigio, Pinot Bianco, and Sauvignon. Three distinct areas of wine produc-tion exist in the Veneto:

- ✔ Verona, the western province, which itself has two sepa-rate vineyard areas, the Lake Garda area (home of Bardolino and Bianco Custoza), and the Lessini hills area north and east of the city of Verona (home of Valpolicella and Soave).

- ✔ The Central Hills, around Vicenza and Padua

- ✔ Eastern Veneto, around Venice and Treviso

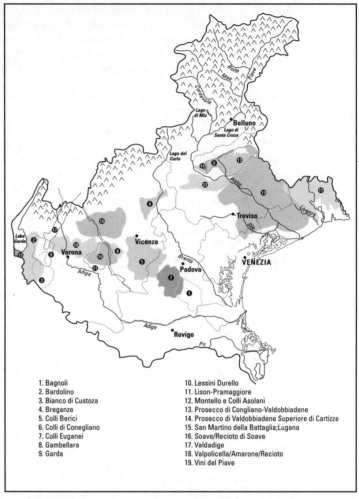

1. Bagnoli
2. Bardolino
3. Bianco di Custoza
4. Breganze
5. Colli Berici
6. Colli di Conegliano
7. Colli Euganei
8. Gambellara
9. Garda
10. Lessini Durello
11. Lison-Pramaggiore
12. Montello e Colli Asolani
13. Prosecco di Congliano-Valdobbiadene
14. Prosecco di Valdobbiadene Superiore di Cartizze
15. San Martino della Battaglia;Lugana
16. Soave/Recioto di Soave
17. Valdadige
18. Valpolicella/Amarone/Recioto
19. Vini del Piave

Figure 7-2: The vineyards of Veneto are clustered in the southwest and the east-central parts of the region.

Verona's major wines

From west to east, the four important DOC wine zones of the province of Verona are Bardolino *(bar doe LEE no)*, Bianco di Custoza *(b'YAHN co dee coos TOH't zah)*, Valpolicella *(vahl poh lee t'CHELL ah)* and Soave *(so AH vae.)*

Although all these wines are mass-produced today, you can still find hand-crafted examples of each by seeking out the wines from our recommended producers. IGT wines from this area carry the designations "Veronese" or "Provincia di Verona."

Bardolino

The *classico* zone, the original vineyard area for Bardolino, is the hillsides around the town of Bardolino and nearby villages, located on the eastern shores of beautiful Lake Garda, Italy's largest lake. Grapes from this area make Bardolino at its best: a light-bodied, pale-ruby, delicate wine, with lively aromas and flavors reminiscent of cherries, a slightly tart aftertaste, and a perfect balance of acidity.

Unfortunately, DOC regulations allow grapes for Bardolino to be grown north and south of the *classico* zone (extending into the Bianco di Custoza area in the south), and farther east of the lake area. Outside of the *classico* zone, the wine tends to be thinner and more neutral in character, especially when it's made by large, industrial wineries.

Look for wine with the DOC Bardolino Classico or Bardolino Classicio Superiore (a bit fuller, with one more degree of alcohol), from the following producers (listed in our rough order of preference):

Guerrieri-Rizzardi, especially its Tacchetto	Fratelli Zeni
	Le Fraghe
Bertani	Santa Sofia
Masi's La Vegrona	Cavalchina
Corte Gardoni's Le Fontane	Le Vigne di San Pietro
Lamberti	

The four main grape varieties that make up Bardolino, all native to Verona, are Corvina (35 to 65 percent), Rondinella (10 to 40 percent), Molinara (10 to 20 percent), and Negrara (up to 10 percent); Corvina is the finest of the four; the best Bardolino wines use high percentages of Corvina.

A dry rosé version of Bardolino, called Chiaretto *(key ah RET toh),* is delightful in the summer when served chilled. There's also sparkling Bardolino, and a Bardolino *novello* (sold a few months after the harvest, just like Beaujolais Nouveau), a specialty of the Lamberti house. Both the red and Chiaretto version of Bardolino are light-bodied enough to accompany fish and seafood as well as light meat entrées, pasta, and pizza. The local specialty around Lake Garda, lake trout, works just fine with Bardolino. Drink Bardolino when it's young and fresh, definitely within three years of the vintage — but younger if possible. Retail prices for Bardolino range from less than $10 for the basic wines up to $15 for single-vineyard versions.

Bianco di Custoza

Bianco di Custoza is a dry, light-bodied, somewhat character-ful white wine named for Custoza, a village southeast of Lake Garda and southwest of Verona. The standard quality of Bianco di Custoza is surprisingly high for such an inexpensive white wine (retailing for $10 to $12), making it one of the really good white wine values in Italy. It's been called the white version of Bardolino, and like its Lake Garda neighbor, it's best when consumed within two or three years of the vintage. Its main grape varieties are Trebbiano Toscano (35 to 45 percent), the native Garganega (20 to 40 percent), and Tocai Friulano (5 to 30 percent). A sparkling style also exists.

Look for the following producers of Bianco di Custoza (listed in our rough order of preference):

Corte Gardoni	Cavalchina
Le Tende	Montresor
Santi	Le Vigne di San Pietro
Lamberti	Santa Sofia

Just like Romeo and Juliet

According to legend, the historic city of Verona was the home of a certain young man named Romeus, and a fair (very) young maiden named Giulietta. In fact, you can view Juliet's (alleged) balcony in Verona, and visit her home for a small fee. At any rate, Verona is worth a visit; it's not only the center of a large wine-producing region but also the home of Italy's gigantic wine fair, VINITALY, which takes place there every April. Sitting in Verona's central square (the Piazza Bra), next to the Roman arena, sipping Valpolicella and munching pizza, is one of our favorite things to do in Italy.

Valpolicella and Amarone

Valpolicella and its sturdier brother, Amarone della Valpolicella, are the two most important red wines in the Veneto area. Like Bardolino, the best Valpolicella wines come from the original *classico* zone — in this case, the western part of the steep, terraced Monti Lessini hillsides north of Verona, the area historically known as Valpolicella. Valpolicella-Valpantena identifies wines, such as Bertani's, whose grapes come from the Pantena Valley.

Valpolicella is made from three of the same varieties as Bardolino, in slightly different percentages: Corvina (40 to 70 percent), Rondinella (20 to 40 percent), and Molinara (5 to 25 percent). Valpolicella has similar aromas and flavors to Bardolino (tart cherry fruit, with a slightly bitter aftertaste), but it tends to be a bit darker in color and slightly more full-bodied. At four million cases annually, Valpolicella's production is twice that of Bardolino, and so it's easier to find a good producer's Valpolicella than a good Bardolino.

It's no secret that the quality of both Valpolicella and Bardolino has suffered from over-production on the part of industrialized wineries and cooperatives. But you can find increasingly good examples of these wines, primarily from quality-conscious, family-owned wineries, many of which we recommend in this chapter. For example, Allegrini, one of the leaders in the quality revival in Valpolicella, makes a fine, well-balanced Valpolicella Classico (about $11 to $12). But Allegrini has abandoned the Valpolicella DOC for its other wines, in order to have more freedom in blending (the wines now carry the designation IGT Veronese). The outstanding single-vineyard wine called La Grola, a wine well-worth its $18 price, contains some Merlot and Syrah, for example, and La Poja is made entirely from the best Veronese red grape variety, Corvina. Considered one of Italy's best red wines, La Poja retails for about $60 (it was less than half that price before it was "discovered").

In good vintages, some of the grapes for Valpolicella are set aside to make the two special wines of the district: the dry Amarone (*ah mah ROE nae*) della Valpolicella and the sweet Recioto (*reh CHO toh*) della Valpolicella. Especially ripe bunches of grapes, primarily Corvina, are spread out on mats in cool, dry rooms for three to four months, where they become partially shriveled, and their juice, very concentrated. The grapes are fermented until the wine is dry to make Amarone, the far more popular style; it's a rich, heady, robust red wine with 14 to 16 percent alcohol, that needs about ten years to mature, and can age for 20 years or more. For the sweet Recioto della Valpolicella, fermentation is stopped so that natural sweetness remains in the wine; this style can also be sparkling. Hearty Amarone is definitely a wine for the wintertime; accompany it with full-flavored roasts, game, or mature, hard cheeses, such as Asiago or Parmesan.

Amarone is a labor-intensive wine and consequently, a good one is never inexpensive. Prices range from about $30 to $75 for wines from the best producers, with most between $45 and $60. If you see an Amarone priced at $20 or less, avoid it; it won't be a true example of this fine wine.

Another variation of Valpolicella is a group of wines made by the *ripasso (ree PAH so)* method, which are actually beefed-up Valpolicellas. In this process, regular Valpolicella undergoes a second fermentation in contact with the deposits from the fermentation of Amarone; the resulting wine develops deeper color, more glycerine, richer texture, and more tannin. *Ripasso* is a winemaking technique, not a legal designation; the word generally appears only on a wine's back label, if at all. Three fine examples of *ripasso* wines are Masi's Campo Fiorin, Bertani's Catullo, and Allegrini's Palazzo alla Torre; all from the Valpolicella area, but not Valpolicella DOC.

A glorious Bardolino

We had our best Bardolino ever a few years ago, in the town of Bardolino, when we took a day off from the VINITALY wine fair to visit a few wineries. Sitting by Lake Garda, nibbling chunks of spicy salami, we drank a Guerrieri-Rizzardi Bardolino from the Tacchetto vineyard. It was young and fresh, and absolutely delicious. That it was a single-vineyard Bardolino from the *classico* zone was a big factor in its quality, but perhaps even more important was its youth: The wine was a 1996, and we drank it in April, 1997. You might have to visit the Veneto to drink Bardolino that young. One more good reason to go there!

We recommend numerous producers from the Valpolicella zone. Those in Class One are our favorites for both Valpolicella and Amarone, and we list them in our rough order of preference; our Class Two producers appear in alphabetical order:

Class One
Allegrini
Quintarelli
Dal Forno
Bertani
Le Ragose
Masi
Brigaldera
Bolla (Valpolicella Classico
  Le Poiane)
Tommasi

Class Two
Stefano Accordini
Brunelli
Ca' del Monte
Campagnola

Michele Castellani
Corte Rugolin
Corte Sant'Alda
Ferrari
Guerrieri-Rizzardi
Montresor
Angelo Nicolis e Figli
Pasqua
Santa Sofia
Santi
Fratelli Speri
Fratelli Tedeschi
Venturini
Zenato
Fratelli Zeni

Soave

Verona's final major DOC wine is Soave — Italy's most famous white wine, along with Pinot Grigio. Soave wines from the *classico* zone, in the hills above the towns of Soave and Monteforte d'Alpone (east of Verona), offer the highest quality; most other Soaves reflect the neutral, insipid style that cheapened the name of Soave and caused it to be frequently maligned. At its best, Soave is a fruity, very dry, fresh, straw-colored wine with class and character; in the hands of a fine producer, such as Gini, Pieropan, or Anselmi, it's one of Italy's best inexpensive white wines. (Most good Soave wines retail in the $10 to $15 range; a few single-vineyard Soaves cost a bit more.)

Soave's main grape variety is the local Garganega; up to 15 percent of Trebbiano di Soave, Chardonnay, Pinot Bianco, and/or Trebbiano Toscano is also permitted. A sweet **Recioto di Soave** (which recently became Veneto's only DOCG wine), from partially dried grapes, also is made, in still or sparkling form. Like Bardolino and Valpolicella, most Soave is at its best when it's young, within three years of the vintage. (The best producers' Soave wines can last much longer, however.)

Two incredible Soaves, both probably 100 percent Garganega, are Gini's La Froscà and Pieropan's La Rocca. Both retail in the $18 to $21 range, and are well worth that price.

Soave is now a huge wine zone (up to six million cases annually). Take care in choosing a producer. We recommend Soave Classico or Soave Classico Superiore wines from the following producers. The first three producers are in a class by themselves; we name them in our rough order of preference. The remaining producers are listed alphabetically:

Class One
Gini
Pieropan
Anselmi

Class Two
Bertani
Bisson
Bolla (Soave Classico Tufaie)
Campagnola
La Cappuccina
Ca' Rugate

Guerrieri-Rizzardi
Inama
Lamberti
Masi
Montresor
Pasqua
Umberto Portinari
Pra
Santa Sofia
Santi
Suavia

Other Verona-area DOC wines

A relatively new DOC zone called **Durello** lies in the eastern Lessini hills, north of the Soave region. Durello is a dry wine, with quite high acidity, made primarily from a local variety called Durella. It's also made in a *frizzante* and sparkling style.

Part of the Lugana area — which we cover in Chapter 6, in the Lombardy section — extends into the southwestern edge of the Verona province, on the south shore of Lake Garda. A leading Veronese producer of Lugana is Zenato.

A new DOC area, called **Garda Orientale** *(GAHR dah oh ree en TAH lae)*, extends slightly into Lombardy, south of Lake Garda. The wines are mainly varietals: reds are Cabernet (from both Cabernet varieties), Cabernet Franc, Cabernet Sauvignon, Merlot, Pinot Nero, Marzemino, and Corvina; whites are Garganega (still or fizzy), Pinot Bianco, Pinot Grigio Chardonnay, Trebbianello, Riesling, Welschriesling (dry or semi-dry, and labelled Riesling Italico), Cortese, and Sauvignon. Garda Orientale Spumante is a sparkling wine from Pinot Bianco, Chardonnay, and Riesling.

Wines of the Central Hills

The Central Hills area of the Veneto is east of Verona and west of Venice, in the provinces of Vicenza and Padua. This area has five DOC zones, one of which, Breganze, is the most important.

Breganze

The Breganze *(breh GAHN zae)* district, north of the city of Vicenza, occupies foothills sheltered by the Asiago plateau (part of the Alps) to the north, with a river on each side. It has a mild climate, and is capable of producing well-structured red wines as well as fine whites.

Breganze Bianco, the basic white, is mainly (at least 85 percent) Tocai Friulano, and Breganze Rosso is mainly Merlot. The Breganze DOC also covers four varietal reds (Cabernet — entirely from both Cabernet varieties), Cabernet Sauvignon, Pinot Nero, and Marzemino, and four white varietals (Pinot Bianco, Pinot Grigio, Chardonnay, and Sauvignon) as well as Vespaiolo, a white wine from Vespaiola, a local, aromatic white variety. Torcolato is a dessert wine made from semi-dried Vespaiola grapes.

One producer dominates the area — Fausto Maculan, one of Italy's best wine producers. Maculan makes an array of internationally-styled and traditional red and white wines, as well as two of Italy's finest dessert wines. His Breganze Bianco DOC, called Breganze di Breganze (about $15), is clean, fresh, and dry, with hints of peach aromas and flavors. Maculan's Brentino di Breganze (also $15), is a traditional Breganze Rosso. His most impressive dry wines are his three Cabernets: the single-vineyard Fratta (an old-vines blend of both Cabernets, with some Merlot), the single-vineyard Cabernet Sauvignon Palazzotto and the Cabernet Sauvignon Ferrata (all retailing for $47 to $50).

Maculan also makes two Chardonnays, a Merlot, and several other dry wines, but his pride and joy are his two acclaimed dessert wines, Torcolato and Acininobili. The Torcolato comes in half-bottles and sells for $27 to $30; the wine is aged in small barrels until it's golden- colored, with intense aromas and flavors of honey and dried fruit, such as apricots. The even richer Acininobili is made similarly, but its grapes are affected with *botrytis cinerea,* as in Sauternes. The resulting wine, which comes in half-bottles and retails for $85 to $90, compares favorably to a great Sauternes.

Gambellara

Gambellara *(gahm bel LAH rah)* is a wine which is very similar to Soave; this is no big surprise, because it's just east of the Soave zone, and uses very much the same white grape varieties: Garganega, with up to 20 percent Trebbiano di Soave and/or Trebbiano Toscano. But since this wine is not much known outside the Veneto, it retails for only about $7 or $8! The Gambellara zone also produces a sweet Recioto di Gambellara, a still or sparkling wine made from semi-dried or dried grapes; and a Vin Santo di Gambellara, a golden-colored dessert wine (see Chapter 8 for more on Vin Santo).

Two producers to look for are Zonin (Italy's largest private wine company, whose headquarters are in the town of Gambellara) and the La Biancara winery, which makes two Gambellara Classicos, Sassaia and I Masieri — both excellent values.

Colli Berici

Colli Berici *(COH lee BEH ree chee)* is a large, historic vineyard area south of Vicenza whose wines are virtually unknown outside the region. Its two main wines are the dry white Garganega and a curious, dry red varietal wine, Tocai Rosso (sometimes called Barbarano if the grapes are more than minimally ripe), whose ripe raspberry flavors suggest that the grape is related to Grenache. This DOC covers four other white varietal wines (Tocai Italico, Sauvignon, Pinot Bianco, and Chardonnay), a Cabernet, and a *spumante*. Producers to look for are Conti da Schio, Villa dal Ferro, and Ca' Bruzzo.

Colli Euganei and Bagnoli

These two wine zones are in the vicinity of the city of Padua — one zone, Colli Euganei *(COH lee ae yu GAH nae),* southwest of Padua, and another, Bagnoli *(bahn YO lee),* south of it.

Vineyards in the beautiful Euganei hills make semi-sweet and bubbly wines that are popular locally, not only in Padua, but also in Venice. The whites are a Bianco mainly from Garganega, Prosecco, Tocai Friulano, and Sauvignon; Fior di Arancio ("orange blossom") from Moscato Giallo, which also has a *passito* style, from dried grapes; and six varietals: Chardonnay,

Moscato, Pinello, Pinot Blanc, Tocai Italico, and Serprino (Prosecco). Red wines are a basic Rosso (from Merlot, the two Cabernets, Barbera, and Raboso Veronese grapes), Rosso *novello*, Cabernet, Cabernet Franc, Cabernet Sauvignon, and Merlot.

Vignalta is the leading producer; look for its Colli Euganei Rosso, made mainly from Merlot. Also, the Fior d'Arancio of La Montecchia, Ca' Lustra, and Borin, as well as Borin's dry white, Colli Euganei Bianco, are all worth trying.

Bagnoli, or Bagnoli di Sopra ("Upper Bagnoli") is a newly created DOC zone directly east of the Colli Euganei area. It covers nine wines. Except for three — a varietal Merlot, a dry red called Friularo from the Raboso Piave variety, and Bagnoli Cabernet (from Cabernet Franc, Cabernet Sauvignon, and Carmenère, together or singly) — the wines are all blends with complicated formulas. The dry red Rosso is 15 to 60 percent Merlot, at least 15 percent Cabernet Franc and/or Cabernet Sauvignon and/or Carmenère, and at least 15 percent Raboso. The dry or semi-dry Bianco contains at least 20 percent of the following varieties: Chardonnay; Tocai Friulano and/or Sauvignon; and Raboso (red grapes vinified without their skins). The dry or semi-dry Rosato is at least 50 percent Raboso, and up to 40 percent Merlot. A sweet red *passito* is mainly Raboso. A white *spumante* (dry) or rosé *spumante* (dry or semi-dry) both have at least 40 percent Raboso with at least 20 percent Chardonnay.

Wines of eastern Veneto

Venice itself is surrounded by marshland, but north, west, and northeast of this magical city are alluvial plains and hillsides covered with vines. The two main wines of this area are Pinot Grigio and Prosecco — a wonderful, inexpensive sparkling wine that has earned worldwide acceptance and recognition. But Merlot and both Cabernets are also important wines here. Five DOC wine zones are mainly in the two provinces of Treviso and Venezia. IGT wines from eastern Veneto can carry the designation "Veneto Orientale."

Prosecco di Conegliano-Valdobbiadene

Prosecco di Conegliano-Valdobbiadene *(pro SAE co dee co nael YAH no vahl doh bee AH deh nae)* takes its tongue-twisting name from two towns north of the Piave River and south of the Alps: Valdobbiadene, in the cooler, hillier west, and Conegliano, in the east, near the Adriatic Sea. Both areas are sheltered by the Alps, making the climate ideal for the Prosecco vines which proliferate between and around the towns.

Prosecco sparkling wine, which comes both in *frizzante* (slightly sparkling) and *spumante* (fully sparkling) styles, is at its crispest, more refined best in the cooler hills around Valdobbiadene. (Usually, Prosecco labels list only one of the two towns as part of the DOC name.) Wines from a small area of steep hills around Valdobbiadene are entitled to the desig- nation Superiore di Cartizze, or Cartizze *(cahr TEET zae);* these wines are theoretically the finest Prosecco — when made by a quality producer who's controlling his crop levels.

Most Prosecco nowadays is dry, fully-sparkling bubbly made by the tank fermentation method rather than the Champagne or bottle fermentation method (see Chapter 15 of *Wine For Dummies* for an explanation of these two production meth- ods); the shorter tank process is preferable in this case because it preserves the freshness and flavor of the grape. Variations include a small amount of dry, still Prosecco, and a sweeter (*amabile* or *dolce*) style of sparkling Prosecco. Prosecco is generally soft more than crisp, and has aromas and flavors that are floral, slightly peachy, and somewhat remi- niscent of almonds. Look for Prosecco that's labelled *Brut* if you want the driest version. Most Prosecco retails in the $10 to $15 range.

We alphabetically list our recommended producers of Prosecco:

Adami	Col Vetoraz
Astoria Vini	Nino Franco
Desiderio Bisol & Figli	Gregoletto
Bortolomiol	Mionetto
Canevel	Ruggeri & C.
Carpenè Malvolti	Zardetto
Le Case Bianche	Zonin

The new **Colli di Conegliano** DOC zone overlaps much of the Prosecco di Conegliano-Valdobbiadene area. This name applies to still (non-sparkling) wines. Only four types exist, but each has a complicated blend of grapes. The dry Bianco derives mainly from a variety that's a Riesling-Pinot Bianco cross, Pinot Bianco itself, and Chardonnay. The dry Rosso is mainly Cabernet Franc, Cabernet Sauvignon, Marzemino, and Merlot. Torchiato di Fregona is a sweet white from dried Prosecco, Verdiso, Boschera, and other varieties, grown in the eastern part of the zone. Refrontolo Passito is a sweet (or *frizzante*) red from dried Marzemino grapes grown in the zone's center.

Montello e Colli Asolani

Montello e Colli Asolani *(mon TEL lo ae COH lee ah so LAH nee)*, is a wine zone south of the Piave River and northwest of the city of Treviso. The zone's best area is the slopes of Il Montello. Even though this DOC applies to Prosecco in all forms — dry or semi-dry; still, *frizzante,* or fully sparkling — the specialties are red wines. The three reds are a blended Rosso (minimum of 85 percent Merlot, Cabernet Franc, and/or Cabernet Sauvignon), Cabernet, and Merlot. Besides Prosecco, other white wines of the area are Chardonnay, Pinot Bianco (both made as still or sparkling wines), and Pinot Grigio.

The zone's most renowned wine estate is Venegazzù, owned by the Loredan Gasparini family; the estate makes primarily Cabernet blends, including one called Venegazzù, which retails for about $25. A winery to watch is Serafini e Vidotto; its acclaimed Bordeaux blend, Il Rosso dell'Abazia, about $35, is one of the best wines of its kind in Italy.

Piave

The Piave *(pee AH vae)* DOC sometimes goes by the name Vini del Piave. The Piave River cuts through the center of this very large district, and most of the zone is the plains of the river basin, with some vineyards in the hills. Piave's three most distinctive wines — the vivid, intense red varietal Raboso and the two lively varietal whites, Verduzzo and Tocai Italico — are gradually giving way to seven international varietals: Cabernet Sauvignon, Cabernet, Merlot, and Pinot Nero for red wines; Chardonnay, Pinot Bianco, and Pinot Grigio for whites. A leading producer in the zone is Ornella Molon Traverso, where the husband-wife team, Ornella Molon and Giancarlo Traverso, make a fine Piave Cabernet and Piave Merlot.

Lison-Pramaggiore

The Lison-Pramaggiore *(LEE sohn prah mahj JOH rae)* zone is in the easternmost part of the Veneto, near the Adriatic Sea, extending slightly into the Friuli region. It has 12 DOC wines. But it's most renowned for one wine — Pinot Grigio — and one wine house, Santa Margherita, whose headquarters are here, but whose wine carries either the Alto Adige DOC or the Valdadige DOC (which applies to vineyards in both the Verona province and the Trentino-Alto Adige region). The Santa Margherita name has become synonymous with Pinot Grigio, and the brand is greatly responsible for the popularity of the Pinot Grigio category. Santa Margherita's Pinot Grigio is not the quality it was when the company was small, however. Now a million-plus case wine house, Santa Margherita has become almost as popular for its Chardonnay, which has either the Alto Adigo DOC or the IGT designation, Veneto Orientale (Eastern Veneto). Russolo, in the area of the town of Pramaggiore, is another wine house of note.

The Lison-Pramaggiore name covers seven varietally-labelled white wines (Tocai Italico, Pinot Bianco, Chardonnay, Pinot Grigio, Riesling Italico, Sauvignon, and Verduzzo). It also covers varietal Merlot, Cabernet Franc, Cabernet Sauvignon, Cabernet, and Refosco. Technically, any wines of these wines may be vinified as sparkling wines.

Friuli-Venezia Giulia: The Great White Way

Tucked away in the northeast corner of Italy is another region that you wouldn't describe as typically "Italian" — whatever *that* is. Friuli-Venezia Giulia *(FREE oo lee veh NET zee ah JHOO lee ah)* was once part of the Venetian Republic, and its eastern sections were part of the Austro-Hungarian Empire until after World War I. Because this region is situated at the crossroads of Slavic countries, Germanic countries, and the rest of Italy, it has been influenced by many cultures. Its best wines are white — in fact, they are indisputably the best white wines in Italy. If you were to visit the eastern province of Gorizia, next to Slovenia, you'd find that most people's surnames are Slavic, and that Serbo-Croatian is spoken as commonly as Italian.

Friuli-Venezia Giulia is usually simply called Friuli. (The name "Venezia Giulia" happens to be the region's only IGT designation.) All Friuli's vineyards are in the southern half of the region; the Alps take up its entire northern section (see Figure 7-3). The Veneto is to the south and west, the Adriatic Sea is also to the south, Austria makes up its northern border, and Slovenia lies on its eastern flank. Friuli produces the equivalent of about 12.2 million cases of wine each year, about 62 percent of which is DOC, a percentage third only to Piedmont and Trentino-Alto Adige in Italy. But, most tellingly, Friuli's grape yields per acre (about 3.5 tons, on the average) are much lower than either Trentino-Alto Adige or Veneto, and are among the lowest in Italy, especially in the region's eight DOC zones. Friuli is a quality-conscious wine region. And yet most Friulian wines retail in the $14 to $24 price range — excellent prices for the quality.

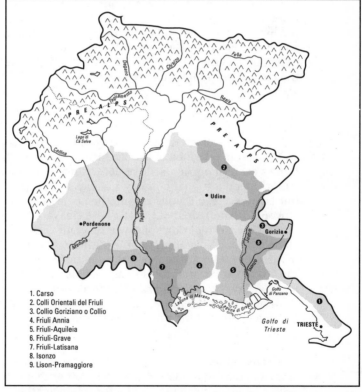

1. Carso
2. Colli Orientali del Friuli
3. Collio Goriziano o Collio
4. Friuli Annia
5. Friuli-Aquileia
6. Friuli-Grave
7. Friuli-Latisana
8. Isonzo
9. Lison-Pramaggiore

Figure 7-3: The vineyards of Friuli-Venezia Giulia are all in the southern part of the region.

The wines of Friuli

Friuli is considered the birthplace of modern white wine in Italy. In the 1960's, producers in this region were pioneers in fermenting the juice of white grapes without the grape skins — creating cleaner, fresher, lighter-colored white wines that didn't oxidize rapidly. Surprisingly, though, red wine still accounts for 40 percent of Friuli's DOC wine production, because Merlot predominates in the largest DOC zone, in the vast, gravelly plains of western Friuli. But in Friuli's two best wine zones, Collio Goriziano (usually known as Collio) and Colli Orientali del Friuli, well over two-thirds of the DOC wines are white.

Friuli now has eight DOC wine zones. Also, a small part of the Lison-Pramaggiore DOC zone of the Veneto (discussed in the previous section) extends into the Pordenone province in southwest Friuli. Of the eight Friuli wine zones, Collio and Colli Orientali del Friuli — often abbreviated as Colli Orientali — are the most important, due to the quality and renown of their wines.

The wines of Collio

The Collio or Collio Goriziano *(COH lee oh go ree zee AH no)* zone is in the province of Gorizia in southeast Friuli. Across Friuli's eastern border is Slovenia, and many of Collio's vineyards extend into that country, mindless of the political border. (As a result, you can find the name Collio on bottles of Slovenian wine.) Most of Collio's best vineyards are located around the town of Cormons, where an ideal, temperate microclimate exists: This area is in the pathway between the cool breezes from the Adriatic and the sheltering foothills of the Alps to the north, and the soil in the hills around Cormons, marl (a clay-like soil) and sandstone, is very suitable for grape growing. This is the finest white-wine area not only in Friuli but in all of Italy; Collio makes five times as much white wine as red wine.

Ironically, 30 years ago, most Collio grape growers sold their grapes in bulk to industrial wineries, rather than making and selling wine themselves. Two factors changed this situation: the sudden international popularity of Pinot Grigio — which gave them a ready market for a variety they had plenty of — and the pioneering work of winemaker Mario Schiopetto, who set an example by commercializing his own excellent wines.

Today, Collio and the nearby Colli Orientali del Friuli area might very well have a larger concentration of fine wineries than any other DOC wine zone in Italy. (One exceptional Collio winemaker, Silvio Jermann, pronounced *YER mahn,* makes a blended white wine from five different varieties, called Vintage Tunina, that's consistently rated Italy's finest white wine. For a wine of its quality, Vintage Tunina is reasonably priced at $35 to $40, but scarce; it also usually needs about 10 years to mature.)

Collio's wines are quite rich and full-bodied for Italian white wines. Among white varieties, the rich Tocai Friulano excels here, but Pinot Bianco, Pinot Grigio, Sauvignon Blanc, Chardonnay, and two local varieties, Ribolla Gialla *(ree BO lah JHAL lah)* and Malvasia Istriana *(mahl vah SEE ah ees tree AH nah),* also do well. (All these varieties are produced as varietal wines under the Collio DOC.) Cabernet Franc and Merlot are the leading red varieties; Collio Rosso, a blend of Merlot, Cabernet Franc, and/or Cabernet Sauvignon, is a popular red wine.

Other Collio DOC wines are the following: Bianco (dry white, from 45 to 55 percent Ribolla Gialla, 20 to 30 percent Malvasia Istriana, 15 to 25 percent Tocai Friulano, and eight other white varieties optional); Müller Thurgau; Picolit (semi-dry or sweet white); Riesling; Welschriesling; Traminer Aromatico; Cabernet; Cabernet Sauvignon; and Pinot Nero. Varietal wines from Collio derive 100 percent from the named grape.

The wines of Colli Orientali del Friuli

Colli Orientali del Friuli *(COH lee or ee en TAH lee del FREE oo lee)* is north and west of Collio. Almost all of the vineyards are in the southern part of this DOC zone, directly north of Collio, and so the two zones for the most part share similar climate and soil. As a result, Tocai Friulano, Pinot Bianco, Pinot Grigio, Sauvignon, and Chardonnay all do well here. But subtle differences in microclimate and customs exist: Among white varieties, Ribolla Gialla is more important here, as are two varieties quite the specialty of Colli Orientali: Picolit, which makes a famous dessert wine, and Verduzzo, which makes dry, semi-dry, and sweet styles of wine. The three grapes produce varietal wines under the Colli Orientale de Friuli DOC.

Red varieties are more important here than in Collio, as well. (White wine production outnumbers red by only a two to one ratio.) Besides making heartier, varietally-labelled versions of Merlot and both Cabernets, Colli Orientali winemakers specialize in one regional favorite red wine — the traditional, sturdy Refosco, from the grape of the same name — and two red wines from varieties indigenous to Colli Orientali, the elegant Schiopettino *(skee oh peh TEE noh,* also known as Ribolla Nera) and the once almost-extinct Pignolo, which makes a dark-colored, aromatic, tannic, intensely fruity dry wine.

Other Colli Orientali DOC varietal wines are the following: Malvasia Istriana; Riesling; Traminer Aromatico; Cabernet; Pinot Nero; and Tazzelenghe (a dry, purplish-red). The DOC also provides for a Bianco, Rosso and Rosato, each based on one or more varieties of the appropriate color.

Colli Orientali del Friuli also has three distinct sub-districts; wines made from grapes grown in these sub-districts may use the sub-district name on their labels. The three districts are the following:

- **Ramandolo** *(rah MAHN doh loh):* In the extreme northern part of Colli Orientali, Ramandolo is renowned for its sweet dessert wine, Verduzzo di Ramandolo. Two leading producers in this area are Giovanni Dri and Fratelli Coos.

- **Cialla** *(CHAL lah):* In the central part of the zone, this district specializes in sweet or semi-sweet Picolit, dry Ribolla Gialla, and Verduzzo (dry, semi-dry, and sweet). Other wines that can carry the Cialla appellation are Cialla Bianco (dry white; can be made from one or more white varieties of the zone); Cialla Rosso (dry red; can be made from one or more red varieties of the zone); Cialla Refosco dal Peduncolo Rosso; and Cialla Schiopettino. Ronchi di Cialla is a leading producer in the Cialla zone.

- **Rosazzo** *(roh SAHTZ zoh):* In the south, this area is especially identified with Ribolla Gialla; in fact, this variety is thought to have originated in the vineyards of the historic abbey, Abbazia di Rosazzo, over 1,000 years ago. Other wines that carry the Rosazzo appellation are Rosazzo Bianco (dry white; can be made from one or more white varieties of the zone); Rosazzo Rosso (dry red; can be made from one or more red varieties of the zone); Rosazzo Picolit (semi-dry or sweet white); and Rosazzo Pignolo (dry red). Abbazia di Rosazzo and Livio Felluga are two leading wineries which have vineyards in Rosazzo.

Recommended producers of Collio and Colli Orientali wines

We name our recommended producers of Collio and Colli Orientali del Friuli wines alphabetically, in two categories (Class One are the standout producers):

Class One

Giralamo Dorigo (Colli Orientali)

Livio Felluga (Collio; Colli Orientali)

Gravner (Collio)

Jermann (Collio)

Le Due Terre (Colli Orientali)

Miani (Colli Orientali)

Ronco dei Rosetti, of Zamò (Colli Orientali)

Ronco dei Tassi (Collio)

Russiz Superiore, of Marco Felluga (Collio)

Mario Schiopetto (Collio)

Venica & Venica (Collio)

Villa Russiz (Collio)

Class Two

La Boatina (Collio)

Bastianich (Colli Orientali)

Borgo Conventi (Collio)

Borgo del Tiglio (Collio)

Ca' Ronesca (Collio)

Paolo Caccese (Collio)

La Castellada (Collio)

Castello di Spessa (Collio)

Collavini (Colli Orientali)

Conte Attems (Collio)

Conte D'Attimis-Maniago (Colli Orientali)

Conti Formentini (Collio)

Fratelli Coos (Colli Orientali)

Giovanni Dri (Colli Orientali)

Marco Felluga (Collio)

Walter Filliputti, at Abbazia di Rosazzo (Colli Orientali)

Gradnik (Collio)

Livon (Collio)

Ascevi-Luwa (Collio)

Francesco Pecorari (Collio)

Perusini (Colli Orientali)

Petrucco (Colli Orientali)

Pighin (Collio)

Isidoro Polencic (Collio)

Prà di Pradis (Collio)

Doro Princic (Collio)

Puiatti (Collio)

Radikon (Collio)

Rocca Bernarda (Colli Orientali)

Paolo Rodaro (Colli Orientali)

Roncada (Collio)

Ronchi di Cialla (Colli Orientali)

Ronchi di Manzano (Colli Orientali)

Ronco delle Betulle (Colli Orientali)

Ronco del Gnemiz (Colli Orientali)

Specogna (Colli Orientali)

Torre Rosazza (Colli Orientali)

Tenuta Villanova (Collio)

La Viarte (Colli Orientali)

Vigne dal Leon (Colli Orientali)

Volpe Pasini (Colli Orientali)

Zamò & Zamò (Colli Orientali)

The wines of Isonzo and Carso

Like Collio and Colli Orientali, the Friuli Isonzo *(ee SOHN zoh)* — or Isonzo del Friuli — and the Carso *(CAR so)* DOC zones are in the eastern part of Friuli — specifically, the southeast (see Figure 7-3). The Isonzo zone is directly south of Collio. The hilly terrain ends in Collio, and so Isonzo consists of plains, but alluvial deposits from the Isonzo River make this area quite suitable for grapes. As it's closer to the sea, Isonzo has more of a maritime climate than Collio, with more rainfall. The northwest part, closest to Cormons, is the best vineyard area. Isonzo has a number of good producers; we rate it right below Collio and Colli Orientale del Friuli as a prime source of good white and red wines. The best Isonzo whites are Sauvignon (especially); Chardonnay; fine, dry Malvasia Istriana; Tocai Friulano; and Pinot Bianco (also sparkling). Merlot is Isonzo's best red wine. All varietal wines in this zone are 100 percent of the named variety.

Other Isonzo DOC wines (many in dry, semi-sweet and sparkling styles) are the following: Moscato Giallo; Moscato Rosa; Pinot Grigio; Riesling and Welschriesling; Verduzzo; Gewürztraminer; Cabernet, Cabernet Franc, and Cabernet Sauvignon; Franconia (dry red); Refosco dal Peduncolo Rosso (dry red); Schioppettino (dry red); Pinot Nero; Vendemmia Tardiva (late-harvest white from Tocai Friulano, Pinot Bianco, Chardonnay, and Verduzzo, together/singly); Bianco (40 to 50 percent Tocai Friulano, 25 to 30 percent Malvasia Istriana and/or Pinot Bianco, and 25 to 30 percent Chardonnay); Rosso (60 to 70 percent Merlot, 20 to 30 percent Cabernet Franc and/or Sauvignon, plus up to 20 percent Pinot Nero and Refosco); and Rosato (same varieties as the Rosso).

Vie di Romans is the standout producer in Isonzo. (Vie di Romans was formerly named Stelio Gallo, a family name, but following a lawsuit brought by E & J Gallo of California, winemaker-owner Gianfranco Gallo was forced to re-name his estate.)

The Carso wine zone is in the extreme southeast part of Friuli. It extends south of Isonzo down the Istrian peninsula to the city of Trieste, the capital of the Friuli region. As in Collio, Carso's eastern border is Slovenia. With the Adriatic Sea on the west, Carso's climate is clearly maritime. Carso's claim to fame, wine-wise, is that it's the home of a unique grape variety, the red Terrano, related to Refosco. In a specific sub-zone of

Carso, Terrano makes wines of piercing acidity, quite popular with the locals in Trieste, who enjoy it with Slavic and other hearty cuisine. The wine is definitely an acquired taste. Other notable Carso wines are a Carso Rosso, with a minimum of 70 percent Terrano, and the dry white Malvasia Istriana, at its almondy, honeyed best here on the Istrian peninsula. Other Carso wines are the following: Chardonnay; Pinot Grigio; Sauvignon; Traminer; Vitovska (dry white; believed to be of Slavic origin); Cabernet Franc; Cabernet Sauvignon; Merlot; and Refosco dal Peduncolo Rosso.

Recommended Isonzo and Carso producers

We recommend the following producers of Isonzo and Carso wines (listed alphabetically):

Borgo San Daniele (Isonzo)	Pierpaolo Pecorari (Isonzo)
Castelvecchio (Carso)	Ronco del Gelso (Isonzo)
Mauro Drius (Isonzo)	Sant' Elena (Isonzo)
Edi Kante (Carso)	Tenuta di Blasig (Isonzo)
Eddi Luisa (Isonzo)	Gianni Vescovo (Isonzo)
Masut da Rive (Isonzo)	Vie di Romans (Isonzo)
Lis Neris-Pecorari (Isonzo)	

Other Friuli DOC wines

Four Friuli wine zones are in the central and western part of the region — **Grave del Friuli** *(GRAH vae del FREE oo lee)*, **Friuli Aquilea** *(ah kwee LAE ah)*, **Friuli Latisana** *(lah tee SAH nah)*, and **Friuli Annia** *(AHN nee ah)*. Known collectively as the Adriatic Basin zones, they are in the plains, where the alluvial soil consists primarily of sand and gravel. Pordenone, in the western part of Grave del Friuli (Friuli's largest DOC zone by far), is the major city.

The wines of these zones are made from the same varieties as in the other Friuli DOC zones, but they are lighter in body and have less finesse. More red wines come from these four zones than the eastern zones, especially wines made from Merlot. Cabernet Franc, Cabernet Sauvignon, Cabernet, and the local Refosco are also popular. Most of the white wines are varietally-labelled: Tocai Friulano, Pinot Bianco, Pinot Grigio, Chardonnay, Verduzzo (in dry, semi-dry, and sweet forms), and others — often in *frizzante* or even *spumante* styles. Varietal wines are 90 percent from the named variety in the Friuli Annia and Friuli Latisana zones, 85 percent in the other two zones.

Other DOC wines from these four zones are the following (many come in multiple styles, such as *frizzante*, *novello*, or *spumante*):

- ✔ **Grave del Friuli:** Bianco (Chardonnay and/or Pinot Bianco); Rosso and Rosato (Cabernet Franc and/or Cabernet Sauvignon); Riesling; Sauvignon; Gewürztraminer; Pino Nero; Spumante (dry sparkling white, from Chardonnay, Pinot Bianco, and Pinot Nero).

- ✔ **Aquileia:** Rosato (70 to 80 percent Merlot, with 20 to 30 percent of both Cabernets, and two Refoscos — Nostrano and Peduncolo Rosso); Riesling; Sauvignon; and Traminer.

- ✔ **Latisana:** Gewürztraminer; Malvasia Istriana; Sauvignon; Rosato (mainly Merlot); Franconia (dry red); Pinot Nero; Riesling; and Spumante (dry or semi-dry, from Chardonnay, and/or Pinot Bianco, and/or Pinot Nero).

- ✔ **Annia:** Bianco, Rosso, and Rosato (dry wines, from any varieties of the appropriate color); Sauvignon; Malvasia Istriana; and Spumante (from Chardonnay and/or Pinot Bianco).

We recommend the following producers in these four Friuli DOC zones (listed alphabetically):

Borgo Magredo (Grave del Friuli)

Emiro Cav. Bortolusso (Annia)

Ca' Bolani (Aquileia)

Cabert (Grave del Friuli)

Forchir (Grave del Friuli)

Mangilli (Grave del Friuli)

Mulino delle Tolle (Aquileia)

A. Vicentini Orgnani (Grave del Friuli)

Pighin (Grave del Friuli)

Plozner (Grave del Friuli)

Tenuta Beltrame (Aquileia)

Vistorta (Grave del Friuli)

Part III
The Wine Regions of Central Italy

LUNGAROTTI

RUBESCO°
— VIGNA MONTICCHIO —
1 9 9 2

NOBIL CASA
CONTINI BONACOSSI

Villa di Capezzano

Carmignano

DENOMINAZIONE DI ORIGINE CONTROLLATA
E GARANTITA

1998

1991

FONTODI
Chianti Classico
Denominazione di origine controllata e garantita

PRODUCED AND BOTTLED BY
AZIENDA AGRICOLA FONTODI
PANZANO - ITALIA
PRODUCE OF ITALY

750 ML
ALC. 13% BY VOL.

In this part . . .

When we think about Italy, we invariably daydream about Tuscany, with its incomparable cities, Florence, and Siena . . . And when we dream about Tuscany, we think of Chianti Classico — unless we're thinking about Chianti's big brother, Brunello di Montalcino, or any of Tuscany's other great wines.

But you'll see that the wine wonders of Central Italy don't stop there. A short trip south takes you to Umbria, where you can experience the white wine, Orvieto, in its new and improved version — or visit Lungarotti, one of Italy's great producers, in Torgiano. Then on to Marche on the Adriatic Coast in the east, where you'll be amazed how good Verdicchio has become! Just south of Marche is Abruzzo, home of one of Italy's most popular, and affordable, red wines, Montepulciano d'Abruzzo. Before leaving Central Italy, you must stop in the Eternal City, Rome, where you can sip cool Frascati by the Spanish Steps and watch the thirsty tourists go by.

Chapter 8

The Wines of Tuscany

●●●●●●●●●●●●●●●●●●●●●●●●●●●●●●●●●●●●●●

In This Chapter

▶ The many faces of Sangiovese

▶ Chianti's new heights of quality

▶ Super-Tuscans galore

▶ Tuscany's happening coastline

●●●●●●●●●●●●●●●●●●●●●●●●●●●●●●●●●●●●●●

*I*f someone were to poll wine lovers regarding their favorite Italian regions, we'd bet that Tuscany would come in first. Besides making Italy's most famous wine — Chianti — Tuscany is home to one of Italy's most prestigious wines, Brunello di Montalcino, and the whole, exciting category of Super-Tuscan wines. Tuscany is also tourist heaven. With the cities of Florence, Siena, and Pisa; quaint medieval towns such as San Gimignano and Montalcino; storybook castles; and the stirringly beautiful hills of the Tuscan countryside, Tuscany is one of Europe's best destinations for art, architecture, history, natural beauty, great food, and fine wine.

If you've been to Tuscany, your pulse might be racing now, as you recall the magic and wonder of the region. Whether you've experienced Tuscany first-hand or not, though, we hope that our enthusiasm for the wines of Tuscany will infect you, and that the wines will bring you as much pleasure as they bring us.

The Big Picture of Tuscany

One particular church in Florence contains the graves of Amerigo Vespucci, Dante, Galileo, Verrazzano, Macchiavelli, and Michaelangelo — enduring testimony to Tuscany's leadership in the realms of science, politics, world discovery, art, and literature during the Middle Ages. In the realm of wine,

Tuscany is no less a leader. Italy's most recent wine renaissance began in Tuscany in the early 1970s, when producers of Chianti decided to show the world once and for all that Tuscan wines deserve to be taken seriously; their quality movement changed the face of wine all over Italy.

Tuscany (including its seven islands) is Italy's fifth largest region, covering a territory slightly smaller than New Hampshire. It sits on Italy's western coast, surrounded by Emilia-Romagna to the north, Umbria to the east, and Lazio to the south; except for a small border with Liguria in the northwest, Tuscany's entire western border is the Tyrrhenian Sea, part of the Mediterranean (see Figure 1-1).

The Apennine Mountains separate Tuscany from Emilia-Romagna in the north, and smaller mountains line the region to the west and south, but Tuscany is more hilly than mountainous. The region's interior is particularly hilly, and some areas of high elevation also exist near the coast. The altitude of the hills tempers the summer heat, which can otherwise be sweltering. (An air-conditioned hotel and mosquito repellent are absolute requisites for a summertime stay in Florence.)

Tuscany has plenty of vineyard land: In all of Italy, only Sicily and Apulia have more acres planted with vines. But seven regions of Italy produce more wine than Tuscany does. Tuscany's hillside vineyards and poor soils are geared toward quality rather than quantity of production. Volume-wise, Tuscany produces more DOC wine than any other region except Piedmont and Veneto, and many of Tuscany's IGT-level wines are extremely high in quality.

About 50 percent of Tuscany's wine production is DOC or DOCG. Tuscany has six DOCG wines and 29 DOCs (depending on how you count them); the vast majority (80 percent) of this classified-level production is red wine. The six DOCG wines are the following:

- ✔ **Chianti** *(key AHN tee)*
- ✔ **Chianti Classico**
- ✔ **Brunello di Montalcino** *(brew NEL lo dee mahn tahl CHEE no)*

✔ **Carmignano Rosso** *(car mee NYAH no)*

✔ **Vino Nobile di Montepulciano** *(VEE no NO bee lae dee mahn tae pool chee AH no)*

✔ **Vernaccia di San Gimignano** *(ver NAHCH cha dee san gee me NYAH no)*

Of these wines, only Vernaccia di San Gimignano is white. Figure 8-1 depicts Tuscany's DOC/G zones.

Sangiovese is the main red grape variety of Tuscany, not just quantitatively but also qualitatively speaking. Many clones of Sangiovese exist; besides broad families of Sangiovese, such as the top-quality Sangiovese Grosso and the ordinary Sangiovese di Romagna, numerous local clones have evolved in each of the districts where the grape has traditionally grown, in response to local conditions. Sangiovese's many mutations explain why it has several different names or nick-names in Tuscany, such as Brunello, Prugnolo Gentile, and Morellino.

The next most important red variety in quality terms is Cabernet Sauvignon; this variety has grown in the region for at least 250 years, but has become especially popular since the late 1970s. Numerous other red varieties exist, including native varieties such as Mammolo, Canaiolo *(cahn eye OH lo)*, Malvasia Nera, and Colorino, and international varieties such as Merlot (like Cabernet, increasingly popular with growers), Pinot Noir, and Syrah.

Trebbiano is the leading white variety of the region in terms of acreage planted — and the main reason that Tuscan white wines are far less exciting than the reds. But Vermentino, a characterful and increasingly popular variety, is common in Tuscany's coastal areas, in blends and alone. The highest qual-ity white wines derive from the Vernaccia grape, grown around San Gimignano, and from international varieties such as Chardonnay, which has grown in Tuscany for about 150 years, but has been particularly fashionable in the last two decades.

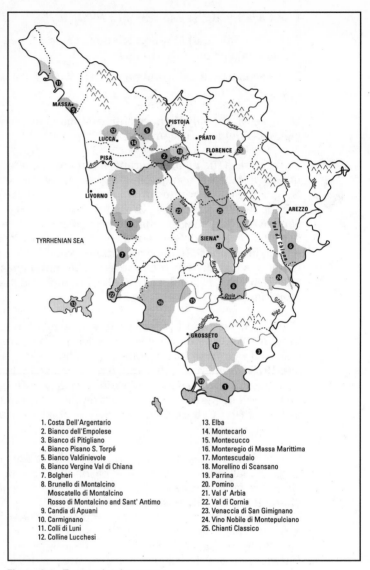

1. Costa Dell'Argentario
2. Bianco dell'Empolese
3. Bianco di Pitigliano
4. Bianco Pisano S. Torpé
5. Bianco Valdinievole
6. Bianco Vergine Val di Chiana
7. Bolgheri
8. Brunello di Montalcino
   Moscatello di Montalcino
   Rosso di Montalcino and Sant' Antimo
9. Candia di Apuani
10. Carmignano
11. Colli di Luni
12. Colline Lucchesi
13. Elba
14. Montecarlo
15. Montecucco
16. Monteregio di Massa Marittima
17. Montescudaio
18. Morellino di Scansano
19. Parrina
20. Pomino
21. Val d' Arbia
22. Val di Cornia
23. Venaccia di San Gimignano
24. Vino Nobile di Montepulciano
25. Chianti Classico

Figure 8-1: Tuscany's wine zones.

The Land of Chianti

Chianti is not just Tuscany's most famous wine — it's Italy's most famous wine, and one of the most famous wines in the entire world. But Chianti is not just one type of wine. The name embodies wines from several sub-zones, which vary quite a lot in richness and quality; it also covers wines for drinking young, and ageworthy wines; inexpensive ($8 a bottle) wines and pricey ($60) wines. What these wines have in common is that they're all red, and they're all based on the Sangiovese grape.

The collective Chianti zone is by far the largest classified wine zone in Tuscany. It's situated mainly in the central part of the region, with one sub-zone (Chianti Colli Pisane) extending farther west, toward the sea. The collective territory produces about eight million cases of Chianti wine per year, along with various white wines, other types of red wine, and dessert wine. Some of these other wines are DOC wines from zones that overlap the Chianti area, such as Pomino, while others are IGT-level wines, such as the so-called Super-Tuscan wines.

The range of Chianti wines

Two separate DOCG designations apply to Chianti wines today: One is Chianti Classico DOCG, for wines from the area between Florence and Siena; the other is Chianti DOCG, for all other Chianti wines. The Chianti DOCG includes wines from six sub-zones, which carry the name of their sub-zone on their labels, as well as wines *not* from a specific sub-zone, which are simply labelled "Chianti."

Since 1996, both Chianti and Chianti Classico are 75 to 100 percent Sangiovese, with up to 10 percent Canaiolo and up to 6 percent of two white varieties (Trebbiano and Malvasia); other red varieties may constitute up to 15 percent of the blend. In practice, Chianti can be entirely Sangiovese, or can be entirely from red varieties, and the addition of as much as 15 percent Cabernet Sauvignon —popular with Sangiovese — or Merlot is entirely legal.

The flexibility that wine producers have in their grape variety selection is one of the reasons that Chianti wines vary in weight and intensity. Simple, inexpensive wines for drinking young are likely to have some white grapes in their blend, while richer wines are made entirely from red grapes; the richest wines are mainly Sangiovese, often with Cabernet Sauvignon, and come from the finest vineyard areas.

Chianti Classico

Chianti Classico is not only the heartland of Tuscany — the original Chianti area, situated at the very center of Tuscany — but it is also the emotional heart of the region. The zone is populated by serious and skilled winemakers who care deeply about their land and their wines, and who infect wine lovers all over the world with their passion.

Becoming passionate about Chianti Classico is not the least bit difficult once you visit the area. It's one of the most timeless and unspoiled places in Italy — hilly landscapes of vines, olive groves, stately cypress trees, wooded areas, old farmhouses, and lordly castles. When we first visited there in 1975, we had the spooky feeling that we were witnessing the same beauty and tranquility that must have inspired the Roman poet Virgil two thousand years earlier. Today, the area still thrills us.

The zone and its wines

Chianti Classico is an area of approximately 100 square miles, situated between the cities of Florence and Siena (see Figure 8-2). It encompasses four communes, or communities, in their entirety — Greve, Radda, Gaiole, and Castellina — as well as portions of five others. More than 700 grape growers farm the 24,700 acres of vineyards in this area.

Although this is not a tremendously large area, the Chianti Classico zone is quite varied in soil and climate because of altitude differences (vineyards are generally from 820 to nearly 2,000 feet high) and varying distance from the Arno River, which flows through Florence. The soil in the southern part of the area is stony and hard in some parts, clayey in others, while soil in the north, closer to Florence, is richer. Higher elevations are cooler. The southernmost part, Castelnuovo Berardegna, is warmer than most of the other parts of the zone. This diversity of climate and soil — together with the flexibility regarding grape varieties that the DOCG regulation provides, and varying winemaking styles — creates a stunning array of wines.

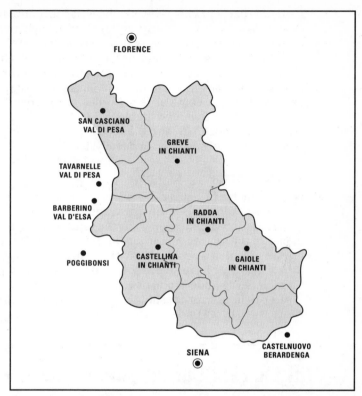

Figure 8-2: Chianti Classico is a wine zone between Florence and Siena.

As generalizations go, most Chianti Classico wines are medium-bodied rather than full-bodied, firm rather than soft, with a medium amount of dry tannin, and medium to high acidity. Tart cherry or ripe cherry are the main aroma/ flavor descriptors, sometimes with delicate floral or nutty notes. One characteristic of Chianti that strikes us is that the wines are fairly inexpressive in the front of your mouth; all their action happens in the middle and rear. They're completely different from most New World reds, whose richness is evident as soon as you put them in your mouth.

For several years now, we've tried to peg the styles of Chianti Classico wines to the specific commune where the grapes grow. Our experimentation has had some limited success: We've come to expect wines from Castelnuovo Berardegna to be richer and riper, Gaiole wines to be firm and structured,

Panzano (part of Greve) wines to be well-concentrated, and Castellina wines (our favorite style) to have finely-tuned aromas and flavors. But generalizations are difficult, we've discovered, because of the varying altitudes within each area. Nevertheless, we look forward to the day when serious wine lovers are as conversant in the communes of Chianti Classico as they are in the communes of Bordeaux. (See our book *French Wine For Dummies,* published by Hungry Minds, Inc., for more on those.) Chianti Classico is a world-class wine region worthy of such detailed analysis.

Clones, vintages, and aging

Another factor bringing diversity to the wines of Chianti Classico — and temporarily frustrating our attempts to make generalizations about them — is the range of Sangiovese clones in the vineyards. During the 1960s and 1970s, most growers planted a prolific clone that makes fairly low-alcohol, thin wines; they have since replanted with several newly-identified or newly-understood clones that produce wines of greater richness. As a result, the nature of Chianti Classico wines is changing under our very noses, so to speak.

Will the real Chianti please stand up?

The land of Chianti has an ancient winemaking legacy. Grape growing and winemaking have existed there since the 8th century B.C. (two centuries before winemaking came to Southern France). The name "Chianti" applied to wine as early as 1398 — although in those early days, "Chianti" was also a white wine — and several wine producers who exist today can trace their companies' lineage back to the 14th century.

In 1716, the Grand Duke of Tuscany declared Chianti a wine of protected origin. But what actually was and wasn't the territory of Chianti remained a contentious subject among producers until the early 20th century. Some wanted to restrict the use of the name Chianti to a fairly small area known as Chianti in the early 15th century, while others wanted the right to use the famous name for their own wines from outlying areas. Factions formed, all of them using "Chianti" as part of their name. In 1932, a governmental decree finally put the matter to rest by recognizing all of the so-called Chianti zones as Chianti, but distinguishing the various areas with specific sub-zone names, such as Chianti Classico, Chianti Colli Fiorentini, and so forth.

Vintages also vary quite a lot in Chianti Classico, but variations in soil and microclimate throughout the zone can offset some vintage variations. (Vineyards in warmer areas can do well in cool years, for example.) Some recent years, such as 1990 and 1997, have been unusually warm and dry, bringing greater ripeness to the grapes and atypical weight and richness to the wines.

In good vintages, most producers make a *riserva* version of their Chianti Classico; *riserva* wines are generally made from a producer's best grapes, and they must age for at least 27 months at the winery, as well as have at least 12.5 percent alcohol compared to the minimum 12 percent for regular Chianti Classico. *Riservas* are capable of aging longer after they are released, too. A Chianti Classico Riserva from a good producer in a good vintage can be very enjoyable even 15 years from the vintage date, while a basic Chianti Classico is best consumed within ten years.

In addition to making both *riserva* and regular styles, many producers make single-vineyard Chianti Classicos — usually *riserva*-level. These single-vineyard wines are generally the most expensive Chianti Classicos of all: They range from $35 to $60, compared to $25 to $45 for *riservas* and $15 to $30 for basic Chianti Classico wines.

Many single-vineyard wines from the Chianti Classico zone aren't technically Chianti at all, however. This area was the hotbed of Super-Tuscan wine production (see the section "Super-Tuscan Wines — the Winds of Change," later in this chapter) all through the 1980s and 1990s, and many producers dedicated their best grapes, from their best vineyards, to these non-DOC, designer wines. Some producers continue this practice. But since 1996, when the DOCG law sanctioned the production of Chianti Classico from Sangiovese alone (or blended), several producers have brought their best wines back into the Chianti Classico fold. An emerging trend is for producers to make two Chianti Classicos, labeling the best one (usually a *riserva*) with the full name of their property, and the other wine with a shorter version of that name. For example, the Castello Brolio winery, owned by Barone Ricasoli, labels one wine as Castello Brolio and another as simply Brolio; Castello di Volpaia does the same.

Our favorite Chianti Classico producers

Most Chianti Classico producers are wine estates — fairly small operations that own vineyards and make wines from their own grapes; each estate typically makes two or three Chianti Classico wines — a basic version, a *riserva,* and a single-vineyard, for example. The names of these estates often begin with *castello* (castle), *fattoria* (pronounced *fah toh REE ah,* meaning farm), or *podere* (pronounced *poh DAE rae,* meaning property). Most bottles of Chianti Classico carry a neck-band with a black rooster on it, the trademark of a voluntary consortium that has promoted the region's wines since 1924.

Some large producers own vineyards in the zone but also make wines from purchased grapes; these wines are usually less expensive than estate-bottled wines. Some large producers own several estates, and make wines at each of them (Ruffino, for example, owns estates in Greve, Panzano, and Castellina, and bottles the production of some of them separately), as well as making wines that are blended from their holdings throughout the *classico* zone. (Antinori's Tenute Marchesi Antinori Riserva is an example of a blended Chianti Classico.)

The average quality level of Chianti Classico wines is quite high, and we therefore admire the wines of many dozens of producers. We divide our favorite producers into two groups; the producers in each are listed alphabetically, and the name of the commune where they are located is listed for each.

Class One
Barone Ricasoli, formerly Castello di Brolio (Gaiole)
Castellare di Castellina (Castellina)
Castello dei Rampolla (Panzano)
Castello di Ama (Gaiole)
Castello di Fonterutoli (Castellina)
Castello di Volpaia (Radda)
Fattoria di Felsina (Castelnuovo Berardegna)
Fontodi (Panzano)
Isole e Olena (Barberino Val d'Elsa)

Marchesi Antinori (San Casciano Val di Pesa)
La Massa (Panzano)
Monsanto (Barberino Val d'Elsa)
Podere Il Palazzino (Gaiole)
Ruffino (various estates)
San Giusto a Rentennano (Gaiole)

Class Two
Badia a Coltibuono (Gaiole)
La Brancaia (Castellina)
Carpineto (Greve)
Castell'in Villa (Castelnuovo Berardegna)

Castello d'Albola (Radda)
Castello di Cacchiano
  (Gaiole)
Castello di Gabbiano
  (Mercatale Val di Pesa)
Castello di Querceto (Greve)
Castello di Verrazzano
  (Greve)
Le Corti (San Casciano Val di
  Pesa)
Dievole (Castelnuovo
  Berardegna)
Agricoltori del Chianti
  Geografico (Gaiole)
Castello di Lilliano
  (Castellina)
Machiavelli (San Casciano Val
  di Pesa)
Melini (Poggibonsi)
Nittardi (Castellina)

Nozzole (Greve)
Poggerino (Radda)
Poggio al Sole (Tavarnelle Val
  di Pesa)
Querciabella (Greve)
Riecine (Gaiole)
Riseccoli (Greve)
Rocca di Castagnoli (Gaiole)
San Fabiano Calcinaia
  (Castellina)
San Felice (Castelnuovo
  Berardegna)
Vecchie Terre di Montefili
  (Panzano)
Vignamaggio (Greve)
Villa Cafaggio (Panzano)
Cecchi-Villa Cerna
  (Castellina)
Viticcio (Greve)

Chianti

The Chianti DOCG designation applies to all Chianti wines other than those made from grapes grown in the Chianti Classico area. This appellation covers wines from six specific sub-zones, as well as wines from peripheral areas. Wines from individual sub-zones may carry the name of that sub-zone on their labels, while wines from the other areas, or wines combining grapes from more than one sub-zone, simply carry the appellation Chianti DOCG. Chianti Superiore is another designation within the Chianti DOCG; it applies to wines made from grapes grown within the provinces of Florence or Siena but not within the Chianti Classico area.

The best Chianti wines are those from specific sub-zones; these sub-zones are the following:

- **Chianti Colli Pisane** *(COH lee pee SAH nae):* The western-most area, in the province of Pisa

- **Chianti Colli Fiorentini** *(fee or en TEE nee):* Literally, "Florentine hills," north of Chianti Classico, in the province of Florence

✔ **Chianti Colli Senesi** *(seh NAE see)*: The Siena hills, the southernmost part

✔ **Chianti Colli Aretini** *(ah rae TEE nee):* The Arezzo hills, in the eastern part of the zone

✔ **Chianti Montalbano** *(mon tahl BAH no):* The northwest part of the zone

✔ **Chianti Rufina** *(ROO fee nah):* The northeastern part of the zone

Of these areas, the Rufina zone probably ranks highest for the quality of its wines — and is also the one area whose wines are generally available in the U.S. (It's also the area whose name most confuses wine drinkers; Rufina *(ROO fee nah),* the zone, has nothing to do with Ruffino *(roof FEE no),* the wine producer.) The Rufina area is slightly more mountainous, and less gently-hilly, than the *classico* zone. Its microclimate is cooler at night than that of the *classico* zone, and the grapes ripen more slowly because of this day-night temperature variation. Traditionally, most Chianti Rufina was relatively light-bodied and made to be enjoyed young, but since the mid-1980s, producers have also made richer, more serious and more ageworthy wines. Some Rufina wines, such as the best of Selvapiana and Frescobaldi, are among the finest of all Chiantis.

If the Rufina zone has any competition within the Chianti DOCG, it comes from Chianti Colli Senesi. This is a large area — the largest of the six sub-zones — extending west and south of the *classico* zone. It encompasses vineyards around San Gimignano, Montalcino, and Montepulciano, among others; each of these areas is famous for other wines (Vernaccia di San Gimignano, Brunello di Montalcino, and Vino Nobile di Montepulciano, all described later in this chapter), but some producers make Chianti Colli Senesi as well. The warmer microclimate of the southern part of Colli Senesi enables producers to make relatively full-bodied Chianti wines.

The most common Chianti DOCG wines on the U.S. market are inexpensive ($6 to $12), fairly light-bodied wines under the basic Chianti appellation. Many of these are made by producers in the *classico* zone who purchase less expensive grapes (or wine) from beyond the Chianti Classico borders specifically to make a competitively-priced wine.

Piero Antinori: a Tuscan leader

In 1966, Piero Antinori's father retired, and named his 28-year-old son Piero managing director and president of the prestigious Marchesi Antinori wine firm. It was a position Piero was destined to fill, as the 25th generation of the Antinori family to run the business — which was officially registered in the Florence Vintners' Guild in 1385. (Seeing the family's 15th-century Palazzo Antinori, on Piazza Antinori in downtown Florence, brings a visceral sense of the company's history and heritage.) And so, you might say that Piero Antinori inherited an established business. But in 1966, Antinori was one of a half dozen leading producers of Chianti. Now, 35 years later, the Marchesi Antinori firm is regarded as not only one of the most important wineries in Italy, but also one of the wine world's best and most consistent. An Antinori Chianti — any one of the many which the winery produces at various price levels — is always well-made. Antinori also owns Prunotto Barolo, makes a fine Vino Nobile (La Braccesca) and Brunello (Pian delle Vigne), has a winery in Bolgheri producing excellent wines, makes a

great white wine from Umbria called Cervaro della Sala, has a new project in Puglia, a project in Hungary, plus a co-produced red wine from Washington state called Col Solare and a winery in Napa, Atlas Peak, which makes Sangiovese.

But Piero's most notable achievement was undoubtedly his role in helping to create the so-called Super-Tuscan wines, and in doing so, saving the Tuscan wine business. Not until a producer of Antinori's stature put his reputation on the line and made a wine that ignored the Chianti Classico DOC blending regulations (a 1971 Tignanello, a Sangiovese-Cabernet blend, which he released in 1978), did the downward spiral of Tuscan wine, instigated by cheap and lackluster Chianti, finally end. Other producers followed, making their own designer wines which gained international recognition in the 1980s and 1990s. The DOC/G commission finally refined the grape blend for Chianti. Today, Tuscany and its wines are in better shape, quality-wise, than in any other time in its history, thanks in no small way to Piero Antinori.

Because Chianti Classico truly dominates the export market for all types of Chianti, our list of recommended producers of Chianti DOCG is short. We list these producers alphabetically, with their sub-zone:

Fattoria di Basciano (Rufina)
Tenuta di Capezzana
  (Montalbano)

Castello di Farnatella
  (Colli Senesi)

Marchesi de' Frescobaldi
(Rufina)
Chigi Saracini (Colli Senesi)
Fattoria Selvapiana (Rufina)

Fattoria di Manzano
(Colli Aretini)
Fattoria di Petrolo
(Colli Aretini)

Pomino, San Gimignano, and other Chianti neighbors

Certain areas within the Chianti zone have their own DOC/G designations for other types of wine. These are really distinct wines that have nothing to do with Chianti itself, but we discuss them here because their vineyards are in the Chianti area.

Vernaccia di San Gimignano

San Gimignano *(sahn gee me N'YAH no)* is a charming medieval town that's famous for its towers. The vineyards east of San Gimignano lie within the Chianti Colli Senesi area, but the local pride is the DOCG white wine, Vernaccia *(ver NAHTCH chah)*.

Vernaccia di San Gimignano is Tuscany's finest type of white wine — and has been, for seven centuries. It derives at least 90 percent from the Vernaccia grape variety, which is famous only here. Generally, Vernaccia is a fairly full-bodied, dry, soft white, with honey, mineral, and earthy flavors, but it sometimes is quite fruity. Characterful white wine is not easy to find in central Italy, and so we encourage you to try Vernaccia di San Gimignano.

The wine varies quite a lot in style according to its winemaking: Some producers ferment or age the wine in small French oak barrels, which gives the wine a toastiness or a creaminess that it doesn't otherwise have, while other producers make the wine un-oaked, so that the mineral aromas and flavors shine through more clearly. Some producers make more than one Vernaccia wine, each a different style.

Vernaccia di San Gimignano was the very first wine to become DOC, in 1966. Much more recently, **San Gimignano** (without the "Vernaccia") became a DOC designation for red, rosé, and Vin Santo wines (see the section, "Vin Santo," a little later in this chapter). San Gimignano Rosso is at least half Sangiovese, and can be labelled "Sangiovese" if that grape is at least 85 percent of the blend; a *riserva* has at least two years of aging. A *novello* also comes mainly from Sangiovese, while a *rosato* is 60 percent Sangiovese, with up to 20 percent Canaiolo, up to 15 percent of other red varieties, and up to 15 percent white varieties — either Trebbiano, Malvasia, and/or Vernaccia. The Vin Santo can be white (from Malvasia, Trebbiano, and Vernaccia) or pink (mainly from Sangiovese); we describe Vin Santo later in the chapter.

We recommend the following producers of Vernaccia di San Gimignano, listed alphabetically:

Baroncini	Palagetto
Vincenzo Cesani	Giovanni Panizzi
Fattoria di Cusona (or Guicciardini Strozzi)	Fattoria Il Paradiso
	San Donato
Casale-Falchini	Fattoria San Quirico
La Lastra	Signano
Melini	Teruzzi & Puthod
Montenidoli	Fratelli Vagnoni
Mormoraia	

Pomino

Pomino *(po MEE no)* is a tiny enclave within the Chianti Rufina area. This hilly zone, with its sandy soil and particularly benevolent climate, is a stronghold of French grape varieties in Sangiovese land. Vittorio degli Albizi, whose family came from Auxerre in France's Chablis region, planted Chardonnay, Merlot, and other French varieties here in the mid-1800s. His heirs later married into the Frescobaldi family, and Frescobaldi — a major producer in the Chianti Rufina zone — is now the main landowner in Pomino.

In the 1960s, some Pomino vineyards were replanted with typical Tuscan varieties; DOC regulations therefore permit both nationalities of grapes. Pomino Rosso derives from Sangiovese, Canaiolo, Cabernet Sauvignon, Cabernet Franc, and Merlot, with other varieties (Frescobaldi uses Pinot Nero); a *riserva*-level has three years' aging. Pomino Bianco comes mainly from Pinot Bianco, Chardonnay, and Trebbiano grapes, with other varieties, such as Pinot Grigio. Pomino may also be made as a Vin Santo — dry, medium-sweet or sweet, white or red.

We have consistently enjoyed the wines of Pomino, both red and white; the whites are full-bodied and rich, and among the best white wines of Tuscany. In addition to Frescobaldi, another fine producer of Pomino is Fattoria Petrognano, which is owned by the owner of Selvapiana, another good Chianti Rufina producer. Expect to pay $18 to $27 for Pomino.

Vin Santo

Vin Santo *(vin SAHN toh)* di Chianti Classico is the DOC name for a traditional Tuscan dessert wine made within the Chianti Classico zone — although several Vin Santos exist, DOC and not, from different parts of Tuscany and elsewhere in Italy.

Vin Santo ("holy wine") is made by drying grapes for several months before pressing them, to concentrate their sugar; the wine from these grapes is then aged in small barrels for several years, sometimes re-fermenting in the process, and developing characteristics of oxidation, such as a nutty aroma and an amber color. Vin Santo wines range from dry to sweet, depending on the individual wine. They're sometimes pink, if red grapes are part of the blend.

Vin Santo di Chianti Classico must come mainly from Trebbiano and Malvasia, but other grapes, red or white, are allowed; the wine ages in barrels for at least three years, or four years for *riserva*. Many producers make it, but in small quantities.

Other DOCs of Central Tuscany

Two other DOC zones are nestled with the Chianti area. **Val d'Arbia** *(vahl DAR bee ah),* or Arbia Valley, takes its name from the Arbia River which flows through the Chianti Classico zone; the Val d'Arbia DOC zone overlaps part of Chianti Classico and also extends southeastward of it. Bianco Val D'Arbia is a white wine based on Trebbiano, Malvasia, and Chardonnay, with up to 15 percent of other grapes, such as Pinot Grigio. It's a dry, light- to medium-bodied white; it can also be a dry, medium-sweet, or sweet Vin Santo.

The territory of the DOC zone called **Colli dell'Etruria Centrale** *(COH lee del ae TROO ree ah chen TRAH lae)* corresponds to the combined Chianti and Chianti Classico zones. The name means "hills of central Etruria," with reference to the ancient Etruscan name for central Italy. The appellation applies to white, red, rosé, and Vin Santo wines. This DOC serves multiple purposes — in some cases providing a DOC haven for wines with a different grape blend from Chianti (white wines, and reds with more than 15 percent of non-traditional grapes, for example), in other cases enabling producers to de-classify wines that don't make the grade for Chianti. The Rosso (and Rosato) is mainly Sangiovese, with Cabernet Sauvignon, Cabernet Franc, and Merlot (no more than 10 percent of any one), and Canaiolo, Trebbiano, and Malvasia (for a total of 10 percent max). The formula for the Bianco and the Vin Santo is no less creative: half Trebbiano, with 5 percent Malvasia and 10 to 45 percent of Pinot Bianco, Pinot Grigio, Chardonnay, and Sauvignon — and up to 15 percent of other local varieties. In time, perhaps this DOC will come to signify a specific style of red or white wine, but for now, it's a catch-all.

Monumental Montalcino

In terms of international renown, the Montalcino *(mon tal CHEE no)* area is Tuscany's second most important wine zone, after Chianti Classico. In terms of quality, however, it's Tuscany's star.

Montalcino is a small medieval town that perches at 1,850 feet altitude, atop a hill in the province of Siena. The first time we left Chianti Classico and drove south to Montalcino we couldn't find it, because the approach to the town is so unassuming that we kept passing it by. The grandeur of Montalcino's wines led us to expect a prodigious town summoning itinerant wine lovers like a beacon, but in reality, Montalcino is an isolated community that stands apart from the cosmopolitan parts of Tuscany in space and in spirit.

The Montalcino wine district is a hilly, densely wooded area surrounding the town, which sits slightly northeast of the district's geographic center. The climate is generally warmer and dryer than Chianti Classico's, and has few extremes because of the tempering influence of the sea to the southwest and the sheltering effect of Mount Amiata, Tuscany's highest peak, to the southeast. Soils are varied from one end of the district to the other, and from lower altitude vineyards (490 feet) to higher (up to 1,640 feet). The particular climate, soils, altitudes, and hillside aspects of the vineyards combine to create a singular effect: that Montalcino is the finest location on earth for the Sangiovese grape.

Brunello di Montalcino

Montalcino's signature wine is Brunello *(brew NEL lo)* di Montalcino, a hefty red wine made entirely from Sangiovese. (Brunello is the local, but unofficial, name for Sangiovese.) In the isolated hills of Montalcino, Sangiovese ripens more and better than elsewhere in Tuscany, giving wines with more color, body, extract, tannin, and richness than other wines based on the same variety.

Not that other Sangiovese wines are necessarily based on exactly the same grapes, however: The various clones of Sangiovese that grow in Montalcino are believed to be distinct from those elsewhere in Tuscany, because they evolved in response to the conditions of Montalcino. In the mid 1800s, a local named Clemente Santi isolated the clones most suited to making a high-quality, ageworthy, 100-percent Sangiovese wine, in an age when easy-to-drink, blended wines were the norm in Montalcino, as in Chianti. The wines of his grandson, Ferruccio Biondi-Santi, and a handful of other producers became celebrated during the second half of the 19th century, and affirmed the special synergy that Brunello and Montalcino share.

Today, about 200 grape growers — mostly small farmers — exist in Montalcino, and Brunello di Montalcino is considered one of Italy's two best wines (the other is Barolo; see Chapter 5). It was the first wine to earn DOCG status, in 1980, and it is generally among Italy's most expensive wines. But production is small: Only about 333,000 cases of Brunello di Montalcino are made each year.

Although the Montalcino district is small, the wines are not uniform in style. The grapes ripen in very different ways in different parts of the zone. For example, in the northern and eastern vineyards, grapes ripen more slowly because of north-facing hillsides, higher altitude, more rain, or cooler temperatures than in the southern and western part of the zone; wines from these areas can be more perfumed, a bit lighter in body and harder than those from the southern areas, where warmer temperatures, intense sunlight and maritime breezes enable the grapes to producer richer wines with riper and more intense aromas and flavors. But the zone is even more complex than this example implies.

Aging and ageability

Since its earliest conception, Brunello di Montalcino has been a wine for aging. Some wines from good vintages not only can age for 50 years or more, but in fact *need* a couple of decades to lose the fire of youth and become harmonious. The DOCG regulations echo the wine's potential by requiring that Brunello age for four years before it can be released — the longest minimum aging period for any wine in Italy; Brunello di Montalcino Riserva, made from a producer's best wines in very good vintages, must age five years before release. For at least two of these four or five years, the wine must age in oak barrels or casks.

Traditional-minded producers age their wine for three years or more in large, old casks, producing more austere wines, while the most avant-garde producers age some of their Brunello in small barrels of French oak (and practice other non-traditional winemaking techniques) to fix a certain fruitiness in their wine. In either case, almost every Brunello is best with *at least* ten years of age from the vintage.

Despite the privileged climate of Montalcino, vintage differences do exist. Since World War II, the Montalcino zone has averaged about five very good to outstanding vintages per decade. By the time that all the Brunellos from the 1990s have been released, in 2004, that decade will probably prove to have exceeded the historical average, with three outstanding vintages (1990, 1995, and 1997) and perhaps five very good vintages (1991, 1993, 1994, 1998, and 1999).

Tasting wines from these great vintages carries a price, however. Brunello from the 1995 vintage costs about $40 to $75 a bottle at retail, and 1995 *riservas* cost up to $100 or more.

Recommended Brunello producers

Here we name our favorite producers of Brunello di Montalcino. We list them alphabetically:

Altesino
Argiano
Castello Banfi
Fattoria dei Barbi
Biondi-Santi (expensive)
Camigliano
Campogiovanni

Canalicchio di Sopra
Capanna
Tenuta Caparzo (especially, the single-vineyard La Casa)
Casanova di Neri
Fattoria del Casato

Case Basse of Soldera
  (very expensive)
Castelgiocondo
Cerbaiona
Ciacci Piccolomini
Col d'Orcia
Costanti
Tenuta Friggiali
Fuligni
La Gerla
Gorelli
Il Greppone Mazzi
Lisini
Il Marroneto
Mastrojanni

Tenute Silvio Nardi
Siro Pacenti
Pertimali di Angelo Sassetti
Pertimali di Livio Sassetti
La Pieve di Santa Restituta
La Poderina
Poggio Antico
Poggio Salvi
Il Poggiolo
Il Poggione
Salvioni-La Cerbaiola
Talenti- Pian di Conte
La Torre
Uccelliera
Val di Suga

Other wines of Montalcino

Once upon a time, the Montalcino zone made only one DOC
wine. Today this area has three DOC wines to accompany its
flagship Brunello di Montalcino DOCG: Rosso di Montalcino,
Moscadello di Montalcino, and Sant'Antimo *(sahnt AHN tee mo)*.

The authorized vineyard zone for these three wines is precisely the same as that of Brunello di Montalcino, but the
wines differ from Brunello either because of their grape varieties or their aging. Moscadello di Montalcino, for example, is
a sweet white wine made from the Muscat grape; this type of
wine was traditional in the area, but had all but disappeared
until Castello Banfi revived the style by planting Muscat
grapes in Montalcino in the early 1980s.

Rosso di Montalcino

Rosso di Montalcino is linked to tradition only in that its existence, since 1984, has helped preserve the traditional long
aging of Brunello di Montalcino — by giving producers an
outlet for wines that they prefer not to age so long. In other
words, Rosso di Montalcino is a baby Brunello, made from the
same grape variety (100 percent Sangiovese) grown in the
same territory, but aged less than Brunello is (minimum one
year instead of four years). It is similar to Brunello in its
aromas and flavors, but is fresher, lighter-bodied, and easier to
enjoy young. Of course, the diminutive of a blockbuster can

still be substantial, and some Rosso di Montalcino wines are fairly serious wines; others are lighter.

Producers can grow grapes specifically to make Rosso di Montalcino (using their younger vines, for example), or they can relegate grapes originally intended for Brunello to the Rosso category if a vintage is less than ideal; they can even decide at some point during the aging period to bottle their Brunello-in-waiting early, as Rosso. In effect, Rosso di Montalcino enables producers to declassify grapes or wines that they believe are unsuitable for Brunello for whatever reason, as well as enabling them to make a younger, more approachable wine, if that's their goal. It was the first DOC wine to give producers such a flexible, viable alternative to their traditional wine.

Rosso di Montalcino doesn't command the price or prestige that Brunello does. But Rosso isn't cheap: Prices range from $20 to $30 at retail. Nevertheless, it's a great means of experiencing what Sangiovese can do in Montalcino. About 70 percent of Brunello producers make a Rosso, at least in some vintages. Depending on the vintage, we recommend drinking Rosso di Montalcino three to ten years from the vintage date.

Sant'Antimo

Since the late 1970s, some producers in the Montalcino area — like their counterparts elsewhere in Tuscany — have grown Cabernet, Merlot, and other internationally-famous varieties for the production of Super-Tuscan wines (see the section "Super-Tuscan Wines — The Winds of Change," later in this chapter). In 1996, Italian authorities approved a new DOC designation, Sant'Antimo, for these wines and similar wines not made from the traditional Sangiovese grape.

Sant'Antimo wines take their name from a beautiful local abbey reputedly built by Charlemagne in the 9th century. The wines include a Bianco and a Rosso, as well as varietally-labelled wines: Chardonnay, Sauvignon Blanc, Pinot Grigio, Pinot Nero, Cabernet Sauvignon, and Merlot.

Because the Sant'Antimo DOC is new, it isn't commonly seen yet on the U.S. market. Castello Banfi uses the appellation for its varietal wines, as well as for its two flagship blended red wines from the Montalcino zone, Summus (a blend of Sangiovese, Cabernet, and Syrah) and Excelsus (Merlot and

Cabernet). On the other hand, Frescobaldi does not use the Sant'Antimo DOC for its Lamaione Merlot, preferring to designate that wine as IGT Toscana instead.

The "Noble Wine" of Montepulciano

The second red Tuscan wine to attain DOCG status in 1980, Vino Nobile di Montepulciano *(VEE no NO bee lae dee mahn tae pul chee AH no)*, has a proud history dating back to the 17th century, when the local wine of the Montepulciano territory was dubbed "noble" because it was a favorite of noblemen. In more recent times, the producers of the Montepulciano zone have worked hard to maintain an elite image for their wine, in the face of stiff competition from both Chianti Classico and Brunello di Montalcino. But Vino Nobile's day might finally have come (again): The Montepulciano zone now seems to have attained a "critical mass" of serious producers, and the wines today are finer than we remember their being in the last 30 years.

The Montepulciano district is a small area around the ancient town of Montepulciano, in southeastern Tuscany (see Figure 8-1). It's an area of fairly open hills crowned by the old town, which sits at an altitude of 1,968 feet. Vineyards occupy slopes down to 820 feet in altitude, the soils of which vary from sandy to clay or rocky, depending on the precise location within the territory. The variety of altitudes and soils provides built-in diversity for the wines; local authorities have in fact identified 20 distinct (but unofficial) sub-zones within the district.

Despite the fact that the Montepulciano area is quite inland, the climate is strongly influenced by the sea, with breezes to keep the air dry and the grapes healthy. The grapes in question are mainly Prugnolo Gentile *(prew N'YOH lo jen TEE lae)*, a local clone of Sangiovese, which constitutes 80 to 100 percent of the wine. Up to 20 percent of "other recommended varieties" of the area are also allowed; traditionally, the soft Canaiolo and the perfumed Mammolo were the blending partners, but these days producers are increasingly using international varieties such as Cabernet or especially Merlot.

Just like Chianti Classico, Vino Nobile di Montepulciano has reinvented itself since the mid-1980s. The wine has changed from a multi-faceted blend (of Sangiovese, Canaiolo, Mammolo, other red varieties, and white varieties) to a straightforward red wine based largely on Sangiovese. Renovation of some of the vineyards has resulted in riper grapes that make a darker, richer wine. And changes within the wineries — notably the use of French oak barrels — have further beefed up the wines' intensity. The regulation requiring the wine to age for two years in oak (or three years, for the *riserva* version) has come under review, with an eye to shortening the aging time. "Foreign" investment, from Swiss owners as well as famous Chianti houses such as Antinori and Ruffino, has also given the zone new impetus — as has the recent, exceptional 1997 vintage.

Vino Nobile is still in transition. Some wines today are soft, rich wines with creamy, plummy fruit flavors and toasty oak notes, while others are relatively lean but smooth with firm tannin and gentle almondy and red fruit flavors. In general, they range in price from about $18 to $30, with some single-vineyard wines costing slightly more.

Other Montepulciano DOC wines

Rosso di Montepulciano is a DOC wine from the same territory as Vino Nobile, and the same grape varieties, but the wine can age as little as five months before release from the winery. As in the Montalcino zone, some producers make their Rosso from specific vineyard sites, while others make Rosso from whichever grapes or wines they deem not suitable for Vino Nobile. Rosso di Montepulciano tends to sell for $12 to $15.

Vin Santo di Montepulciano is the third DOC that applies to the same territory. It's a white — actually gold or amber — dessert wine (see the section, "Vin Santo," earlier in this chapter) made at least 70 percent from Malvasia, Grechetto, and/or Trebbiano, with other local whites permitted. An amber-red style, called Occhio di Pernice *(OKE kee oh dee per NEE chae)*, meaning "eye of the partridge," contains at least 50 percent Sangiovese. While the white must age three years — or four, to be considered *riserva* — the red wine must age eight years.

The most famed and sought-after Vin Santo, not only of Montepulciano, but of all of Tuscany as well, is that of Avignonesi; its bouquet, complexity of flavors, and length on the palate are truly remarkable; sadly, it's made in minute quantities and is expensive.

Montepulciano-area producers

We list here our favorite producers of Vino Nobile di Montepulciano and Rosso di Montalcino, arranged alphabetically:

Avignonesi	Il Macchione
Poderi Boscarelli	Poliziano
La Braccesca	Redi
La Calonica	Massimo Romeo
Fattoria del Cerro	Salcheto
Contucci	Tenuta Trerose
Dei	Tenuta Valdipatta
Fassati	Villa Sant'Anna
Lodola Nuova	

Carmignano

Carmignano *(car mee N'YAH no)* is Tuscany's least known red DOCG wine. The tiny production area is ten miles west of Florence (see Figure 8-1), about in the middle of Tuscany along the region's east-west axis. Only a handful of companies make wine here, in a vineyard area of only about 270 acres. Although the area is cool, relatively low altitudes enable Sangiovese grapes to ripen well.

One of Carmignano's claims to fame is that Cabernet Sauvignon — the modern darling of the Chianti crowd — has traditionally been grown in the zone. While other Tuscan producers had to petition for changes in their regulations to permit them to use Cabernet in their blend, Carmignano producers used Cabernet Sauvignon and/or Cabernet Franc since the get-go, when they gained DOC status in 1975. Perhaps that's one reason why the blend for Carmignano hasn't changed drastically in recent years, as it has for other classic Tuscan reds. Carmignano derives primarily from Sangiovese, along with Canaiolo and the two Cabernet varieties.

When Carmignano was a DOC wine, all its types — red, rosé, and Barco Reale *(BAR co rae AH lae),* a young style — had equal status. But in 1990, red Carmignano left its peers behind to become a DOCG wine. Carmignano DOCG can be *riserva* if it ages three years before release.

A separate DOC exists for Barco Reale di Carmignano, a fresh, youthful red wine made from similar varieties as DOCG Carmignano; this DOC also covers a rosé wine and two styles of Vin Santo, a white and a pink.

We love Carmignano because it can be so utterly harmonious and graceful — like the aged Tuscan reds of decades ago that first made us appreciate Chianti. Villa di Capezzana is our favorite producer, and its wines are the most elegant of the area. Ambra, another good producer, makes considerably riper, plumper wines. Fattoria Artimino is also very good.

Super-Tuscan Wines — The Winds of Change

The category of so-called Super-Tuscan wines is a mixed bag of wines from all over Tuscany, mainly red but also white. It's a completely unofficial category; in fact, according to how wines are normally classified in Italy (see Chapter 3), the category of Super-Tuscans doesn't even exist. But for 20 years now, wine lovers and wine professionals have used the term to refer to certain wines from Tuscany.

What are these wines? They are expensive wines ($45 and up) of small production, usually internationally-styled (with fairly pronounced fruitiness and lots of oakiness), usually made from grape varieties or blends that aren't traditional in Tuscany, and carrying fanciful names. When winemakers began fashioning Super-Tuscan wines in the late 1970s and early 1980s, these wines also had in common the fact that they were all technically only *vini da tavola* with no geographic designation smaller than "Tuscany." (Chapter 3 explains the significance of *vini da tavola.*) They were not DOC wines, and the designation IGT did not yet exist.

To grasp exactly what Super-Tuscan wines are, consider their origins. Thirty years ago, Chianti had to contain at least

10 percent of white varieties in its blend, and Sangiovese could be no more than 70 percent of the wine; Chianti's image was low, and its market was depressed. Some producers felt they could make a better wine (and receive a higher price for it) by using unconventional grape varieties or blends, and winemaking methods borrowed from places such as Bordeaux, that produce high quality wines. These new wines didn't qualify as DOC Chianti, and so they were labelled as *vino da tavola di Toscana*. The most common blends were Sangiovese and Cabernet Sauvignon, or wines that were entirely Cabernet or entirely Sangiovese.

The trend of Super-Tuscan wine production spread beyond the borders of Chianti Classico to every corner of Tuscany, as winemakers sought to show off their talent and make profitable wines. (Actually, the first Super-Tuscan wine didn't come from the Chianti zone but from Bolgheri, near the Tuscan coast, but the movement gained its impetus in Chianti.) It even spread to other parts of Italy, where today you can find a few Super-Veneto wines, for example, or Super-Piedmonteses — although they're never really called that.

(Confusingly enough, the trend of making non-DOC/G wines has also spread to lower price categories; some Chianti producers make $7 to $12 wines labeled "Sangiovese" rather than "Chianti," for example, in order to take advantage of the recognition that Sangiovese has gained among wine lovers. These inexpensive wines are *not* Super-Tuscans, however.)

The Super-Tuscan trend accomplished a huge amount of good for Tuscany and particularly for Chianti Classico, because it forced wine professionals around the world to take Tuscan wines seriously. It also forced modifications of the Chianti and Chianti Classico regulations, in 1984 and in 1996, so that outdated practices, such as using white grapes in the blend, are no longer required.

Today, under the new DOCG regulations, many of the Super-Tuscan wines from within the Chianti Classico zone can actually qualify as DOCG Chianti Classico; some producers are bringing their wines back under the Chianti umbrella, while others are not. (The entire production of the excellent producer, Montevertine, for example, is still all non-DOC.) But all Super-Tuscan wines today are now IGT-level wines, because "Tuscany" is an official IGT designation.

No official or even complete listing of all Super-Tuscan wines exists. We wanted to be the first to do it, but the task is overwhelming. Besides, a lot of confusion exists over what is and isn't a Super-Tuscan wine today, because some of the original Super-Tuscan wines, such as Sassicaia *(sas ee KYE ah),* are now DOC wines. (See the section, "Bolgheri," later in this chapter for more on Sassicaia.) That's part of the difficulty in having an unofficial category. The best we can do is to list here some of our favorite Super-Tuscan wines (some of which are DOC wines), in alphabetical order, along with their grape/s and producer (when we list Cabernet, we refer to Cabernet Sauvignon):

Brancaia, Sangiovese-Merlot (La Brancaia)

Cabreo Il Borgo, ⅘ Sangiovese, ⅕ Cabernet; La Pietra, Chardonnay (Ruffino)

Camartina, Cabernet - Sangiovese; Batàr, Chardonnay (Querciabella)

Cepparello, Sangiovese (Isole e Olena)

Cerviolo, 40-30-30 percent Sangiovese-Merlot-Cabernet (San Fabiano)

Flaccianello della Pieve, Sangiovese (Fontodi)

Fontalloro, Sangiovese, (Fattoria di Felsina)

Grattamacco, Sangiovese, Malvasia Nera, Cabernet (Grattamacco)

Lamaione, Merlot (Marchesi de' Frescobaldi)

Masseto, Merlot (Tenuta dell'Ornellaia)

Ornellaia, mainly Cabernet Sauvignon; some Merlot, Cabernet Franc (Tenuta dell'Ornellaia)

Il Pareto, Cabernet (Nozzole)

Percarlo, Sangiovese (San Giusto a Rentennano)

Le Pergole Torte, Sangiovese (Montevertine)

Prunaio, mainly Sangiovese (Viticcio)

Sammarco, ⅘ Cabernet; ⅕ percent Sangiovese (Castello di Rampolla)

Sassello, Sangiovese (Castello di Verrazano)

Sassicaia, 75-25 percent Cabernet Sauvignon-Cabernet Franc (Tenuta San Guido)

I Sodi di San Niccolò, mostly Sangiovese; some Malvasia Nera (Castellare di Castellina)

Solaia, 80-20 percent Cabernet -Sangiovese (Antinori)

Tignanello, 80-20 percent Sangiovese-Cabernet (Antinori)

La Vigna di Alceo, mainly Cabernet; some Petite Verdot (Castello di Rampolla)

Tuscany's "Hot" Coast

The central hills of Tuscany have been *the* scene of the wine action for generation upon generation, but today Tuscany's coastal areas are emerging as major production zones for fine wine. Wine producers from Tuscany's interior and from other regions of Italy have invested in vineyards and wineries along the coast, and wineries that already existed there have hired famous winemaking consultants to help them improve the quality of their wines.

If you were to travel through Tuscany in the company of winemakers, you'd hear a lot of talk about an area called Maremma *(mah REM mah)*. Technically, Maremma is a stretch of land that extends from six miles north of the town of Bolgheri southward into the region of Latium. (Long ago, it was a hotbed of malaria because of mosquito colonies in the coastal marshes.) The name is still used to refer to that whole coastal area, but increasingly, in wine terms, Maremma refers just to the province of Grosseto — Tuscany's southernmost province, where Maremma Toscana is an IGT designation.

Bolgheri

The Bolgheri DOC zone sits about in the middle of the Tuscan coast in the province of Livorno; it takes its name from the small, walled town of Bolgheri. Sassicaia, the original Super-Tuscan wine, is made here in vineyards of the Tenuta San Guido estate (owned by Marchese Incisa della Rochetta, cousin of the Antinori brothers). These vineyards are an official sub-zone of Bolgheri, specifically Bolgheri-Sassicaia DOC. Sassicaia, a blend of Cabernet Sauvignon and Cabernet Franc, was first made in 1944, and commercialized in 1968.

Bolgheri *(BOHL gheh ree)* is a fairly small wine zone with fewer than 1,000 acres of vineyards. Although the coast itself is flat, the land quickly rises into hills, where the vineyards are located; sea breezes create a particular microclimate for these hills. The Bolgheri DOC covers a range of wines, including blended whites from Trebbiano, Vermentino, and Sauvignon; varietal Vermentino (Antinori has a good one) and Sauvignon; reds and rosés from Cabernet, Merlot, and Sangiovese; and a pink Vin Santo. Many Bolgheri wines are unremarkable, but the finest are quite good.

Apart from the Tenuta San Guido estate which makes Sassicaia, other Bolgheri properties of note are Ornellaia *(or nel LYE ah),* owned by Lodovico Antinori, who makes a first-rate blended red under the estate name, a blockbuster Merlot called Masseto, and a thoroughly enjoyable Sauvignon called Poggio alle Gazze; Tenuta Guado al Tasso, owned by the Piero Antinori family, with their top wine here a Cab/Merlot blend called Guado al Tasso; Grattamacco; and Ca' Marcanda, a new property built by Angelo Gaja of Piedmont, whose first wines will reach the U.S. in late 2001.

Val di Cornia

Other coastal DOC wines in the province of Livorno come from an area called Val di Cornia *(vahl dee COR nee ah),* situated south of Bolgheri where the land juts into the sea. In our experience, the distinction between DOC and Super-Tuscan wines is still confused in this area, because DOC is a fairly new designation here — but some of the wines can be impressive, however you categorize them. The Val di Cornia DOC applies to light- and medium-bodied whites made mainly from Trebbiano, with Vermentino and other white varieties, including Pinot Grigio and Pinot Bianco; rosés and reds almost entirely from Sangiovese, with Cabernet Sauvignon, Merlot, and other varieties; and a *riserva*-level red, aged for three years. Four of the major sub-zones of Val di Cornia — whose names appear on wine labels — are Suvereto, San Vincenzo, Campiglia Marittima, and Piombino.

Val di Cornia producers whose wines we have admired include Tua Rita, Gualdo del Re, Villa Monte Rico, Le Volpaiole, Podere San Michele, Lorella Ambrosini, Montepeloso, Jacopo Banti, and Azienda Agricola Rigoli.

Grosseto's new frontier

Eight DOC wines hail from Grosseto, Tuscany's southernmost and largest province. As proof of how "happening" the Grosseto area is, consider that four of these eight DOCs are less than five years old.

Monteregio di Massa Marittima *(mahn tae RAE gee oh dee MAHS sah mah REET tee mah)* is a very hilly area extending inland from the coast in the northern part of the Grosseto province; Massa Marittima is one of the towns there. DOC regulations provide for a Vermentino, and for a Rosso, regular or *riserva,* that's 80 percent Sangiovese; for the future, producers are hoping to reduce Sangiovese to 50 percent to enable more use of varieties such as Cabernet, Merlot or Syrah. This area has attracted investment from numerous winemakers from Tuscany, elsewhere in Italy, and France.

Partially overlapping that zone and extending farther inland is a new DOC zone (1998) called **Montecucco** *(mahn tae KOOK coh).* This area makes a varietal Vermentino and Sangiovese, as well as a blended white (60 percent Trebbiano) and blended red (60 percent Sangiovese). Two even newer DOCs are Capalbio and Sovana. **Capalbio** *(cah PAHL bee o)* features a varietal Vermentino, Sangiovese and Cabernet Sauvignon, a blended white (at least half Trebbiano) and a blended red (at least half Sangiovese). **Sovana** *(so VAH nah)* is a red wine zone, with varietal wines from Sangiovese, Cabernet Sauvignon, Merlot and Aleatico, and a blended Rosso that's half Sangiovese.

Another DOC area, **Costa dell'Argentario** *(COHS tah del lar jen TAH ree oh),* occupies islands and an adjoining coastal area just north of the border with Latium. The wine from this resort area is a soft, dry, varietally-labelled white from the Ansonica grape variety (a grape that's very big in Sicily, where it's called Inzolia). The tiny **Parrina** *(pah REE nah)* zone lies just north; it makes a white based mainly on Trebbiano, Ansonica, and/or Chardonnay, as well as red and rosé wines based mainly on Sangiovese, and a *riserva*-level red with three years aging.

Morellino *(moh rael LEE no)* is the name used for the Sangiovese grape in the hilly vineyard area around the town of Scansano *(scahn SAH no),* in the central part of the Grosseto province. The dry, fragrant wine, **Morellino di Scansano,** derives from this variety; a *riserva*-level, with two years aging, also exists. Although this is not a new DOC zone, the wine is somewhat in transition because of all the new action in Grosseto in general. For example, Jacopo Biondi-Santi is selling a high-end Scansano, made at his new Castello di Montepo property, for $45 a bottle — making an emphatic quality statement. Other Morellino di Scansano wines, such as Moris Farms and Cantina del Morellino di Scansano, sell in the $12 to $15 range. Le Pupille and Massa Vecchia are two other good producers from this area whose wines are available in the U.S.

Overlapping the eastern half of the Morellino di Scansano zone
and extending south and eastward to Latium is the DOC zone
of **Bianco di Pitigliano.** This soft, dry white derives 50 to 80
percent from Trebbiano grown on volcanic soil, along with
numerous other grapes such as Greco, Malvasia, Verdello,
Grechetto, Chardonnay, Sauvignon Blanc, Pinot Blanc, and
Welschriesling.

Other Tuscan Wines

In the interests of completeness, we describe here the remaining nine DOC wines of Tuscany, most of which come from the
western part of the region. Although these wines are not
common on the U.S. market at the moment, Tuscany is so hot
that you might conceivably see any of them in the not-too-dis-
tant future. These nine DOCs are the following:

- ✔ **Bianco di Valdinievole** *(vahl dee nee AE voh lae):* This
  wine comes from an area just west of the Chianti
  Montalbano zone; it's a dry, sometimes slightly *frizzante*
  white mainly from Trebbiano, with Malvasia, Canaiolo
  Bianco, Vermentino, and other grapes. Also Vin Santo.

- ✔ **Montecarlo:** Named after a community east of the city of
  Lucca, this DOC has possibly the most interesting blend
  of grapes of any in Tuscany: It covers a dry, delicately flavored white wine (Trebbiano, Semillon, Pinot Grigio,
  Pinot Bianco, Vermentino, Sauvignon, and Roussanne);
  also a dry red wine (Sangiovese, Canaiolo, Ciliegiolo,
  Colorino, Malvasia Nera, Syrah, Cabernet Franc, Cabernet
  Sauvignon, and Merlot), which becomes *riserva* with two
  years of age; and a white or pink Vin Santo.

- ✔ **Colline di Lucchesi** *(co LEE nae dee loo KAE see):* The
  "Lucca Hills" Rosso derives from Sangiovese, Canaiolo,
  Ciliegiolo, Colorino, and three white varieties; a dry, deli-
  cate Bianco derives from Trebbiano, Greco or Grechetto,
  Vermentino, and Malvasia.

- ✔ **Candia dei Colli Apuani** *(CAHN dee ah dee CO lee ap oo
  AH nee):* A dry or off-dry, aromatic white wine mainly
  from Vermentino and Albarola. This is Tuscany's north-
  western-most DOC zone (not counting Colli di Luni, a
  Ligurian area that spreads slightly into Tuscany; see
  Chapter 5).

- **Bianco dell'Empolese** *(bee AHN co del lem poh LAE sae):* From a tiny area north of the town of Empoli, on both sides of the Arno River, a dry white or a Vin Santo primarily from Trebbiano.

- **Bianco Pisano di San Torpè** *(pee SAH no dee sahn tor PAE):* This zone overlaps much of the Chianti Colli Pisane area; the local dry white and Vin Santo derive mainly from Trebbiano.

- **Montescudaio** *(mahn tae skoo DYE oh):* A dry white or Vin Santo from Trebbiano, Malvasia, and Vermentino grapes grown directly south of the Pisano San Torpè area, close to the sea.

- **Elba:** Because of its long history of grape growing, the island of Elba has a DOC designation that permits numerous types of wine to be made under the name Elba: a dry Bianco (mainly Trebbiano); a bottle-fermented, sparkling Bianco; a dry to semi-sweet Ansonica; a sweet, unblended Ansonico Passito; a Rosso mainly from Sangiovese, which may become *riserva* with two years of age; a Rosato, also mainly from Sangiovese; a semi-sweet red Aleatico; and a white or pink Vin Santo.

- **Bianco Vergine Valdichiana** *(VER gee nae vahl dee kee AH nah):* The Chiana Valley sits at the eastern foot of Tuscany's central hills, bordering on Umbria; the light, youthful dry white wine from this area comes mainly from Trebbiano — as does its *spumante* style and its slightly sweet *frizzante naturale* style.

Chapter 9

The Wines of Central Italy

In This Chapter

▶ The all-Italian region

▶ Verdicchio on the march

▶ Rugged Abruzzo and its Montepulciano

▶ Forgotten Molise

▶ The region around Rome

Many of the wines of Central Italy, both red and white, are particularly good values. Some of the white wines — such as Orvieto, Verdicchio, and Frascati — are old friends to wine drinkers, but now they're new, in a sense, because they're better made today than they have ever been — particularly Verdicchio. Other wines of Central Italy are new to wine lovers; Sagrantino di Montefalco, for example, a red DOCG wine from Umbria, is practically unknown in the U.S., despite the fact that it's a pretty terrific wine. Which is one of the reasons we've written this book!

Umbria: The Inland Region

Umbria *(OOM bree ah)* has the distinction of being Italy's only region that is surrounded entirely by Italy. Most other regions manage to touch a sea, or — in the case of a few northern regions — another country. But Umbria is centered within Italy. Tuscany is Umbria's neighbor to the northwest, and Rome is a two-hour drive southwest from Umbria's southern border (see Figure 9-1). The region's eastern border is entirely occupied by Abruzzo.

Other than its capital — the busy, industrial city of Perugia, home of one of Italy's finest universities — Umbria is sparsely populated. The Apennine Mountains take up much of the land. But tourists (present company included!) do flock to the town of Assisi, near Perugia, where once lived St. Francis of Assisi, friend of animals and nature.

Winewise, Umbria is in Tuscany's shadow. Many of its grape varieties are the same as Tuscany's, and no matter how good the wines are, there's no competing with Tuscany's international recognition. (Chapter 8 covers Tuscan wines.) Umbria's main claim to wine fame is that it's the home of the historic hilltop town, Orvieto, and the white wine of the same name. But even in Orvieto, large Tuscan producers such as Antinori and Ruffino make much of the wine.

Umbria is blessed with a similar climate to Tuscany's: warm and dry, but cool enough, thanks to the Tiber River and its tributaries flowing through the region. The soil is mainly calcareous clay and sand, with plenty of limestone, always good for vines. Considering its natural resources, Umbria has not nearly realized its potential as a wine region. But in the last decade, Umbria has made significant progress. The region's most well-known red wine — Rubesco Riserva, the Torgiano Rosso Riserva DOCG of Lungarotti, Umbria's first family of wine — continues to be admired throughout the world. And lately, Umbria's other DOCG wine, the red Sagrantino di Montefalco, is finally getting some belated attention beyond the borders of Umbria.

Umbria has always been known as a white wine region. Twenty-three percent of its wines are DOC or DOCG, and a high percentage of this wine is white — mainly Orvieto — made by large wineries or cooperatives. But the latest figures reveal that 40 percent of Umbria's wines are now red — a big jump in red wine production over the past decade.

With the debut of three new DOCs in the last few years, Umbria now has 11 DOC wines, in addition to its two DOCG wines. (The majority of these wines hail from the province of Perugia, which occupies the northern two-thirds of Umbria.) But many fine Umbrian wines, especially reds, carry the designation IGT Umbria, because that name has strong recognition. (Umbria's other IGT zones are Allerona, Bettona, Cannara, and Spello.)

UMBRIA WINE ZONES
1. Colli Altotiberini
2. Colli Perugini
3. Torgiano DOCG
4. Montefalco
5. Orvieto

MARCHE WINE ZONES
6. Bianchello del Mentauro
7. Verdicchio dei Castelli di Jesi
8. Rosso Conero
9. Verdicchio di Matelica
10. Vernaccia di Serrapetrona

ABRUZZO WINE ZONES
11. Montepulciano d'Abruzzo
12. Trebbiano d'Abruzzo

LAZIO WINE ZONES
13. Frascati
14. Marino

MOLISE WINE ZONES
15. Biferno
16. Pentro

Figure 9-1: The five regions of Central Italy and their wine zones.

Orvieto

The town of Orvieto *(or vee AE toh)* arises from a rocky hill that towers above the Rome-to-Florence stretch of the *autostrada,* drawing art lovers and wine lovers alike into its medieval majesty. Orvieto is Umbria's — and one of Italy's — most famous white wines.

Umbria's aristocracy

If you'd like living proof of the potential of southern Umbria as a wine zone, look no further than the wines of Antinori's Castello della Sala winery, an ancient castle north of Orvieto that has been in the family for generations. Two specialties are the dry white Cervaro della Sala (about $38), a very good, ageworthy, barrel-fermented wine made from Chardonnay with some Grechetto; and a white dessert wine called Muffato della Sala (about $40 to $42 for a 500 ml bottle), made from Sauvignon and other varieties affected by noble rot. This winery also makes an attractive Chardonnay and a Sauvignon (both about $11 to $12) and a Pinot Nero — all of which carry the Umbria IGT designation. Antinori's Orvieto Classico Campogrande DOC (less than $10) comes from the same winery.

The Orvieto wine zone is a large area in southwest Umbria that extends north to the border of the Perugia province, and south into the Latium region. The original *classico* sub-zone, where the best Orvieto originates, is the middle-third of the area; wines from this part of the zone are named "Orvieto Classico." The special chalky limestone soil, called *tufa,* which predominates in the *classico* area, along with ancient remnants of volcanic soil, gives a unique character to Orvieto Classico wines.

In the Middle Ages, Orvieto was a sweet, golden-colored wine; only in the last 50 years or so has most Orvieto been made *secco* (dry). As recently as the 1970s, we remember Italians telling us to try the *real* Orvieto — Orvieto Abboccato *(ahb boh CAH toh)* — a semi-dry style that was popular in Italy. DOC regulations still permit the production of sweet, or semi-sweet, Orvieto; besides the *secco* style, the wine can be *abboccato,* *amabile (ah MAH bee lae,* semi-sweet), and *dolce* (sweet).

Orvieto is a blended wine that, as of the year 2000, is now at least 60 percent Grechetto (considered its best variety), with up to 15 percent Trebbiano (known locally as Procanico), plus other local white varieties including Verdello, Canaiolo Bianco, and Malvasia. This formula enables producers to make the wine in varying degrees of richness; some producers use as much Grechetto as possible in their wine, to give it fruitiness and weight, for example. The quality in recent years has improved

quite a bit, thanks to grape growing and winemaking experimentation, and the work of Umbrian enologists Riccardo and
Renzo Cotarella.

As evidence of Umbria's new red wine direction, Orvieto now
has a companion DOC red wine, **Rosso Orvietano** *(or vee ae
TAH no),* made in a very large area that includes the entire
Orvieto zone. This new DOC covers a blended Rosso plus
eight varietally-labeled wines. The Rosso derives at least 70
percent from any or all of nine varieties — Aleatico, Cabernet
Franc, Cabernet Sauvignon, Canaiolo, Ciliegiolo, Merlot,
Montepulciano, Pinot Nero, and Sangiovese — with Barbera,
Cesanese, Colorino, and Dolcetto optional. The eight varietal
wines derive from varieties that make up 70 percent of the
blended wine, except for Montepulciano.

Torgiano

Torgiano *(tor gee AH no)* is a town on the east bank of the Tiber
River, across from Perugia. In the northern hills of Torgiano,
which have a rather warm microclimate, both red and white
grape varieties grow to make a DOCG and several DOC wines.

If ever there were an example of one wine producer dominating
and popularizing a wine zone, Torgiano is it. The late Giorgio
Lungarotti made his Cantine Lungarotti not only Umbria's
most renowned winery, but also one of the most prestigious
wineries in all of Italy. His step-daughter, Teresa Lungarotti,
now carries the Torgiano banner. Lungarotti wines are popular
worldwide; of the nearly 220,000 produced annually, over half
are exported. Thanks to Lungarotti, Torgiano earned DOC
status in 1968.

In 1990, one Torgiano wine, the Rosso Riserva, was given the
unusual honor of being singled out for DOCG status. **Torgiano
Rosso Riserva DOCG** is basically just one wine, Lungarotti's
Rubesco Riserva della Vigna Monticchio, the brand's flagship
wine. Torgiano Rosso Riserva is mainly Sangiovese with a small
amount of Canaiolo; Trebbiano, Ciliegiolo, and/or Montepulciano
are optional. It must age at least three years — but Lungarotti's
wine is released *ten* years after the vintage. In good vintages
(refer to Appendix B), Lungarotti's Rubesco Riserva has the
complexity, finesse, and aging ability of top classified growth
Bordeaux wines selling for twice the price or more. (The excellent 1990 Rubesco Riserva retails for about $35.)

Torgiano DOC wines number nine (not counting its one DOCG), of which the blended Rosso and Bianco are the most popular. Torgiano Rosso is basically the same blend as the Rosso Riserva, but ages for a minimum of 18 months; it's best known in the form of Lungarotti's Rubesco, a fine value at $14 to $15 retail. Torgiano Rosato, a dry rosé, has the same blend. Torgiano Bianco is mainly Trebbiano and the local Grechetto. (Lungarotti's version, called Torre di Giano, is a dry, character-ful wine made from 70 percent Trebbiano and 30 percent Grechetto; it retails for $11 to $12.) Torgiano varietal wines are Chardonnay, Cabernet Sauvignon, Pinot Nero, Pinot Grigio, Riesling Italico, and a Spumante, made from Chardonnay and Pinot Nero.

Sagrantino di Montefalco

About 12 miles south of Torgiano, the town of Montefalco is enjoying a revival, as is its leading grape variety, Sagrantino *(sah grahn TEE no)*. This native variety has made red wine locally since the Middle Ages, but that wine was traditionally a sweet wine. In its revived form, it's now mainly a dry, full-bodied wine, and it has won enough acclaim to have been granted DOCG status.

Purplish-ruby Sagrantino is a robust wine that can take some aging. It's also still made as a *passito*. The dry Sagrantino di Montefalco is gaining renown, as producers begin to make it a specialty; retail prices range from $23 to $28.

From the same area also come the **Montefalco DOC** wines. Rosso di Montalfalco is mainly Sangiovese, with some Sagrantino and up to 15 percent other varieties; it retails for $10 to $20. Less seen in the U.S. is the dry white Montefalco Bianco, made mainly from Grechetto and Trebbiano; Adanti's Montefalco Bianco sells for a mere $10 to $11.

Umbria's other DOC wines

All of the wine areas of the Perugia hills are in or near the Tiber (*Tevere* in Italian) River Valley, the Topino River Valley, and the Lake Trasimeno district. The area seems to be awakening from a long slumber. Apart from Torgiano and Montefalco, described earlier in this chapter, these are the DOC wines of the Perugia hills:

✔ **Colli Altotiberini** *(CO lee ahl toh tee beh REE nee):* A long, narrow zone in the hills along both sides of the Tiber River, from northwest Umbria to Perugia. This area has three wines: a dry Rosso (mainly Sangiovese, with 10 to 20 percent Merlot, up to 10 percent white grapes, and up to 15 percent other red varieties); a dry Rosato from the same varieties, but without the 15 percent "other red grapes"; and a dry Bianco (75 to 90 percent Trebbiano, up to 10 percent Malvasia and up to 15 percent other white varieties).

✔ **Colli del Trasimeno** *(CO lee del trah see MAE no):* A large wine zone in western Umbria, in hills surrounding Lake Trasimeno, central Italy's largest lake. The Bianco (mainly Trebbiano; up to 40 percent Malvasia and/or Verdicchio and/or Verdello and/or Grechetto) is comparable to Orvieto; the Rosso is an easy-drinking, fruity, dry red (mainly Sangiovese, up to 40 percent Gamay and/or Ciliegiolo, up to 20 percent white grapes). The two leading producers of Colli Trasimeno wines are La Fiorita-Lamborghini (the famed auto family) and Pieve del Vescovo — both available in the U.S.

✔ **Colli Perugini** *(CO lee peh roo GEE nee):* Hills south of Perugia and west of the Tiber River form this wine zone, an area currently not living up to the potential of its cool microclimate. Three wines are here: a dry Rosso (mainly Sangiovese, with 15 to 35 percent Ciliegiolo and/or Montepulciano and/or Barbera, and up to 10 percent Merlot); a deep-colored, dry Rosato from the same varieties; and a dry Bianco (mainly Trebbiano, with 15 to 35 percent Verdicchio and/or Grechetto and/or Garganega, and up to 10 percent Malvasia).

✔ **Assisi:** This newly created DOC zone centers around the town of Assisi, east of Perugia; one of its interesting wines is a dry, white Grechetto — Umbria's finest white variety; Rosso, Rosato, and Bianco di Assisi DOC wines also exist.

✔ **Colli Martani** *(COH lee Mahr TAH nee):* An underachieving, large zone that includes the hills south of the Torgiano zone on the eastern banks of the Tiber River, and envelops the smaller Montefalco DOC zone. The area has four varietal wines: Grechetto, Grechetto di Todi (made in a sub-zone around the town of Todi), Trebbiano, and one red, Sangiovese.

The area around Orvieto, in southwestern Umbria, has two DOC zones other than Orvieto itself and Rosso Orvietano, both discussed earlier in the chapter. These other wine zones are the following:

- **Lago di Corbara** *(LAH go dee cor BAH rah):* This new DOC is devoted solely to red wines. The Lago di Corbara zone is south of the town of Orvieto and is actually a part of the Orvieto wine zone, around Lake Corbara. The soil here, mainly red clay and tufa, is ideal for red wines. The Rosso wine made here is very much similar to the blend of Orvietano Rosso; three varietal Lago di Corbara wines are Cabernet Sauvignon, Merlot, and Pinot Nero.

- **Colli Amerini** *(CO lee ah meh REE nee):* This southern-most Umbrian DOC zone has five wines, including a white Malvasia, the area's most typical wine. A dry, blended Bianco is primarily Trebbiano, with Grechetto and/or Verdello and/or Garganega and/or Malvasia, and other white varieties; a dry Rosso, *novello,* and dry, full-bodied Rosato are mainly Sangiovese, with Montepulciano and/or Ciliegiolo and/or Canaiolo and/or Merlot and/or Barbera, and other varieties. Most of these wines are made by the fine co-op, Cantina Sociale dei Colli Amerini.

Recommended Umbrian wineries

We list here, alphabetically, our recommended wine producers of Umbria:

Fratelli Adanti
Antonelli
Barberani-Vallesanta
Bigi
Arnaldo Caprai-Val di Maggio
La Carraia
Castello della Sala
Cantina Sociale dei Colli
  Amerini
Còlpetrone
Co.Vi.O. (also known as
  Cardeto)

Decugnano dei Barbi
La Fiorita-Lamborghini
Cantine Lungarotti
Cantina Monrubio (formerly
  Vi.C.Or.)
Pieve del Vescovo
Rocca di Fabri
Tenuta di Salviano
Fratelli Sportoletti
Tilli
Tenuta Le Velette

Marches, on the Adriatic

The Italian name for the Marches region is Marche *(MAHR kae)*, and since we much prefer the name in Italian, we use it throughout this chapter. Marche is in east-central Italy, its rather long eastern border running along the Adriatic Sea. Umbria is Marche's neighbor to the west, Emilia-Romagna is north, and Abruzzo is south (see Figure 9-1). Marche's most important city and its capital is the seaport of Ancona, located in the central part of the coastline.

Much of Marche — about two-thirds — is occupied by the Apennine Mountains, including the entire western part. The rest is mainly hillsides, ideal for grapevines. The weather between the Adriatic Sea and the Apennines is just about perfect most of the time, sunny and mild, with pleasant breezes. A number of rivers course through the hillsides, making their way to the sea, and exert a tempering effect on the climate.

Marche has 11 DOC zones, and one IGT designation, Marche. Its most famous wine is the white varietal wine, Verdicchio *(vair DEEK ee oh)*. The region's two most renowned reds are Rosso Cònero *(ROHS so COH nae ro)* and Rosso Piceno *(ROHS so pee CHAE no)*. The fact that many people outside of Marche still have not heard of these two fine reds is evidence that Marche has a way to go in promoting its wines.

Verdicchio

Marche has two DOC Verdicchio wines:

- ✔ **Verdicchio dei Castelli di Jesi** *(ver DEE key oh dae cahs TEL ee dee YAE see)*, mainly from the province of Ancona, by the sea

- ✔ **Verdicchio di Matelica** *(ver DEE key oh dee mah TAE lee cah)*, from an inland area in the province of Macerata

Verdicchio dei Castelli di Jesi is clearly the most important DOC wine in Marche in terms of production. The vineyard area is mainly in the hills west of the city of Jesi, on both sides of the Esino River. The best, or *classico* area, is west of Jesi, in a hilly area 12 to 18 miles from the Adriatic. The soil here is calcareous clay, with sand, remnants of fossils, and minerals. Wines from the *classico* sub-zone are generally the best wines.

Although producers may blend up to 15 percent Malvasia and/or Trebbiano into their Verdicchio wine, many of them make a 100 percent Verdicchio for quality reasons, and most also make single-vineyard Verdicchios or special cuveés. Verdicchio is an unusual white wine for this part of Italy in that it's capable of aging, and you can find *riserva* versions, although we enjoy its fruity freshness and liveliness when it's young. The wine is totally dry, with fresh appley or lemony flavors, and sometimes a slightly tangy character suggestive of salty sea air. DOC regulations also permit the production of a sparkling and a sweet *passito* version.

Verdicchio di Matelica is sought after because its production is only one-tenth that of Verdicchio di Castelli di Jesi. The Matelica wine zone is in an isolated valley in the foothills of the Apennines in western Marche; the climate here, away from the Adriatic, is more continental, resulting in a somewhat different style of Verdicchio: fresh, delicate, and aromatic in its youth, with good acidity, it is fuller-bodied and longer-lasting than the easy drinking Verdicchio dei Castelli di Jesi.

The comeback wine of the decade

Verdicchio first gained fame in the 1950s when the Fazi-Battaglia winery bottled it in a green amphora-shaped bottle and promoted it as the ideal wine with fish — which it is. The wine caught on, and it was a big success for a couple of decades. The vast increase in sales unfortunately had its downside. The wine slipped badly in quality, and by the late 1970s, you couldn't give it away to the more wine-savvy customers who replaced the less sophisticated winedrinkers of the '50s and '60s. In the 1980s, Verdicchio producers, led by Fazi-Battaglia, moved to improve the quality of their wines, starting with re-planting the vineyards. Fazi-Battaglia hired one of Italy's top wine consultants, Franco Bernabei, to oversee the project. The results have been nothing short of remarkable. Today, Verdicchio is better than ever, and it's selling retail for $8 to $9! We aren't prone to making bold statements, but here is one: *We can't think of any better wine in the world for under $10 than the Verdicchio that's being made today.* It is crisp, full of flavor, un-oaked, and quite delicious. A natural with fish and seafood.

The grape variety requirements for Verdicchio di Matelica are the same as in Castelli di Jesi, and the permitted Trebbiano and Malvasia are also seldom used. Verdicchio di Matelica comes in regular, *riserva,* sparkling, and *passito* versions.

Rosso Cònero and Rosso Piceno

Rosso Cònero is the premium red wine of Marche, made only in a limited area — the hillsides of Monte Cònero, a dramatically beautiful area that provides a striking backdrop to the seaport of Ancona. In this area, Montepulciano is clearly the best red variety, and Rosso Cònero derives at least 85 percent from this grape; up to 15 percent Sangiovese is permitted, but seldom used.

Rosso Cònero might well be the best relatively unknown red wine of Italy; if this wine were from a high-profile region such as Tuscany or Piedmont, it would have been granted DOCG status long ago — as would both Verdicchio wines, for that matter. Rosso Cònero has pronounced herbal and black cherry aromas and flavors, is quite tannic and full-bodied, and improves with age. And yet it retails for $15 to $20, which makes it one of Italy's finest red wine values.

Rosso Piceno, Marche's other important red, has a much larger production than Rosso Cònero; in fact, it's Marche's largest-volume red wine, and second only to Verdicchio dei Castelli di Jesi in total volume. The Rosso Piceno wine zone is the largest in Marche, extending from the Abruzzo border in the south into all of Ascoli Piceno province except the Apennine Mountains, through both Macerata and Ancona provinces — but excluding the smallish Rosso Cònero and Lacrima di Morro d'Alba zones. The best part of the zone is a limited hillside area of 13 communities east of the provincial capital, Ascoli Piceno, extending to the coast.

Rosso Piceno is at least 60 percent Sangiovese, with up to 40 percent Montepulciano, and up to 15 percent of two white varieties, Trebbiano and Passerina. The wine is at its best when a full 40 percent of the lower-cropping Montepulciano is used. Rosso Piceno can be decent, but Rosso Cònero is generally the far superior wine.

Marche's other DOC wines

Marche has seven additional DOC zones:

- **Colli Pesaresi** *(CO lee pae sah RAE see):* This wine zone is in the hills between the coast town of Pesaro and inland Urbino, an art center; this area is just south of Romagna, and so the wines from this area very much resemble Romagna wines (see Chapter 7). The Rosso (or *novello*) is mainly Sangiovese. Colli Pesaresi Focara Rosso is similar to the Rosso except that only Pinot Nero may be blended with Sangiovese. The Bianco is mainly Trebbiano; Colli Pesaresi Roncaglia Bianco may have only Pinot Nero blended with Trebbiano. A visit to the hill town of Urbino is worthwhile, especially in the fall; besides its two museums, Urbino has the largest autumn white truffle market outside of Piedmont.

- **Bianchello del Metauro** *(bee ahn KEL lo del meh TOUW ro):* This smaller wine zone lies within the Colli Pesaresi zone, and it covers 18 communities in the Metauro River Valley. The white Biancame grape variety (locally called Bianchello) does particularly well in this area. The wine resembles Verdicchio with its lively, lemony flavors, and is particularly popular with summer tourists along the Adriatic beaches.

- **Lacrima di Morro d'Alba** *(LAH cree mah dee MOR ro DAHL bah):* The hills west of Ancona, around the community of Morro d'Alba and others, is the zone for this ripe, fruity dry red wine made from the local red Lacrima variety, with up to 15 percent Montepulciano and/or Verdicchio. It does not age well, and is mainly consumed locally.

- **Esino** *(ae SEE noh):* This large, new zone covers all of Ancona province and that part of Macerata province in which Verdicchio dei Castelli di Jesi and Verdicchio di Matelica wines are grown. Esino Bianco is a dry white (still or *frizzante*) from at least 50 percent Verdicchio. Esino Rosso is a dry red made from a minimum of 60 percent Sangiovese and/or Montepulciano; it also comes in a *novello* style.

✔ **Vernaccia di Serrapetrona** *(ver NAHTCH cha dee ser rah peh TRO nah)*: It's a toss-up as to whether the red Lacrima from Morro d'Alba or this red Vernaccia from the Serrapetrona area is the most "different" wine of the region. The Vernaccia we know from Tuscany (see Chapter 8) is a dry white wine; this Vernaccia is not only a naturally bubbly red, but it is also usually made in a semi-sweet or sweet style — although it can also be dry, and it can even be made as a completely sparkling red wine, with fermentation in the bottle as in Champagne! The wine is mainly Vernaccia di Serrapetrona, with up to 15 percent Sangiovese and/or Montepulciano and/or Ciliegiolo; the zone is west of the southern part of the Verdicchio di Matelica zone.

✔ **Colli Maceratesi** *(CO lee ma cheh rah TAE see)*: This dry, light-bodied white wine is made throughout the province of Macerata, as well as in the community of Loreto in Ancona province, usually along the coastal part of this territory. It's mainly Maceratino (a possible variant of Verdicchio), with up to 20 percent Trebbiano and/or Verdicchio and/or Malvasia and/or Chardonnay.

✔ **Falerio dei Colli Ascolani** *(fa LAE ree oh dae CO lee ahs coh LAH nee)*: This dry white wine is made mainly from Trebbiano; up to 25 percent Verdicchio and/or Pecorino and/or Passerina and/or Pinot Bianco may be added, and up to 7 percent Malvasia. The wine zone is the entire province of Ascoli Piceno.

Marche wines to buy

The wines of Marche are still great values, because producers of this region — with the exception of Fazi-Battaglia and Umani Ronchi, both Verdicchio producers — have not really marketed their wines around the world. The three wines to especially look for are the two Verdicchio wines and the excellent red, Rosso Cònero. Bear in mind that ten times as much Verdicchio dei Castelli di Jesi exists than Verdicchio di Matelica — making the latter more difficult to find. We list alphabetically our recommended wine producers in the Marche region:

Belisario (Cantina Sociale di Matelica)
Bisci
Boccadigabbia
Bonci
Brunori
Fratelli Bucci
Le Caniette
Casalfarneto
Colonnara
Tenuta Cocci Grifoni
Fattoria Coroncino
Attilio Fabrini
Fazi Battaglia
Fiorini
Garofoli
Lanari
Conte Leopardi
Mario Lucchetti

Stefano Mancinelli
Fattoria Mancini
Marchetti
Enzo Mecella
La Monacesca
Monte Schiavo
Moroder
Saladini Pilastri
San Biagio
Santa Barbara
Sartarelli
Anzillotti Solazzi
Tavignano
Le Terrazze
Terre Cortesi Moncaro
Umani Ronchi
Velenosi
Villa Pigna
Villamagna

Mountainous Abruzzo

The region is known as Abruzzi *(ah BROOT see)* in English, but we prefer the Italian Abruzzo *(ah BROOT zo)*, and so we use Abruzzo throughout this chapter. Like Marche, Abruzzo is in east-central Italy with the Adriatic Sea as its eastern border. Along with its neighbor to the south, Molise, the Abruzzo region is one of Italy's most mountainous regions, and perhaps the most isolated. (Officially, Abruzzo is 65 percent mountains; 35 percent hills, and 100 percent rugged.) Until recently, the very high, formidable Apennines — which reach about 9,000 feet here, their tallest point in mainland Italy — kept Abruzzo separate from the rest of the country, especially the northern and western parts; Abruzzo historically had little contact with Latium and Rome to the west, and Marche to the north (see Figure 9-1). As for mountainous Molise *(mo LEE sae)* to the south, that region might be even more isolated than Abruzzo!

But Abruzzo's warm, sunny hillsides provide ideal conditions for grapevines. Unfortunately, with the exception of a handful of producers, quantity rather than quality is the goal in the Abruzzese hillsides: Abruzzo's average crop size — almost 8 tons per acre — is the highest in Italy, a country known for some large grape crops! To illustrate the point, Abruzzo has only 38 percent as much vineyard land as Tuscany, but usually makes half again as much wine. Just as in many southern regions of Italy, most of the wine (two-thirds) is made by cooperatives, and much of it is sold in bulk to other producers and co-ops outside the region.

Of the 45 million cases produced in Abruzzo annually, only 17 percent is DOC, and most of that is Montepulciano d'Abruzzo or Trebbiano d'Abruzzo, both inexpensive commercial wines commonly sold as jug wines. (Abruzzo's small DOC production explains why the region has so many IGT designations — nine.) And yet the potential for quality exists. In the hands of a great producer, such as Edoardo Valentini, these two DOC wines can reach uncommon heights of nobility. Like many other regions of Italy which had never before focused on producing quality wines from low-yielding vines, Abruzzo has begun its renaissance. We can look forward to better wines coming from this rugged region in the future.

Abruzzo's vineyards and wines

Most of Abruzzo's vineyards are planted on hillsides, where calcareous clay predominates. The hillsides face the Adriatic, whose breezes ventilate the vineyards during the warm, dry summers. Wine is made throughout Abruzzo's four provinces, but the northern two, Teramo and Pescara, have the most favorable hillside sites, climate, and soil for quality wines. The southern province of Chieti is known for its quantity of wine — in fact, Chieti is the fifth largest wine-producing province in Italy. Little wine is made in the totally mountainous L'Aquila province, home of the regional capital of the same name; Cerasuolo *(cher ah SWO lo)*, a dry rosé wine made from Montepulciano, is the main wine from a few hillsides in L'Aquila.

Montepulciano *(mahn tae pul chee AH no)*, the reigning grape variety of Abruzzo, has absolutely no relation to Vino Nobile de Montepulciano, the DOCG wine from the town of Montepulciano in Tuscany (see Chapter 8). At its best, Montepulciano-the-grape makes a dark, fragrant, tannic, sturdy red wine with naturally low acidity that's capable of aging. It's a prolific variety that grows throughout central Italy and is, in fact, Italy's fifth most planted red variety — after Sangiovese, Barbera, Merlot, and Puglia's Negroamaro.

Montepulciano d'Abruzzo is one of Italy's most popular red wines, primarily because much of it retails for the equivalent of less than $5 a 750 ml bottle, and it's of decent quality. Although it's produced in all four provinces, most of it comes from the prolific vineyards of the warm Chieti province in southern Abruzzo, while most of the better (and somewhat more expensive) Montepulciano d'Abruzzo comes from Teramo and Pescara provinces in the north; much of the dry, deep cherry pink version, Cerasuolo, comes from L'Aquila.

Montepulciano d'Abruzzo and Cerasuolo must be at least 85 percent Montepulciano, with Sangiovese (or other red varieties of the region) optional. In Abruzzo, Montepulciano is far superior to Sangiovese, and many producers use it exclusively. A third version of Montepulciano d'Abruzzo, called Colline Teramane *(cohl LEE nae ter ah MAH nae),* is made from grapes grown only in Teramo and 30 other communities in Teramo province; it must have a minimum of 90 percent Montepulciano, with up to 10 percent Sangiovese permitted.

The other leading wine of Abruzzo is the dry white **Trebbiano d'Abruzzo** *(trehb bee AH no dah BREWTZ zo).* The name of the wine is the same as the name of a local clone of Trebbiano, which is considered finer than Tuscany's Trebbiano grape. Some wines made from Trebbiano d'Abruzzo are so good and so uncharacteristic of Trebbiano (especially in their low acidity) that the grape is believed not to be a Trebbiano at all, but possibly the Bombino Bianco of Apulia. In any case, DOC regulations permit Trebbiano d'Abruzzo wine to be made at least 85 percent from Trebbiano d'Abruzzo and/or Trebbiano Toscano varieties, and most of the mass-market Trebbiano d'Abruzzo wines are so Trebbiano-like in character — pale and crisp, with neutral, modest flavors — that they probably rely heavily on Trebbiano Toscano.

One exception is the "Lord of the Vines," as he is called locally — Edoardo Valentini makes clearly the world's greatest wine from the Trebbiano variety (if that's what it is). Two other Abruzzo producers of note are Masciarelli and Emidio Pepe, both known for their Montepulciano d'Abruzzo and Trebbiano d'Abruzzo. Pepe, a throwback from another time, is renowned for still crushing his grapes by foot (still done for some Porto wine in Portugal's Douro Valley, but practically nowhere else), and for aging his wines *entirely* in bottles — not a barrel in sight; the sediment in his bottles is awesome!

Although Trebbiano d'Abruzzo wine is made in all four provinces, most of it comes from the southern Chieti province; like Montepulciano d'Abruzzo, however, the best Trebbiano wines are made in the two northern provinces, Termano and Pescara.

The newest DOC wine in Abruzzo is **Controguerra** *(cohn tro GWER rah),* which comes from five communities near the Marche border, including Controguerra, whose colorful name means "anti-war." A whole slew of wine styles are permitted: a dry, blended Rosso (at least 60 percent Montepulciano, and at least 15 percent Merlot and/or Cabernet, with up to 25 percent of other red grapes); a *novello* from the same grapes, at least 30 percent of which must undergo *carbonic maceration*, a technique that gives a dark, grapey, low-tannin wine for drinking young; and a blended, dry Bianco (at least 60 percent Trebbiano Toscano, at least 15 percent Passerina, with up to 25 percent other white varieties). Varietal wines are Cabernet (Franc and/or Sauvignon), Ciliegiolo, Merlot, Pinot Nero, and Chardonnay.

The ambitious Controguerra producers also make two bubbly wines and two dessert wines: a dry *frizzante* from the same grape varieties as the Bianco; a dry *spumante* (at least 60 percent Trebbiano Toscano, at least 30 percent Chardonnay and/or Verdicchio and/or Pecorino, and other white varieties); a sweet Bianco *passito* from semi-dried grapes of the same varieties as the *spumante*; and a Rosso *passito,* a fairly sweet red mainly from semi-dried Montepulciano grapes.

Abruzzo wines worth buying

The action in Abruzzo is its native grape, Montepulciano d'Abruzzo, and some of the fine wines made from this variety. But if you can find Valentini's Trebbiano d'Abruzzo, buy it! Also, Cataldi Madonna's Cerasuolo is the best dry rosé in the region. We list our recommended wine producers alphabetically:

Casal Thaulero

Cataldi Madonna

Barone Cornacchia

Illuminati

Marramiero

Masciarelli

Monti

Camillo Montori

Emidio Pepe

Cantina Tollo

Valentini

Zaccagnini

Forgotten Molise

You say you want to get away? Do we have the place for you! Molise *(mo lee sae)* is so remote that even most other Italians have never visited it. Its beaches on the Adriatic are empty, even in the summer (at least that's what we've heard; we've never been there, either). There's no traffic to speak of. And there's only one major winery! Somehow, Molise has earned two DOCs, although no one outside the area has ever heard of one of them.

Molise was actually part of Abruzzo, its northern neighbor, until 1963. But in many ways — such as the climate and many of its wines — Molise looks to the south. Puglia lies to its southeast, and Campania to its southwest and west; its northeastern border is the Adriatic coast (see Figure 9-1). Naples is closer to Molise than Rome is.

Of Italy's 20 regions, Molise ranks 19th in both size and population. (Only the Valle d'Aosta, buried in the Alps of northwest Italy, is smaller and has fewer people.) About 330,000 people live in this mountainous region, where the Apennines are as high as 6,000 feet in the south. Although quite a few hillsides would provide good sites for vineyards, and the climate is mainly sunny and dry, Molise has not really tapped its wine potential. Much of the winemaking that does exist is old-fashioned, to say the least; most of the wine that is not locally consumed is sold in bulk to large wineries in nearby regions. In general, the Italian wine revival has not quite reached Molise yet.

Molise's two DOC wines

Molise's leading grape varieties are those of central Italy: Montepulciano, Sangiovese, and Trebbiano Toscano. But varieties from the South, such as Campania's Aglianico and Greco, and Puglia's Bombino Bianco and Bombino Nero, are also here. Just about four million cases of wine are made annually, but only 2 percent is DOC.

Two wine areas exist: The more important one is in the province of Campobasso, which occupies the eastern two-thirds of the region; the other one is entirely in the Apennine Mountains, in western Molise. The **Biferno** *(bee FER no)* DOC wines, named for the Biferno River, come from the first area, and are the only wines that are known outside of Molise. Biferno Rosso is a dry red (60 to 70 percent Montepulciano, 15 to 20 percent Aglianico, 15 to 20 percent Trebbiano, and other varieties); Biferno Rosato is a dry rosé from the same grapes as the Rosso; and Biferno Bianco is a dry white (65 to 70 percent Trebbiano, 25 to 30 percent Bombino Bianco, and 5 to 10 percent Malvasia).

Molise's other DOC — **Pentro,** or Pentro d'Isernia *(PEN tro dee SER nee ah)* — comes from two separate areas of western Molise. These wines vie for the title of the most obscure DOC wines of Italy. The Pentro appellation covers a dry Rosso (45 to 55 percent Montepulciano, 45 to 55 percent Sangiovese, with other red varieties up to 10 percent); a dry Rosato from same grapes as the Rosso; and a dry Bianco (60 to 70 percent Trebbiano Toscano, 30 to 40 percent Bombino Bianco, and other white varieties optional).

The lone Molise wine producer

Yes, we're only recommending one Molise wine producer, but it's a good one, and its wines are available in the U.S.

Masseria Di Majo Norante is located in Campomarino, near the Abruzzo border. Di Majo Norante is the only established private winery in Molise, making about 200,000 bottles a year of DOC and non-DOC wines. (The non-DOC wines carry the designation IGT Terre degli Osci.) The Di Majo family has always focussed on quality wines; the legendary enologist Giorgio Grai (from Alto Adige) was formerly a consultant here; now the consultant is the renowned Riccardo Cotarella. Wines to try are the Biferno Rosso Ramitello (about $11 or $12, and very good) and Rosso Molì, plus the Biferno Bianco Ramitello and Molì; other wines we recommend are the red Aglianico (about $12), and two white wines: the Greco (about $8 or $9) and the Fiano.

Latium: Rome's Region

Latium, an Italian region that has been a famous wine area since Roman times, is located in west-central Italy, where the Mediterranean Sea forms its rather long western border. At the center of Lazio *(LAH t'zee oh)*, as it's called in Italian, is its capital, Rome, the Eternal City. Tuscany and Umbria are north of Latium, Abruzzo is to the east, and Campania is to the south (see Figure 9-1). With over 5 million people, Latium ranks third in population among Italy's regions, after Lombardy and Campania. The region has plenty of cultivable land for wine, because the Apennines occupy only its eastern part; most of the region is hilly and about one-fifth is plains.

Latium's high-volume production of inexpensive, neutral tasting white wines has tarnished the region's image in the post-World War II era. The most renowned wine of the region, Frascati, has often been the victim of overproduction. But, as in many other regions of Italy, a quality movement is building steam in Latium.

Latium has traditionally been a white wine region; well over 80 percent of its wines, and over 95 percent of its DOC wines, are white. (Malvasia and Trebbiano Toscano dominate this white wine production.) Yet, its dry, warm weather, combined with the volcanic terrain throughout much of the region, are ideal for red wines; some wine producers are beginning to realize the area's potential and are making interesting new red wines. At this point, Latium ranks sixth among Italian regions in wine production with an annual output of about 35 million cases — 17 percent of which is DOC wine. As quality becomes important in Latium, total wine production will probably decrease, but red wine production will increase.

Within the last ten years, the number of Latium's DOC wine zones has jumped from 14 to 24. These zones fall into four general wine areas:

- ✔ The Castelli Romani and Colli Albani hills, south of Rome
- ✔ Northern Latium
- ✔ The South Coast
- ✔ The hills of southeast Latium

Latium's IGTs

If you get your hands on an innovative wine from Latium, it's likely to have the designation IGT Lazio, or perhaps one of the following IGT designations: Civitella d'Agliano, Colli Cimini, Frusinate, or Nettuno.

Frascati and company, from Rome's hills

The most important wine area in Latium is clearly the Castelli Romani and Colli Albani districts, two sets of hills southeast of Rome. The Castelli Romani hills are closer to the city; the Albano hills, named for Lake Albano, are slightly farther south and east. These districts have nine DOC zones, producing 80 percent of Latium's DOC wine, almost all white. This is the home of Frascati, Marino, and other zones that have supplied the citizens of Rome and the rest of the world with oceans of inexpensive wine for the past few decades.

Some producers of both Frascati and Marino have reacted against the colorless, industrial-style wines bearing these names by making more intensely flavored, golden-colored Frascati and Marino that are quite interesting.

Frascati *(frah SKAH tee),* one of Italy's most popular white wines, is made from vineyards around the hill town of Frascati and three other Castelli Romani communities; it's at least 70 percent Malvasia di Candia and/or Trebbiano, with up to 30 percent Greco and/or Malvasia del Lazio, and up to 10 percent other varieties. Although Frascati is usually dry (labeled *secco* or *asciutto*), it can also be made fairly sweet *(amabile)* or sweet *(canellino);* it's also made in *novello* and *spumante* versions. Wines exported to world markets — such as the Fontana Candia and Gotto d'Oro brands — are usually inexpensive, light-bodied, and fairly dry.

The **Marino** *(ma REE no)* zone is adjacent to the Frascati area, to its west. Marino is made on the western slopes of Castelli Romani, extending to the southern outskirts of Rome. It derives up to 60 percent from Malvasia Bianca di Candia, 25 to 55 percent from Trebbiano (any of three clones), 15 to 45 percent from Malvasia del Lazio, and up to 10 percent from Bonvino and/or Cacchione. It can be dry *(secco)*, semi-dry *(abbocato)*, semi-sweet *(amabile)*, or *dolce;* it can also be *spumante.*

When Marino is mass produced, it looks and tastes very much like similarly-produced Frascati — colorless and insipid. But in the hands of a quality producer such as Paola Di Mauro (and her consulting oenologist, Riccardo Cotarella), the wine shows how full-bodied and complex it can be — such as her Marino called Colli Picchioni Oro.

A third important DOC zone of this area, production-wise, is **Colli Albani**, the second-largest source of wine in Latium after Frascati. Most Colli Albani wine is inexpensive, dry white wine made in large co-ops from up to 60 percent Malvasia di Candia, 25 to 50 percent various clones of Trebbiano, and 5 to 45 percent Malvasia del Lazio, with up to 10 percent other white grapes; it can be made in various sweeter versions, as a *spumante* or *novello.*

The remaining six DOC zones of this area are the following, arranged roughly in the order of their proximity to Rome, from closest to farthest:

- ✔ **Castelli Romani:** A new umbrella DOC covering all of Castelli Romani and Colli Albani, Rome itself, and parts of Latina province to the south. The Bianco is mainly Malvasia and Trebbiano, and can be *secco, amabile, frizzante*, or *novello;* the Rosso and Rosato are at least 85 percent Cesanese and/or Merlot and/or Montepulciano and/or Sangiovese and/or Nero Buono; both wines can be dry, sweet, or *frizzante,* and the Rosso can also be *novello.*

- ✔ **Montecompatri Colonna** *(mon tae com PAH tree co LOHN nah):* This small area adjoins Frascati on the east, around Montecompatri, Colonna, and other communities. The wine may carry the name of Montecompatri, Colonna, or both. It's very similar to Frascati, made from Malvasia Bianca di Candia and/or Malvasia del Lazio, with at least 30 percent Trebbiano, and up to 10 percent Bellone or Bonvino optional. It can be *secco, amabile, dolce*, or *frizzante.*

✔ **Colli Lanuvini** *(CO lee lah nu VEE nee):* From vineyards on the southern slopes of the Colli Albani area, stretching south to the Aprilia zone (described later in this chapter), a dry white wine mainly from Malvasia di Candia and/or Malvasia del Lazio, with at least 30 percent various clones of Trebbiano, and up to 10 percent other white grapes; Colli Lanuvini can also be a semi-sweet *(amabile)* wine.

✔ **Zagarolo** *(zah gah RO lo):* From vineyards northeast of Castelli Romani, a dry or *amabile* white wine from the same varieties as in the nearby Montecompatri Colonna zone, made in small quantities.

✔ **Genazzano** *(jeh nahtz ZAH no):* East of Zaragolo, Genazzano is one of Latium's newest DOC wines. The zone produces a dry white as well as a dry red wine; the Bianco is mainly Malvasia di Candia, Bellone, Bombino, Trebbiano Toscano, and Pinot Bianco; the Rosso is mainly Sangiovese and Cesanese.

✔ **Velletri DOC** *(vehl LEH tree):* In the southeastern slopes of Colli Albani, this wine zone produces both dry and sweet white and red wines. Velletri Bianco is from the same varieties as Montecompatri Colonna, and can be a dry, *amabile,* or *dolce* wine, as well as a dry or sweet sparkling wine; a dry or *amabile* Rosso is 20 to 45 percent Sangiovese, 30 to 35 percent Montepulciano, at least 15 percent Cesanese, and up to 10 percent Bombino Nero and/or Merlot and/or Ciliegiolo.

Northern Latium wines

The Tiber River, flowing from Umbria in the north, on its way to Rome and the Mediterranean, cuts northern Latium in two; just a little amount of wine is made east of the Tiber in mountainous Rieti province; most is produced around the lakes of Viterbo province in the north, and along the coastline of Roma province, north of Rome. Not counting a bit of the Orvieto zone in the north — which we cover earlier in this chapter in the Umbria section — northern Latium has eight DOC wines, the most well-known of which is Est! Est!! Est!!! di Montefiascone *(mon tae fee ahs CO nae).*

We refuse to repeat in detail the undoubtedly apocryphal story of how this wine received its name; it involves a Flemish bishop on his way to Rome and a page he sent ahead to find a good wine spot — which Montefiascone supposedly was. ("Est" is Latin for "It is," or "This place rocks.") In any case, the modest, dry white wine of Montefiascone has never lived up to all those exclamation marks. It's made in the volcanic hillsides around the craterous lake, Lago di Bolsena, from 65 percent Trebbiano, 20 percent Malvasia Bianca, and 15 percent Rossetto (also known as Trebbiano Giallo). It's also made in an *abboccato* (semi-dry) style.

We describe the remaining seven DOCs of Northern Latium in the following list. In a nutshell, most of their wines are light-bodied whites from Malvasia and Trebbiano, although a little red wine exists, too. These DOCs are the following:

- ✔ **Aleatico di Gradoli** *(ah lae AH tee co dee GRAH doh lee):* This sweet red, varietal dessert wine comes from the northwestern hillsides of Lago di Bolsena, carrying over into the Est! Est!! Est!!! di Montefiascone DOC zone a bit.

- ✔ **Colli Etruschi Viterbesi** *(CO lee ae TRUE ski vee ter BAE see):* Several blended wines and ten varietally-labeled wines come from this large zone encompassing most of northern Lazio. The blended wines are Rosso, Rosso *novello,* and Rosato (from Sangiovese and Montepulciano — in dry, sweet, and *frizzante* versions) and Bianco (from Trebbiano Toscano, or Procanico, as it's called locally, and Malvasia — in dry, sweet, and *frizzante* styles). The ten varietals are Procanico, Grechetto, Rossetto (dry or sweet), Moscatello (dry or sweet), Moscatello Passito, Sangiovese Rosato (dry or sweet), Greghetto, Montepulciano, Canaiolo, and Merlot. Many of these come in *frizzante* and *novello* versions.

- ✔ **Vignanello** *(veen yah NEL lo):* A relatively new area making Rosso and Rosato from Sangiovese and Ciliegiolo; Bianco from Trebbiano and Malvasia; varietal Greco; and a Greco *Spumante.*

- ✔ **Cerveteri** *(cher veh TEH ree):* A long, narrow wine zone which includes the northern outskirts of Rome and six communities north of Rome along the coast, including Cerveteri itself, a coastal resort where the dry white Cerveteri Bianco is quite popular. The wines are Bianco *secco,* Bianco *frizzante,* and Bianco *amabile,* made from

Trebbiano Toscano and/or Trebbiano Giallo, Malvasia di
Candia and/or Malvasia del Lazio, with other white varieties permitted; and Rosso (*secco, novello,* or *amabile*)
and Rosato, made from Sangiovese and/or
Montepulciano, Cesanese, and other red varieties.

✔ **Tarquinia** *(tar KEE nee ah):* Another broad, new DOC
zone encompassing 30 communities in Lazio's two northern provinces; the types of wine and grape varieties of
the Tarquinia DOC wines are exactly the same as those of
Cerveteri.

✔ **Bianco Capena** *(bee AHN coh cah PAE nah):* A dry or
abboccato white wine made in the hills north of Rome,
from three Malvasia clones, three Trebbiano clones, and
up to 20 percent Bellone and/or Bombino.

✔ **Colli della Sabina** *(CO lee del lah sah BEE nah):* A new
DOC on the eastern side of the Tiber River; a dry white
Bianco, *spumante,* and *frizzante* are at least 40 percent
Trebbiano, and at least 40 percent Malvasia; a Rosso,
Rosso *frizzante,* Rosso *novello,* Rosso *spumante,* Rosato,
and Rosato *frizzante* are made from 40 to 70 percent
Sangiovese, 15 to 40 percent Montepulciano, with other
red varieties.

Latium's South Coast

The southern coast of Latium includes three DOC wines —
Aprilia, Cori, and Circeo. With the exception of Cori, the northernmost area, this part of Latium is less blessed with favorable
grape growing conditions than the cooler Castelli Romani and
Colli Albani hills to the northeast. But some exciting wines,
both red and white, many of which are non-DOC, are being
made from low-yielding vines, especially at the Casale del
Giglio winery in Aprilia. These are the zones of Latium's South
Coast:

✔ **Cori** *(COH ree):* This small area is closest to the Colli
Albani hills, and its wines resemble those of the neighboring Velletri. Cori Bianco (up to 70 percent Malvasia di
Candia, up to 40 percent Trebbiano Toscano, and up to 30
percent Trebbiano Giallo and/or Bellone) can be dry,
amabile, or *dolce.* The more distinctive Cori Rosso is a
dry red with 40 to 60 percent Montepulciano, 20 to 40 percent of the local Nero Buono di Cori, and Cesanese.

✔ **Aprilia** *(ah PREE lee ah):* The Aprilia wine zone, between the Colli Albani area to the north and the Mediterranean to the south, is one of the areas of Latium's wine renaissance. Aprilia has three varietal wines, each of which must derive at least 95 percent from its named grape: Aprilia Trebbiano, Merlot, and a dry rosé, Sangiovese.

✔ **Circeo** *(cher CHAE oh):* This new wine zone along the coastline covers six types of wine: Circeo Bianco (dry or *amabile,* made from at least 60 percent Trebbiano Toscano and up to 30 percent Malvasia di Candia, with up to 30 percent other white varieties); Circeo Rosso and Rosato (both of which can be dry, *amabile,* or *frizzante,* made from at least 85 percent Merlot); Circeo *novello* (from the same grapes as the Rosso, but made only as a dry wine); and three varietal wines — Trebbiano, Sangiovese (still or *frizzante*), and Sangiovese Rosato (still or *frizzante*).

Southeast Latium

The Ciociaria *(cho CHA ree ah)* hills of southeast Latium have been producing red wines for some time, based on the local Cesanese *(chae sah NAE sae)* grape; the three DOC wines of the area all derive 90 percent from that variety. Traditionally these wines were sweet and bubbly, but lately the trend has shifted to dry wines. But much of the area's sparse population has left grape growing in favor of opportunities in industry; as a result, two of the three red wines — **Cesanese di Affile** *(ahf FEE lae)* and **Cesanese di Olevano** *(oh lae VAH no)* — have practically disappeared. The third, **Cesanese di Piglio** *(PEE l'yoh),* is the best of the three, but the grapes are difficult to cultivate in the mountainous territory. Look for the Cesanese del Piglio of Massimi Berucci.

There's more promise for Latium's newest DOC wine area, **Atina** *(ah TEE nah)* — or so we've heard. This DOC, in the southern part of inland Latium, is so new that we don't have all the details about its grapes and wines yet, other than that there's a Rosso made mainly from Cabernet Sauvignon, with some Merlot, and a Bianco, made from Sauvignon Blanc, and possibly Sémillon, Malvasia, and Vermentino. Producer Giovanni Palumbo is a leader in making these red and white Bordeaux-style blends.

Latium wine producers

Even though Latium is dominated by large cooperatives, in recent years independent wine producers have made a name for themselves with quality wines and have begun to restore the image of this historic region. Also, some of the large wineries and co-ops have begun making smaller lots of finer wine; the huge Fontana Candida winery, for example, which exports 625,000 cases of wine annually, is making an excellent Frascati Superiore called Santa Teresa, in small quantities.

We list our recommended Latium producers in alphabetical order:

Massimi Berucci
Cantina Cooperativa di
   Cerveteri
Colacicchi
Colle Picchioni-Paola Di Mauro
Falesco
Fiorano
Fontana Candida
Casale del Giglio
Cantina Oleificio Sociale di
   Gradoli

Gotto d'Oro
Casale Marchese
Mazzioti
Mottura
Giovanni Palombo
Castel de Paolis
Tenuta Le Quinte
Villa Simone
Conte Zandotti

Part IV
The Wine Regions of Southern Italy

In this part . . .

Southern Italy is the home of Italy's most prolific wine region, Puglia, and two of Italy's heartiest red wines, Salice Salentino and Primitivo. (You know that a wine called "Primitivo" has to be a brute!) But Southern Italy's best red wine, Taurasi, is in neighboring Campania — seat of the beautiful Amalfi Coast and Naples, the birthplace of pizza. We wind up your tour of Italy's wine regions with a stop in the country's two beautiful island regions, Sicily and Sardinia. Sicily's Greek ruins have always attracted tourists, but the region is also famous for its wine — lots of wine, more than most entire countries! Sardinia, that most isolated of all of Italy's regions, is coming alive, wine-wise, making very affordable reds and whites that are distinctive from the rest of Italy's *vino*. Southern Italy is *hot!*

Chapter 10

The Wines of Southern Italy

In This Chapter

▶ Campania's untapped potential

▶ Sturdy reds from Puglia

▶ Basilicata's Aglianico del Vulture

▶ The rustic wines of Calabria

Southern Italy has a proud wine history. The area has produced wine for over 4,000 years; in 2,000 B.C., when Phoenician traders arrived in what is today the region of Apulia, a local wine industry was already thriving! The Greeks later dubbed Southern Italy, "The Land of Wine." The Romans delighted in the wines of the Campania region.

But that was then. In more recent history, Southern Italy has been perhaps the world's prime example of an underachieving viticultural area. That old bugaboo, overproduction — along with indifference plus political and criminal corruption — conspired to keep Southern Italy from achieving wine greatness. Most of the area's huge production of dark, high-alcohol, low-acid wine was sold in bulk, as blending wine, to wineries in Northern Italy, France, and Germany. Only within the last decade has this area begun its long-awaited wine renaissance, producing fine wines from quality-conscious producers. The future now looks rosy in the land of wine.

Campania: Revival Begins

The region of Campania in many ways embodies Southern Italy. It's the home of Naples, Italy's third largest city and the most bustling metropolis south of Rome. Naples — or Napoli *(NAH po lee)* as the Italians call it — with its famous bay, is one of the world's great seaports — not to mention the birthplace of pizza! (Pizza aficionados tell us that Naples still makes the world's best pizza. If for no other reason, the city is worth a visit.) As in the rest of Italy's South, the weather is generally warm, at least in the low altitudes. Flavorful vegetables, fruits, and grains crowd the countryside, along with grapevines. The people are generally shorter and swarthier than in the North; and they're also usually more outgoing than Northern Italians.

Campania sits along Italy's western coast, on the Tyrrhenian Sea; the region is south of Latium and Molise, west of Puglia and Basilicata, and north of Calabria (see Figure 10-1). Campania has Italy's second-largest population, thanks to thriving Naples. It boasts one of the most beautiful coastlines in the world; the Amalfi Coast and the Sorrento Peninsula, with the nearby isle of Capri, are just some of the renowned coastal attractions.

Campania is so gifted in terms of its climate, soil, and topography that it could be one of the great wine regions of Italy — and perhaps someday it will be. The Romans clearly favored Campania for wine. And yet, just ten short years ago, more than half of the region's DOC wine came from *one* producer! That producer, Mastroberardino, is still the leader in DOC wine production, but today several others have finally joined the ranks of quality-conscious firms willing to tap Campania's tremendous potential. One of their key assets is a red grape variety, Aglianico *(ah l'yee AH nee co)*, which has proven to be one of the great, noble grapes of Italy; also, two white varieties, Fiano and Greco di Tufo, make some of the very best, long-lived white wines in the country. It's safe to say that in a few years, Campania will be regarded as one of Italy's "hot" wine regions.

More than half of Campania's terrain consists of hillsides. The Apennines run along the central and eastern parts of the region; other mountains and hills are in and near the western coastline, including several volcanoes — some of which are not extinct, including the famous Mount Vesuvius (before 79 A.D., there was a city nearby, called Pompeii). The climate is mainly hot and dry near the sea, but can be cool and rainy, especially in the autumn, in the inland Apennines.

Figure 10-1: Southern Italy: The Land of Wine.

Campania produces about 23 million cases of wine annually, only about 8 percent of which is DOC/G wine. (But give the region credit for its progress: ten years ago, less than 2 percent of Campania's wine was DOC/G, the lowest percentage in Italy.)

Campania now has one DOCG wine (in 1993, Taurasi was awarded DOCG status), along with 18 DOC wines, which are scattered throughout its five provinces. These 19 wines can be grouped geographically into four areas:

- The Irpinia hills of Avellino, in central Campania
- The coastal hills and islands around Naples
- Southern Campania
- The northern hills of the region

The wines of Avellino

Campania's three greatest wines come from the Irpinia hills around the city of Avellino, the capital of the Avellino province: the red Taurasi, and two DOC whites, Fiano di Avellino and Greco di Tufo.

Until recently, the only winery that mattered in Avellino was Mastroberardino, owned by a family that has produced wine for about 300 years. Since the 1970s, Antonio Mastroberardino has been responsible for dramatic improvements not only in the wines of Avellino, but also in the wines of the coastal hills area; his brother, Walter, ran the business end of the winery.

But two things happened in the past decade to alter the fine wine scene in Avellino. Feudi di San Gregorio, another very good, but smaller, producer, whose consulting enologist is the renowned Riccardo Cotarella, began producing wines that challenged Mastroberardino's monopoly. Even more devastating, the two Mastroberardino brothers, in the classic Italian tradition, had a bitter feud and split up their property. (Is there another country in the world which has more feuding brothers in the wine business than Italy?) Walter and his viticulturist son, Paolo, took some of the best vineyards for their own winery, Terredora di Paolo (or simply, Terredora). The Mastroberardino winery — now called Antonio, Carlo e Pietro Mastroberardino — once made well over 90 percent of Avellino's Taurasi wines, but now that figure will necessarily dwindle.

Taurasi

Mastroberardino's 1968 Taurasi Riserva won so much acclaim worldwide that it brought this massive red wine — and its noble grape variety, Aglianico — attention it had never before received. Taurasi *(touw RAH see)* is a wine that demands aging, not unlike the other great Italian reds — Barolo, Barbaresco, and Brunello. In good vintages, this complex, powerful, and tannic wine is at its best after 15 to 20 years.

Taurasi's vineyard area is the hills around the community of Taurasi and 16 others, northeast of Avellino. The wine must be at least 85 percent Aglianico, with up to 15 percent other red varieties, but in practice, most of the better Taurasi wines are 100 percent Aglianico. Taurasi must age for at least three years before being released, at least one of which is in wood; Taurasi Riservas must age for at least four years (including at least 18 months in wood). Taurasi wines retail in the $32 to $40 price range. Mastroberardino's finest Taurasi is the single-vineyard "Radici"; other good Taurasi wines are made by Feudi di San Gregorio and Terredora.

Fiano di Avellino

At its best, Fiano di Avellino is Southern Italy's top dry white wine — and one of the best in the entire country. It's a delicately-flavored wine with aromas of pear and toasted hazelnuts, which become more pronounced with age. Unlike most dry white wines, Fiano di Avellino is best with at least five or six years of aging, and will be fine for up to 15, in good vintages.

The DOC zone for this wine is the hills around Avellino and 25 other communities, a few of which are in the Taurasi DOCG zone; the best Fiano vineyards are in the hills around Lapio. Fiano di Avellino must have at least 85 percent Fiano grapes, with the balance Greco and/or Coda di Volpe and/or Trebbiano Toscano. Fiano di Avellino wines retail for about $18 to $24. Wines to look for include Terredora's single-vineyard Terre di Dora, Mastroberardino's single-vineyard Vignadora or Radici, and Feudi di San Gregorio's Pietracalda.

Greco di Tufo

The name Greco di Tufo *(GREH co dee TOO foh)* applies to both a white grape variety and a DOC wine. The Greeks introduced the Greco variety to Italy over 2,000 years ago. It flourishes in many parts of Italy, but the particular clone (called Greco di Tufo) that grows around the hillside village of Tufo and seven other communities directly north of Avellino is undoubtedly the best. "Tufa" or "tufo" is a type of calcareous rock deposited by springs or lakes; the tufaceous and volcanic soil of the Tufo area makes an auspicious environment for this grape.

Greco di Tufo is a far more prolific grape than the difficult-to-grow Fiano. Even though the wine's DOC zone is about one-third the size of Fiano di Avellino's, much more Greco di Tufo is made — in fact, it's Campania's largest-production DOC wine. Greco di Tufo is similar to Fiano di Avellino; the differences are that Greco di Tufo wines are more intensely fruity and crisper; Fiano di Avellino wines are more subtle and a bit softer. Greco di Tufo also ages well, but not quite so long as Fiano; Greco di Tufo is usually ready to drink after three or four years, but can age for at least 10 to 12 years. Greco di Tufo wines must derive at least 85 percent from Greco, with the balance Coda di Volpe. Look for the Greco di Tufo wines of Feudi di San Gregorio, Mastroberardino — especially the single-vineyard Vignadangelo — and Terredora. Greco di Tufo retails for about $17 to $23.

Wines of the coastal hills and islands around Naples

When hundreds of thousands of uncritical tourists descend on your shores every year and buy up all your wine, you don't have to aim for greatness. Perhaps this is the main reason that the coastal hills and islands around Naples haven't made much quality wine in the past. Certainly the area has the right ingredients: a warm, dry climate, and soil rich in tufa and volcanic ash. (Actually, these conditions favor red wine production more than white, but the vacationing tourists favor cool, white wines, and that style has therefore predominated.) Now, some producers are joining the quality wine movement, despite their two nemeses: Naples' urban sprawl and the easy tourist *lira* (dollar).

This area has seven DOC wines. Three of them, Ischia, Capri, and Vesuvio, are longstanding. Ischia *(EES key ah)* actually became Italy's second DOC wine, in 1966. And that's not the only history this wine has going for it: The Greeks planted grapes on this island in 770 B.C. Not much wine is made today, but white wines dominate production, with D'Ambra Vini d'Ischia making the island's best. Ischia Bianco is mainly Forastera, with Biancolella and other white grapes; the same varieties also make a Bianco *spumante,* and each of these two grapes makes a varietal wine. Ischia Rosso is a dry red mainly from Guarnaccia (in the Grenache family) and Piedirosso (known locally as Pér'e Palummo); Piedirosso also makes a varietal wine and a *passito.*

Capri *(CAH pree),* the island at the end of the Sorrento Peninsula, is such a wealthy tourist mecca that vineyards or winemaking don't get much attention. Capri's extremely limited vineyards are on terraced slopes with calcareous soil, and overlook the sea. Capri has two wines: Capri Bianco (mainly Falanghina and Greco, with up to 20 percent Biancolella); and Capri Rosso (mainly Piedirosso).

Lacryma Christi del Vesuvio *(LAH cree mah CHREE sti de veh SOO vee oh),* also called Vesuvio, comes from vineyards on the slopes of Mount Vesuvius, east of Naples, overlooking the Bay of Naples. The area has great volcanic soil, but had very little quality wine until Mastroberardino came along. Vesuvio's wines can be white, red, or rosé. The basic wines, with less than 12 percent alcohol, carry the simpler Vesuvio DOC, while the white, red, or rosé wines from riper grapes are Lacryma Christi ("tears of Christ") del Vesuvio The Bianco is mainly Verdeca and Coda di Volpe, with up to 20 percent Greco and/or Falanghina; the Rosso and Rosato are mainly Piedirosso and Sciascinoso, with up to 20 percent Aglianico. All three Lacryma Christi wines can also be *spumante.*

Since 1990, four new DOC wine areas have joined these three:

- ✔ **Campi Flegrei** *(CAHM pee FLEH grae):* The Campi Flegrei zone includes parts of the city of Naples, the coastal town of Pozzuoli, and four other communities situated around (hopefully) extinct volcanoes near Naples. Of Campania's newer DOC zones, this area has the most promise — if Naples doesn't gobble it up. Campi Flegrei Bianco is a dry white made mainly from Falanghina, Biancolella, and Coda di Volpe varieties; Campi Flegrei Falanghina is a dry white varietal — or a *spumante* — derived at least 90 percent from that variety. Campi Flegrei Rosso is a dry red (or *novello* style) mainly from Piedirosso, Aglianico, and Sciascinoso grapes. Campi Flegrei Piedirosso — dry or *passito* — must contain at least 90 percent of this variety

- ✔ **Costa d'Amalfi** *(COHS tah dah MAHL fee):* The hills above the Amalfi Coast in Salerno province are the striking setting for vineyards that now produce better wine than ever, doing justice to their newly-awarded DOC status. Wines from vineyards in three sub-zones — Furore, Ravello, and Tramonti — can add these names to their labels; one exceptional producer in the Furore and Ravello sub-zones for both red and white wines is Marisa Cuomo.

The Costa d'Amalfi DOC features Bianco, Rosso, and Rosato wines. The Bianco is at least 60 percent Falanghina and Biancolella; the Rosso and Rosato are at least 60 percent Piedirosso and Sciascinoso.

✔ **Penisola Sorrentina** *(peh NEE so lah sor ren TEE nah):* The Sorrento Peninsula zone juts out at the southernmost part of Naples province, and borders the Amalfi Coast to the south. Parts of the area can name their wines with a sub-zone name; these include two villages on the north side of the peninsula, Lettere and Gragnano (for dry red wines), as well the town of Sorrento, for red and white wines. Both Lettere and Gragnano were known for their fizzy red wines, but have lost many of their vineyards due to Naples' expansion. Penisola Sorrentina Bianco is mainly Falanghina, Biancolella, and/or Greco; the Rosso and Rosso *frizzante naturale* are mainly Piedirosso, Sciascinoso, and/or Aglianico.

✔ **Asprinio di Aversa** *(ahs PREE nee oh dee ah VEHR sa):* This wine zone in the plains north of Naples makes a dry white wine from at least 85 percent Asprinio grapes; in its more popular form, Asprinio di Aversa is a dry *spumante,* from 100 percent Asprinio. Aversa has been a declining wine area that hopes the blessing of DOC status can revive it.

Southern Campania

The rugged, rocky hills of Southern Campania are known as the Cilento Hills — an unspoiled area, with remnants of ancient Greek towns, a spectacular coastline extending to the neighboring region of Basilicata, and mountains (part of the Apennine chain) preserved as a national park. In this beautiful, natural setting, robust red grapes such as Aglianico thrive, along with the white Fiano and Moscato. (Luigi Maffini, makes fine varietal Fiano wines in this area under the Paestum IGT.)

Southern Campania boasts two formal wine zones that make a total of ten wines. **Cilento** *(chee LEN toh)* is Campania's largest DOC zone; it occupies the region's southern coastal area and extends well inland. Four types of Cilento wine exist: a dry Rosso (60 to 75 percent Aglianico, 15 to 20 percent Piedirosso and/or Primitivo, 10 to 20 percent Barbera); a dry Rosato (70 to 80 percent Sangiovese, 10 to 15 percent Aglianico, and 10 to

15 percent Piedirosso and/or Primitivo); a Bianco (60 to 65 percent Fiano, 20 to 30 percent Trebbiano Toscano, 10 to 15 percent Greco Bianco and/or Malvasia Bianca); and an Aglianico.

Castel San Lorenzo *(CAHS tel sahn lo REN zo)* is a new DOC zone inland from the Cilento area that has three blended wines and three varietals. Castel San Lorenzo Rosso and Rosato are dry wines mainly (80 percent) from Barbera and Sangiovese; the Bianco is a dry white mainly (80 percent) from Trebbiano Toscano and Malvasia Bianca. The three varietal wines are Barbera, a sweet Moscato Bianco, and a Moscato *spumante*.

Campania's northern hills

Northern Campania is dominated by the Apennine Mountains and their foothills; it includes some historic wine districts, such as Falerno del Massico, on the coastline, which dates back to Roman times, and quite a few new, developing wine areas. The climate varies considerably. The coastal area of Falerno is warm, and produces plump wines redolent of fruit; wine zones further inland have a cooler Apennine-influenced climate, and more austere wines. Northern Campania now has seven DOC wines:

- ✔ **Falerno del Massico** *(fah LER no del MAH see co):* These vineyards occupy the slopes of Monte Massico, near the Latium border to the north; the name Falerno goes back to the Romans, who revered the white wine of this area. Today, three styles of Falerno del Massico exist: a Bianco (most likely made from a different variety than it was 2,000 years ago), a Rosso, and a Primitivo (one of the rare varietal Primitivo wines outside of Puglia). The Bianco is a dry white entirely from Falanghina, the area's best white variety; the Rosso is a dry red primarily from Aglianico, with 20 to 40 percent Piedirosso, and up to 20 percent Primitivo and/or Barbera; and the Primitivo has up to 15 percent Aglianico and/or Piedirosso and/or Barbera. Villa Matilde and Fontana Galardi are two leading wineries.

- ✔ **Gallucio** *(gahl LOO cho):* This brand new wine zone in northern Campania, on the Latium border, is directly north of Falerno but farther inland, where the climate is cool and the terrain is hilly. Gallucio's vineyards occupy the hills around an extinct volcano, where the soil is rich in minerals. The wines are similar to Falerno's, but tend to be a bit lighter and have more aromatic finesse. Gallucio wines include a Rosso and Rosato based mainly on Aglianico, and a Falanghina Bianco.

✔ **Solopaca** *(so lo PAH cah):* This wine zone in north-central Campania is in a valley between two mountain ranges, and is named for the village of Solopaca. Six types of wine carry the Solopaca DOC: a Rosso, Rosato, Bianco, two varietal wines, and a *spumante*. Solopaca Bianco is a dry white made from Trebbiano Toscano, Falanghina, Coda di Volpe, Malvasia Toscana, and Malvasia di Candia, with other white varieties optional; the Rosso and Rosato are dry wines made from Sangiovese and Aglianico, with up to 30 percent Piedirosso and/or Sciascinoso with other varieties optional. There's a red Aglianico and white Falanghina; the *spumante* is at least 60 percent Falanghina.

✔ **Taburno** *(tah BUR no):* Named after the Taburno mountain range, south of Solopaca. Taburno has a varietal Aglianico (Rosso or Rosato), Falanghina, Greco, and Coda di Volpe (all whites), and Piedirosso. Blended wines include a dry Bianco, mainly (70 percent) from Trebbiano Toscano and Falanghina; a Rosso, mainly (70 percent) from Sangiovese and Aglianico; and finally, a dry *spumante*, mainly from Coda di Volpe and/or Falanghina.

✔ **Sant'Agata dei Goti** *(sahnt AHG ah tah dae GO tee):* A Bianco, Rosso, *novello*, and Rosato — all from the same varieties (no, we didn't make a mistake!). Those varieties are Aglianico and Piedirosso, both reds (other non-aromatic red varieties may be added); the Bianco is made using only the colorless juice of the grapes, and not their red skins. Five varietal wines include two dry red wines (Aglianico and Piedirosso), two dry whites (Greco and Falanghina), and one sweet white (Falanghina *passito*), all of which are at least 90 percent of the named variety. The production zone is west of Taburno.

✔ **Guardiolo** *(gwar dee OH lo):* Guardiolo Bianco is a dry white made mainly from Malvasia Bianca di Candia and Falanghina; a Rosso and Rosato are mainly Sangiovese. Guardiolo Aglianico is a dry red with at least 90 percent of that variety, and Guardiolo Falanghina is a dry white 90 percent varietal, with Malvasia Bianca and/or other white

> grapes; a *spumante* is a dry sparkling wine made from the same varieties as the Falanghina. Vineyards are in high hills around the village of Guardia Sanframondi, within the eastern part of the Solopaca area.
>
> ✔ **Sannio** *(SAHN nee oh):* This is a new, general wine zone covering the entire Benevento province, as a catch-all designation for wines outside the province's other DOC zones.

IGT wines from Campania can carry the following regional names, depending on where in the region their vineyards are located: Beneventano, Colli di Salerno, Dugenta, Epomeo, Irpinia, Paestum, Pompeiano, Roccamonfina, and Terre del Volturno.

Campania wines worth buying

Our recommended wine producers in Campania are listed alphabetically:

Antonio Caggiano	Michele Moio
Cantina Grotta del Sole	S. Molettieri
La Caprense	Montevetrano
Marisa Cuomo	Mustilli
D'Ambra Vini d'Ischia	Ocone
De Concilus	San Giovanni
De Lucia	Terredora
Feudi di San Gregorio	Antica Masseria Venditti
Galardi	Villa Matilde
Luigi Maffini	Villa San Michele
Mastroberardino	

Apulia: Italy's Wine Barrel

Apulia, or Puglia *(POO l'yah),* as the Italians call it, is truly Italy's wine lake, producing between 100 and 130 million cases of wine annually. If Puglia were a country, it would be the seventh-largest wine-producer in the world! About 80 percent of Puglia's wine is red, but less than 4 percent of it is DOC; most of it is unremarkable wine made by large-volume cooperatives that's shipped north in bulk to improve the less robust red wines of cooler climes.

One of the reasons that Puglia produces so much wine — besides its wine-friendly sunny, dry climate — is its lack of mountains. It's the only southern region that's practically mountain-free, and in fact is Italy's flattest region, consisting mainly of fertile plains, with some hills and plateaus.

In envisioning Puglia, remember that the length of the region does not run north-south, but northwest to southeast; Molise, the Italian region you might envision as north of Puglia, is actually northwest of it, and the Adriatic Sea forms Puglia's northern (and eastern) border (see Figure 1-1). Puglia's neighbors to the west are the regions of Basilicata and Campania; the huge Gulf of Taranto is to the south and southwest. Puglia's Salento Peninsula, the "spike" of the "heel," is the easternmost part of Italy, stretching into the Adriatic towards Greece.

The capital of Puglia is the port city of Bari, on the Adriatic Sea, in the central part of the region. Besides Bari, the four other principal cities are Foggia *(FOJ jah),* Taranto *(TAH rahn toh),* Brindisi *(BREEN dee see),* and Lecce *(LAECH chae)* — each the capital of its province, as is Bari. Foggia is the largest of the five provinces, occupying all of northern Puglia. The Lecce province, the southern half of the Salento Peninsula, boasts the largest vineyard area, and is the scene of most of Puglia's quality winemaking. The city of Lecce itself is an interesting, historic town definitely worth visiting — as is Otranto, a resort town on the Adriatic Sea that's the easternmost community in Italy. Gallipoli, on the western shores of Puglia, on the Gulf of Taranto, is another resort community where you can escape Puglia's summer heat.

Puglia's three major grape varieties are Negroamaro, Primitivo, and Malvasia Nera — all red grapes. These grapes grow mainly on the Salento Peninsula, and most of the wines of that area are made from one, or a blend, of them. Negroamaro and Primitivo, in fact, are Italy's fourth and sixth most-planted red grape varieties — even though they grow mainly just in Puglia. The Malvasia Nera used in Puglia is mainly two particular clones, Malvasia Nera di Lecce and Malvasia Nera di Brindisi.

Puglia has 25 DOC wine zones, one of which — Aleatico di Puglia — extends across all five provinces (but in actuality the wine grows almost entirely in the Gioia del Colle district, south of Bari). This historic specialty is a sweet, high alcohol red dessert wine made from the Aleatico variety, with up to 15 percent other grapes (Negroamaro, Primitivo, and Malvasia Nera). A *liquoroso* version also exists.

Puglia's 24 other DOC zones fall into four general groups, according to their location. From south to north, these areas are the following:

- ✔ The Salento Peninsula, the most important area for quality
- ✔ The "Trulli" district, north of the Salento peninsula
- ✔ Central Apulia, including Castel del Monte, a quality zone
- ✔ The Northern Plains

IGT wines from Puglia can carry the following place names, depending on where their vineyards are located, and the producer's preference: Daunia, Murgia, Puglia, Salento, Tarantino, or Valle d'Itria.

The Salento Peninsula

With its flat, arid plains, palm trees, and cactus plants, the Salento Peninsula resembles a desert area in many places; if not for the cool breezes from the Adriatic Sea, this area would be unbearably hot, especially in the summer. Vines grow in a red soil atop primarily calcareous rock that's particularly ideal for red grapes. Some vineyards bear very small crops of Negroamaro, Primitivo, and Malvasia Nera — particularly compared to typical crop sizes in the rest of Puglia — which reflects the advanced thinking of many local producers, and results in intensely flavored wines.

The Salento Peninsula is Puglia's major wine district; its 11 DOC wines include the renowned Salice Salentino and Primitivo di Manduria. Most of its wines are dark and robust, with ripe flavors and rather high alcohol content. They're made mainly from Negroamaro and/or Primitivo, with Malvasia Nera the third most important grape. (But Aglianico, Campania's noble red grape — and in our opinion the best red variety in Southern Italy — is an emerging presence in the peninsula, either for varietal or, more commonly, blended red wines.)

Salice Salentino

Salice Salentino *(SAH lee chae sah len TEE no)* is Puglia's wine ambassador: It's the one Apulian wine that many winedrinkers abroad have tasted, or at least heard of. It's a dark, robust wine of the South, with all the warm, ripe, even slightly baked, flavors of sun-drenched grapes. It's made mainly from Negroamaro, with up to 20 percent Malvasia Nera.

The late Cosimo Taurino, whose wines have had great success on the U.S. market (and whose son, Francesco, continues his work), favored a lusty style for this wine. He made his Salice Salentino — and his two other, even classier Negroamaro wines, Notapanaro and Patriglione — from extra-ripe grapes, to achieve this style. But even before Taurino, Leone de Castris established Salice Salentino as a major Italian red wine. Today, at Agricole Vallone, enologist Severino Garofano not only makes a fine Salice Salentino but also has come up with Puglia's answer to Amarone (see the Veneto section of Chapter 7 for info on Amarone) — Graticciaia, a blackish, concentrated, high-alcohol red from late-harvested Negroamaro and Malvasia Nera grapes. Basic Salice Salentino retails for $10 to $11, but special, single-vineyard versions run anywhere from $12 to $30, and Graticciaia costs about $35.

Although the main type of Salice Salentino is a red wine, various other styles exist: a *novello;* a refreshing, dry rosé; a Rosato *spumante* (all from the same grape varieties as the Rosso); and even white and sweet versions. Salice Salentino Bianco is mainly (70 percent) Chardonnay, while Salice Salentino Pinot Bianco (still or *spumante*) combines Pinot Blanc with up to 15 percent Chardonnay and Sauvignon. The traditional sweet, high-alcohol red wine of Puglia, Aleatico Dolce (or *liquoroso*), is another style of Salice Salentino.

Primitivo di Manduria

Primitivo di Manduria *(pre meh TEE vo dee mahn DOO ree ah)* is both the name of a DOC wine and the name of a grape. Of the various types of Primitivo grapes, this is the one thought to be genetically the same as Zinfandel. Surely, Primitivo di Manduria wines share certain characteristics with Zinfandel: They're dark in color (although some red American Zins are made in a lighter style), they're usually high in alcohol, and they're rich and opulently fruity. If anything, Primitivo seems to make wines that are bigger in every way than most

Zinfandels, starting with their deep purple color (which is partly due to the fact that the juice of the grapes is dark, rather than colorless).

Primitivo di Manduria wine always comes 100 percent from that grape. (What other variety could compete with it?) It's rich, ripe, and explosively fruity; its *minimum* alcohol content is 14 percent but usually higher. Although it can age for a few years, it's best young.

The Perucci brothers — who make wine under the Pervini (an acronym for "Perucci Vini"), Felline, and Sinfarosa brands — are greatly responsible for the improvement of wines in this DOC zone. Formerly, the wines were rough and rustic — like some rowdy relation you enjoy but try to avoid introducing to polite company. But lately, Primitivo di Manduria wines have taken on an elegance — relatively speaking, since high-alcohol reds trade on power rather than subtlety or finesse — that they didn't previously have. You can find Primitivo di Manduria retailing for $9 to $12 — although Sinfarosa makes one called "Zinfandel," which sells for $20. Primitivo di Manduria also comes in three dessert styles: *dolce naturale* (minimum alcohol, 16 percent); *liquoroso dolce naturale* (minimum alcohol, 17.5 percent); and *liquoroso secco* (minimum alcohol, 18 percent). With two glasses of these wines, you'll eat the whole cake.

Other Salento Peninsula wines

The nine other Salento Peninsula DOC wines are the following:

- ✔ **Brindisi** *(BREEN deh see):* Named after the coastal town of Brindisi, this is a dry, rich red wine (or a rosé) that's mainly Negroamaro, with up to 30 percent Montepulciano and/or Malvasia Nera and/or Susumaniello (a Croatian variety), and Sangiovese. Cosimo Taurino's greatest wine, Patriglione, mainly Negroamaro, is Brindisi's finest wine; Agricole Vallone also makes good Brindisi wines.

- ✔ **Copertino** *(co per TEE no):* These dry red and rosé wines are mainly Negroamaro, with up to 30 percent Malvasia Nera and/or Montepulciano, plus up to 15 percent Sangiovese. The great enologist of the Salento Peninsula, Severino Garofano, consults at wineries in Copertino, and so quality is high here. The vineyards are directly south of the Salice Salentino zone.

✔ **Squinzano** *(skwin ZAH no):* At one time this area near the coast, south of the Brindisi area, was just a source of bulk wines; now it has a higher profile, thanks to Antinori's Vigneti del Sud, a new 1250-acre estate that's growing mainly Negroamaro. Squinzano's two wines are a dry Rosso and a Rosato, both from the same varieties: mainly Negroamaro, with Malvasia Nera and Sangiovese.

✔ **Levorano** *(leh vo RAH no):* Levorano Rosso and Rosato are Negroamaro with up to 35 percent Malvasia Nera and/or Sangiovese and/or Montepulciano, and up to 10 percent Malvasia Bianca. Levorano Bianco (which became Salento's first white DOC wine in 1980) is at least 65 percent Malvasia Bianca, with Bombino Bianco and/or Trebbiano Toscano. This small zone is east of Copertino and Salice Salentino.

✔ **Nardò** *(nar DOH):* Nardò Rosso and Rosato are mainly Negroamaro, with Malvasia Nera and/or Montepulciano. Vineyards are on the western coast of the peninsula, north of Gallipoli.

✔ **Alezio** *(ah LEH zee oh):* The dry Alezio Rosso (or Rosato) is mainly Negroamaro, with Malvasia Nera, Sangiovese, or Montepulciano, together or singly. This small zone is east of coastal Gallipoli. The leading winery is Calò's Rosa del Golfo, which makes one of Italy's best dry rosés, from Negroamaro and Malvasia Nera.

✔ **Matino** *(mah TEE no):* Salento's earliest (1971) and south-ernmost DOC zone, Matino makes two dry DOC wines, a Rosso and Rosato, both wines mainly Negroamaro, with up to 30 percent Malvasia Nera and/or Sangiovese.

✔ **Lizzano** *(leet ZAH no):* Lizzano boasts the most varied range of wines in the Salento Peninsula. They include a dry Rosso and Rosato (still or *frizzante*), and a Rosato *spumante*, all mainly from Negroamaro, with some Malvasia Nera, and other varieties optional, including Montepulciano, Sangiovese and Pinot Nero. A dry, white Lizzano Bianco (also *frizzante*) and Bianco *spumante* are made mainly from Trebbiano and/or Chardonnay and/or Pinot Bianco, with Sauvignon other varieties optional. Varietals are Negroamaro (Rosso or Rosato) and Malvasia Nera (from either the "Lecce" or "Brindisi" clones, or both) The Lizzano zone borders the Gulf of Taranto and overlaps the western part of the Primitivo di Manduria zone.

✔ **Galatina** *(gah lah TEE nah):* A Rosso and Rosato wine based primarily on Negroamaro. This is the newest and smallest DOC zone in Puglia, situated south of Copertino and west of the coastal town of Otranto.

The "Trulli" district

The Trulli district, south of the city of Bari, is an area of valleys and gorges carved by the Itria River. Unique to this area are the unusual, conical-roofed, triangular-shaped stone dwellings, called *trulli,* built to counteract the sometimes harsh heat of the area. We've stayed in them in warm weather, and they're indeed quite cool. (In New York City, an Italian restaurant called I Trulli, owned by a native of Puglia, specializes in Apulian cuisine and wines.) Ironically, considering the heat, two of the four DOC wines of the district are white; they're grown in a belt where the clashing currents of the Adriatic and Ionian Seas bring cool breezes and summer rain.

Puglia's most renowned white wine is **Locorotondo** *(lo co ro TOHN doh).* It's a dry white made mainly from Verdeca with 35 to 50 percent Bianco di Alessano, and Fiano and/or Bombino Bianco and/or Malvasia Toscana optional. A *spumante* style also exists. **Martina Franca** (or Martina) is the other white DOC wine of the Trulli district. It's very similar to Locorotondo, with exactly the same grape varieties. Martina Franca, the community which is the center of this wine zone, is a dramatic, *trulli* hill town, five miles south of Locorotondo.

Vineyards around the ancient town of **Ostuni** *(oh STEW nee),* northwest of the coastal city of Brindisi, make Ostuni Ottavianello — a dry, light-bodied, cherry-red wine made from Ottavianello (France's Cinsault variety) and Ostuni Bianco, a dry white mainly from the local Impigno and Francavilla.

The **Gioia del Colle** *(JOY ah del CO lae)* name applies to six wines made in a fairly large area south of the city of Bari. This is the northernmost zone in Puglia producing a Primitivo DOC wine, a 100 percent varietal. Primitivo is also the main variety (50 to 60 percent) in Gioia del Colle Rosso and Rosato; these two wines also contain Montepulciano and/or Sangiovese and/or Negroamaro, with Malvasia Nera optional. Gioia del Colle Bianco is a dry white from Trebbiano, and other white varieties of the zone. Besides Aleatico di Puglia — which is made primarily in the Gioia del Colle area — two Gioia del Colle Aleaticos are Aleatico *Dolce*, a sweet red, and Aleatico *liquoroso dolce*.

Central Puglia

Castel del Monte is the most important DOC wine in the Bari province of Central Puglia; four other DOC wines are here, either wholly or partly in the Bari area.

Castel del Monte

In the 13th century, the Norman Emperor Friedrich II, then ruler of this region, built a magnificent, octagon-shaped castle on a high plateau (known as the Murge) near the community of Andria, west of the city of Bari. The castle, known as Castel del Monte, remains one of the great sights of Puglia, and gives the name to this rather large wine zone which lies northwest of Bari. The emperor had vineyards planted around the castle, perhaps realizing that the reddish soil, the temperate climate, and the altitude of this dry plateau would favor grapevines; this it does, especially red varieties.

Castel del Monte's best producer is Rivera, a longstanding leader here, whose Rosso Riserva "Il Falcone" is internationally renowned. Recently, the area has attracted outside investment, such as Tuscany's Antinori firm, which, under the name Vigneti del Sud, purchased 250 acres of land here (plus 1,250 acres in the Salento peninsula).

Castel del Monte can be a blended Rosso, Rosato or Bianco wine or one of seven varietal wines. The Rosso is a dry red mainly from Uva di Troia and/or Aglianico and/or Montepulciano, with up to 35 percent other red varieties. The dry Rosato derives from Bombino Nera and/or Aglianico and/or Uva di Troia, and up to 35 percent other red varieties. The Bianco is a dry white mainly from Pampanuto (an indigenous variety) and/or Chardonnay and/or Bombino Bianco, with up to 35 percent other white varieties. Six of the Castel del Monte varietal wines must derive at least 90 percent from the named variety: Pinot Bianco, Chardonnay, Sauvignon, Pinot Nero, Aglianico, and Aglianico Rosato. The seventh varietal, Pinot Bianco da Pinot Nero, is a dry white from Pinot Nero, with up to 15 percent Pinot Bianco.

Other central Puglia wines

The four other central Puglia DOC wines are the following:

- ✔ **Moscato di Trani** *(mohs CAH toh dee TRAH nee):* This is a rare, traditional golden dessert wine that's one of Southern Italy's best sweet wines; it's made from at least 85 percent Moscato di Trani or Moscato Reale grapes, with other Moscato varieties. A sweeter *liquoroso* style also exists. The wine zone is around the coastal town of Trani, north of Bari.

- ✔ **Rosso Barletta** *(ROHS so bar LET tah):* This dry red wine produced around the coastal town of Barletta (north of Trani and Bari) is made primarily from the native Uva di Troia, with Montepulciano and/or Sangiovese, and Malbec.

- ✔ **Rosso Canosa** *(ROHS so cah NO sah):* This dry, difficult-to-find red wine comes from a small zone around the community of Canosa di Puglia, just south of the Castel del Monte zone. Rosso Canosa is very similar to Castel del Monte Rosso; it's mainly Uva di Troia, with Montepulciano and Sangiovese.

- ✔ **Gravina** *(grah VEE nah):* Another little-known DOC wine, Gravina is a delicate, dry white (which can also be *amabile* or *spumante*) from Malvasia del Chianti, with Greco di Tufo and/or Bianco di Alessano, and Trebbiano and/or Bombino Bianco and/or Verdeca optional. The zone is near the Basilicata border in the west, around the town of Gravina-in-Puglia.

The northern plains

The northern plains area in the province of Foggia, known as La Capatanata, is Puglia'a least important wine district. Red wines are mainly made with Montepulciano and Sangiovese grapes, while Bombino Bianco and Trebbiano dominate the whites.

The district's leading DOC zone, and its most prolific, is **San Severo** *(sahn seh VEH ro),* in the northernmost part of Puglia, around the community of San Severo. The Rosso and Rosato wines are both dry, and made mainly from Montepulciano, with some Sangiovese; the Bianco is a dry white made from Bombino Bianco and Trebbiano, with up to 20 percent Malvasia Bianca and/or Verdeca; a *spumante* also exists.

Other DOC wines of the northern plains are the following:

- **Cacce'e Mmitte di Lucera** *(CAH chae ae MEET tae dee loo CHER ah):* This simple red wine, to enjoy young, comes from a zone south of San Severo; made from the local Uva de Troia, with Montepulciano and/or Sangiovese and/or Malvasia Nera, and 15 to 30 percent of white varieties (Malvasia del Chianti and/or Bombino Bianco).

- **Orta Nova** *(OR tah NO vah):* A dry Rosso and Rosato are primarily Sangiovese, with up to 40 percent Uva di Troia and/or Montepulciano, and Lambrusco Maestri and/or Trebbiano optional. This zone lies south of the provincial capital of Foggia, around the community of Orta Nova.

- **Rosso di Cerignola** *(ROHS so dee cheh ree N'YOH lah):* Rosso di Cerignola is a rather scarce, dry red made primarily from Uva de Troia, with Negroamaro, and up to 15 percent Sangiovese and/or Barbera and/or Malbec and/or Montepulciano and/or Trebbiano. The Cerignola zone is south of Orta Nova.

Recommended Puglia producers

Almost all of Puglia's best wines are red, and a large majority of them come from the Salento Peninsula and are based on Negroamaro, Puglia's leading variety — except when they're Primitivo wines. Our recommended wine producers in Puglia are listed alphabetically:

Botromagno
Michele Calò
Candido
Cantele
Cantina del Locorotondo
Cantina Sociale Copertino
D'Alfonso del Sordo
Felline
Leone de Castris
Lomazzi & Sarli
Masseria Monaci
Nugnes
Masseria Pepe

Pervini
Rivera
Rosa del Golfo (also known as Giuseppe Calò)
Sinfarosa
Cosimo Taurino
Torrevento
Agricole Vallone
Valle dell'Asso
Vigneti del Sud (Antinori)
Vinicola Savese
Conti Zecca

Mountainous Basilicata

Basilicata ranks with Molise and Valle d'Aosta as one of the least-known and least populated regions in Italy. The Apennine Mountains occupy most of it, along with some hills and only a small percentage of flat land. Even though Basilicata is very southerly, snow falls all winter in its mountains; its capital city, Potenza, 2,624 feet up, is usually Italy's coldest city, winter and summer. The only truly hot and dry area is the maritime coast in the southeast, where the warm breezes from North Africa waft in from the Ionian Sea.

The Greeks arrived in what is now Basilicata in the 6th or 7th century B.C. and planted grapevines, including what is now Southern Italy's finest variety, Aglianico. Today, the region has only one DOC wine (the least of any region in Italy) — Aglianico del Vulture *(ah l'yee AH nee co del VOOL too rae),* from vineyards around the extinct volcano, Monte Vulture, in northwest Basilicata, near Campania's border.

Before this area earned DOC status in 1971, almost all of Basilicata's Aglianico grapes went to Puglia. Now, a few producers bottle their Aglianico, but wine production in Basilicata has been dominated for some time by one very good producer — Donato D'Angelo. Today, Paternoster is another noteworthy winery.

Basilicata is a paradox — here in Southern Italy, the "Land of Wine," it produces only five million cases of wine annually, one of the country's lowest totals, and it has one of the lowest grape yields per hectare of any of Italy's regions. Basilicata's topography — mostly mountains — and its cool, harsh climate seem to be too much for the vines. The region's one DOC wine amounts to less than 3 percent (about 140,000 cases) of Basilicata's annual production.

Other than Aglianico, the Monte Vulture region produces some IGT-level Moscato and white Malvasia, both mainly sweet and sparkling. In the eastern plains area, around Matera, and in the Ionian plains area in the southeast, some robust, red IGT-level wines are made from Montepulciano, Sangiovese, Aglianico, Primitivo, and Bombino Nero grapes. All these IGT wines carry the designation IGT Basilicata.

Aglianico del Vulture

If it weren't for Aglianico del Vulture, we could have skipped right over Basilicata. But Aglianico del Vulture is a serious wine worth trying. It's mainly a dry, powerful red — but *amabile* and sweet *spumante* versions are also made, although rarely exported.

The wine derives entirely from the austere, tannic Aglianico variety, and like all Aglianico-based wines, it requires aging; when its black-red color starts to turn to ruby, and its blackberry aromas begin to evolve, usually after about five years, you can begin to enjoy the wine.

Basic Aglianico del Vulture ages a minimum of one year at the winery, but wines labeled *vecchio* (old) age for at least three years, and those labeled *Riserva* age for at least five years before release. Aglianico del Vulture wines, especially the *vecchio* and *Riservas*, improve for ten years or more, especially in good vintages (see Appendix B). Most Aglianico del Vulture wines retail for $16 to $20.

Basilicata brands to buy

We list alphabetically only the leading producers of Aglianico del Vulture, the most important wine in the region, in this section, because it's basically the only wine from the region that's exported: Basilium, D'Angelo, Armando Martino, Paternoster, and Francesco Sessa.

Rugged Calabria

Another primarily mountainous region, Calabria is the "ball" and "toe" of Italy's boot, and the southernmost region of the Italian mainland. The Ionian Sea is on its eastern border, the Tyrrhenian is to the west; the island of Sicily is to the southwest, across the narrow Straits of Messina, and Basilicata is across the Apennine Mountains to the north (see Figure 10-1).

Calabria is a poor region, and has lost many of its inhabitants to emigration, primarily to the U.S. and Argentina. Wine is a minor product, less important in the region's economy than olive oil, produce, and grains. The climate along both coastlines is hot and dry, but winters are cold and harsh in the interior mountains, especially in northern Calabria. Most of the region's wines come from the central part of both the eastern and western coasts.

Almost 90 percent of Calabria's annual wine production of nearly 11 million cases is red wine. Only 4 percent of Calabria's wine has DOC status. In fact, only a few independent producers and cooperatives even bottle their wine; much of Calabria's sturdy, high-alcohol wine is sold in bulk to wineries in Northern Italy and nearby countries.

Although 12 DOC wine zones now exist in the region, only one, Cirò, on the east-central coast, has gained any recognition outside of Calabria; most of the other wines are consumed locally. The dominant red variety throughout Calabria is Gaglioppo *(gah l'yee OH po)*, possibly a native grape, but probably of Greek origin. Greco is the major white variety.

Cirò

The Cirò *(chee ROH)* wine zone is in the eastern foothills of the Sila Mountain range (part of the Apennines), and extends to the eastern, Ionian coastline; the Cirò Classico area, the best section, is around the communities of Cirò and Cirò Marina in the northern part of the zone. Vines grow in calcareous, marly soil that also contains lots of clay and sand; summers are hot and dry, and winters are mild, due to the influence of the Ionian Sea.

Ciró comes in red, white, and rosé styles, but the red is the area's best wine. Cirò Rosso and Rosato are dry wines from at least 95 percent Gaglioppo, with Trebbiano and/or Greco Bianco optional. A good Cirò Rosso is full-bodied, powerful, tannic, fruity, and soft; it's at its best when it's consumed within three or four years of the vintage. Cirò Bianco is a dry white from at least 90 percent Greco Bianco, with Trebbiano optional. The *classico* designation is for Cirò Rosso only.

To say that Cirò is spearheading a Calabrian wine resurgence would be overstating the case. Most of Cirò is still bound to the past; many common technological winemaking practices, such as temperature-controlled fermentation, have barely arrived in Calabria. But two Cirò wineries — Librandi and Fattoria San Francesco — have employed enologists and are taking the necessary steps to make quality wine. The basic Cirò Rosso from these wineries retails for a mere $10 to $11, and their *riservas* are $15 to $16.

Other Calabrian wines

In addition to Cirò, Calabria has 11 other DOC wines. Two of them come from the Ionian coast, near Ciró, where the warm, dry climate makes fairly robust wines:

- ✔ **Melissa:** Melissa Rosso and Bianco resemble red and white Cirò, but are not quite up to Cirò's level of quality. The Rosso is mainly Gaglioppo, with Greco Nero and/or Greco Bianco and/or Trebbiano and/or Malvasia Bianca. The dry Bianco is mainly Greco Bianco, with Trebbiano and /or Malvasia Bianca. The Melissa zone is directly south of Cirò.

- ✔ **Sant'Anna di Isola Capo Rizzuto** *(sahnt AHN nah dee EE so la CAH po ritz zoo toh):* This wine, from a zone directly south of Melissa, takes its name from the town of Isola di Capo Rizzuto, once an island, but now part of the mainland because of the filling-in of marshland. A Rosso and Rosato, both dry wines, are mainly Gaglioppo, with Nocera and/or Nerello Mascalese and/or Nerello Cappuccio (Nerellos are Sicilian varieties), and up to 35 percent Malvasia Nera and/or Malvasia Bianca and/or Greco Bianco.

Another seven DOC wines come from the western part of the region. Four of these are generally lighter wines from interior, mountainous areas, in the north of the region. Two are richer wines from coastal areas with warmer climates. And one wine, Savuto, comes from an area that combines both climates. From north to south, these DOC wines are the following:

✔ **Pollino** *(pohl LEE no):* Named for the Pollino mountain range (part of the Apennines), Pollino Rosso is a pale cherry red, dry wine that's best at two to three years of age; it's mainly Gaglioppo, with Greco Nero, and up to 20 percent white varieties optional. Its production zone is near the border with Basilicata.

✔ **Verbicaro** *(vehr bee CAH ro):* The new Verbicaro DOC wines are a red, white and rosé. The dry Rosso and Rosato are primarily Gaglioppo and/or Greco Nero, with a small amount of Malvasia Bianca and/or Guarnaccia Bianca and/or Greco Bianco, and other red grapes optional; the dry Bianco is from Greco Bianco, Malvasia and Guarnaccia Bianca, with other white grapes optional. Their vineyards are primarily in the foothills of the Pollino range in northwest Calabria, west of the Pollino zone, and extending to the western, Tyrrhenian coast.

✔ **San Vito di Luzzi** *(sahn VEE toh dee LOOTZ zee):* These three wines include a dry Rosso and Rosato mainly from Gaglioppo with Malvasia Nera, and the optional addition of Greco Nero, Sangiovese, and other red varieties; and a dry Bianco mainly from Malvasia Bianca and Greco Bianco, with up to 40 percent other white varieties. This is a new, very small wine zone; grapes come from the vineyards around the hamlet of San Vito, which is part of the community of Luzzi.

✔ **Donnici** *(DOHN nee chee):* Donnici is a dry Rosso or Rosato made mainly from Gaglioppo with some Greco Nero and/or Mantonico Nero, and white varieties optional. The Donnici wine zone is directly south of Cosenza, on the western slopes of the Sila Mountain range.

✔ **Savuto** *(sah VOO toh):* Savuto is probably the best of Calabria's mountain wines. The Savuto zone extends to the coast, but most of its vineyards are in the cooler, interior part of the zone, just south of Donnici. Savuto can be a Rosso or Rosato, from 35 to 45 percent Gaglioppo, 30 to 40 percent Greco Nero and/or Nerello Cappuccio and/or Magliocco Canino, up to 10 percent Sangiovese, with up to 25 percent Malvasia Bianca and/or Pecorello.

✔ **Scavigna** *(scah VEE n'yah):* Scavigna Rosso and Rosato are dry wines produced from at least 60 percent Gaglioppo and Nerello Cappuccio, with other red varieties optional; Scavigna Bianco is a dry white from Trebbiano, Chardonnay, Greco Bianco, and Malvasia Bianca, with other varieties optional. This new DOC zone lies south of Savuto on Calabria's western coast.

✔ **Lamezia** *(lah MEH zee ah):* The influence of the Tyrrhenian Sea is evident in these wines, from plains and low hills near the Sant'Eufémia Gulf, where the warmth gives them body. The four Lamezia wines include one white varietal, Greco, and three blended wines: the dry Lamezia Rosso (also *novello*) and Rosato, from Nerello Mascalese and/or Nerello Cappuccio, Gaglioppo and Greco Nero, with Magliocco, Marsigliana, and other red varieties optional; and the dry Lamezia Bianco, from Greco Bianco, Trebbiano, and Malvasia Bianca, with other white varieties.

Calabria's final two wines come from zones in the south of the region, but are so different that generalizations are impossible:

✔ **Greco di Bianco:** Greco di Bianco is an amber-colored sweet wine, with luscious aromas of herbs and citrus; it's made from partially dried Greco Bianco grapes, and has a minimum alcohol content of 17 percent. Unfortunately, very little Greco di Bianco is produced. It comes from a remote wine zone, in the hills behind the town of Bianco, on the Ionian coast.

✔ **Bivongi** *(be VOHN gee):* Bivongi Rosso, Rosato, and Bianco are new DOC wines from a zone in the middle of nowhere, all by itself in the hilly south. The dry red (including a *novello*) and rosé are 30 to 50 percent Greco Nero and/or Gaglioppo, and 30 to 50 percent Nocera and/or Castiglione and/or Calabrese (also known as Nero d'Avola in Sicily), with 10 percent other red, and 15 percent other white, varieties optional. The dry white is 30 to 50 percent Greco Bianco and/or Guardavalle and/or Mantonico Bianco, and 30 to 50 percent Malvasia Bianca and/or Ansonica, with up to 30 percent other white varieties.

IGT wines from Calabria carry the following IGT names, depending on where in the region the vineyards are located: Arghillà, Calabria, Condoleo, Costa Viola, Lipuda, Locride, Palizzi, Pellaro, Scilla, Val di Neto, Valdamato, and Valle del Crati.

Calabrian wines to buy

We can only recommend five producers of Calabrian wines, but this is partially because much of Calabria's limited production of bottled wines never leaves the region. The three private wineries and the two cooperatives that we *do* recommend, listed alphabetically, are the progressive, quality leaders in the region today: Cantine Lamezia Lento and Caparra & Siciliani (both co-ops); Fattoria San Francesco, Librandi, and Odoardi.

Chapter 11

Sicily and Sardinia

• •

In This Chapter

▶ Greek ruins and British traders

▶ More than just dessert(s) wine

▶ Vermentino: Sardinia's modern white wine

▶ Cannonau: the red wine of Sardinia

• •

S icily and Sardinia, the two largest islands in the
Mediterranean Sea, have more in common than their size.
Each has a wine culture that dates back a long time — to the
8th century B.C. for Sardinia, and 4,000 years for Sicily. Each
has been dominated by foreigners for much of its history until
the 19th century. Each has its own language besides Italian
(Sicilian and Sardo), and inhabitants of both islands are
fiercely independent — so much so that they don't like to be
compared. (Sorry about that!) Wine-wise, both Sicily and
Sardinia were primarily suppliers of bulk and jug wines until
about ten years ago. Inexpensive wines are still a big business,
but a quality movement definitely exists on both islands. With
their wonderful climate and terrains, both Sicily and Sardinia
are sure to be prime sources of fine wine in the near future.

Sicilia Leaves the Past

Sicily is not only the largest island in the Mediterranean, but
also Italy's largest region. It has the fourth-largest population
in the country — practically tied with Latium for third. In most
years, Sicily vies with Puglia as Italy's largest producer, with an
average annual production of over 100 million cases, about

one-sixth of Italy's wine. Actually, Sicily has more vineyards than Puglia, but its recent emphasis on quality has reduced crop size, and therefore the amount of wine produced from those vineyards. That said, one province in western Sicily, Trapani *(TRAH pah nee)*, is the volume leader of all of Italy's 94 provinces.

Seventy-five percent of Sicily's wines are made by cooperatives, but smaller, private producers are on the rise: Just ten years ago, co-ops made 90 percent of Sicily's wine. Until the mid-1980s, when Italy's wine revival reached across the Straits of Messina into Sicily (or, more likely, flew in by jet from Turin and Florence), Sicilian producers still emphasized quantity rather than quality.

Besides quantity, Sicily's focus over the past 100 years had been its dessert and fortified wines, such as Marsala. These types of wine are still important, but in the past decade, high-quality dry whites and reds have become the emphasis. White wine exceeds red wine production by nearly three to one — another tradition in this warm island where fish and seafood play a leading role in the local cuisine — but more producers are beginning to concentrate on dry reds.

Sicily's vineyards and wines

Sicily clearly has a Mediterranean climate — hot and dry on the coasts, temperate and moist in the interior. About 85 percent of Sicily is mountainous or hilly; the Apennine Mountains of mainland Italy extend into Sicily, and are especially high in the northeastern part, where Mount Etna is — at 10,705 feet, the highest active volcano in Europe. Most of the wines are made around the coast, where most of the people live (see Figure 11-1).

A white variety, Catarratto Bianco, is by far Sicily's most planted grape, covering more than 40 percent of its vineyards, and is especially prominent in western Sicily. Catarratto Bianco, in fact, is Italy's third most-planted variety, after Trebbiano and Sangiovese. Other white varieties popular in Sicilian vineyards are Trebbiano Toscano, Grillo, and the indigenous Inzolia (also known as Ansonica).

Figure 11-1: Sicily's wine zones are mainly along the coast.

Nero d'Avola is the main red variety, and the primary grape in Sicily's best red wines. The indigenous Perricone (also known as Pignatello) is Sicily's second most popular red variety, but it's mainly used for blending. Nerello Mascalese is starting to be recognized as Sicily's other fine red variety, along with Nero d'Avola.

The DOC concept has come slowly to Sicily. Its wines are about 98 percent non-DOC — and most of the remaining 2 percent is Marsala. But, like dry wines and fine wines, DOC wines are increasing. In fact, the number of DOC wines has risen from nine to 17 over the past 10 years. But Sicily's most famous wine — for the last 200 years — is Marsala.

Marsala

The current version of Marsala, as a largely sweet, fortified wine, was created in 1773, by the British. (Marsala had existed as a sweet wine in Roman times, and as a dry, oxidative wine suggestive of Sherry before the British entered the picture.) Because the Brits spent a good deal of time having wars with the French, they had to look elsewhere (to Portugal, Spain, and Italy) for their wines. But the wines from these far-away countries could not survive the long sea voyages to England; when the Brits got the idea of adding spirits to stabilize the wines, Port, Sherry, Madeira, and Marsala were born.

Marsala's hey-day was the last half of the 19th century, when it was regarded as one of the world's great wines (sweet, fortified wines were very popular at that time). But Marsala fell out of fashion during the 20th century. Until its recent revival, which began in the mid-1980s, the word "Marsala" stirred up images of cheap cooking wine for most people. Marsala was prized for its culinary versatility — it does wonders for that custardy dessert, *zabaglione,* and *vitello marsala* (veal sautéed in a buttery Marsala sauce) is a classic dish — but no one would dream of actually drinking the stuff! What made Marsala's image even worse was the imitation "Marsala" wines that other countries, such as the U.S., produced. Marsala producers themselves — especially major firms such as Florio, Rallo, and Pellegrino — saw to it that much stricter production regulations went into effect in 1986; commercial flavored styles, such as Egg Marsala, are no longer legal, and the wine's average quality has improved. But it's still a confusing type of wine, because it comes in numerous color, sweetness, and age styles.

The vineyard area for Marsala is the entire province of Trapani in western Sicily, excluding Alcamo (another DOC zone), and various islands off the western coast. Marsala can have three hues: *oro* (light golden); *ambra* (amber-yellow); and *rubino* (ruby red). The *oro* and *ambra* derive mainly from two white varieties, Grillo and Catarratto, with Inzolia and Damaschino also permitted; aging turns the wines to deep gold and deep amber. The *rubino,* a far smaller category, derives from red varieties — Pignatello and/or Nero d'Avola and/or Nerello Mascalese — with up to 30 percent of the white varieties that go into *oro* and *ambra* Marsala.

Most Marsala is also made in three different sweetness levels: *secco* (dry), *semisecco* (semi-dry), and *dolce* (sweet). Finally, Marsalas are categorized by their aging. The following types are made:

- ✔ **Fine** *(FEE nae):* Aged at least one year

- ✔ **Superiore:** Aged at least two years

- ✔ **Superiore Riserva:** Aged at least four years

- ✔ **Vergine** *(VER gee nae),* **Soleras,** or **Vergine Soleras:** Aged at least five years

- ✔ **Vergine Soleras Stravecchio, Vergine Soleras Riserva, Soleras Stravecchio,** or **Soleras Riserva:** Aged at least ten years

The last two types are only *secco,* or dry. These are the two most serious types of Marsala, consumed very much like dry Sherry — as *apéritif* wines, or with consommé. Retail prices for Marsala (Sicilian Marsala, that is!) range from $10 up to $40 for the *Vergine* or *Soleras* versions. Pellegrino, Rallo, and Florio are all reliable Marsala producers. De Bartoli is a smaller producer who specializes in *Vergine* and *Soleras* Marsalas.

Other Sicilian wines

The provinces of Trapani, Palermo, and Agrigento *(ah gree JEN toh),* in the western part of Sicily, have nine of the 17 DOC zones in the region, and make 80 percent of the quality wine in Sicily — whether it's DOC, IGT, or *vino da tavola* level. (The latter two categories include many fine wines as well the inexpensive wines you'd expect to see with those designations. The reason? Many Sicilian producers, typically independent, have abdicated DOC status for their wines.) In eastern Sicily, the seven DOC zones produce small quantities.

Only one formal wine zone exists in mountainous central Sicily — **Contea di Sclafani** — and although this is a new DOC area, it's important for the quality of wine produced there. The Contea di Sclafani *(con TAE ah dee sclah FAH nee)* zone is the home of the acclaimed Regaleali winery, owned by the equally renowned Tasca d'Almerita family. The late Count Giuseppe Tasca d'Almerita proved to the world that excellent dry red, white, and rosé wines can be made in Sicily, thanks to the temperate to cool microclimates of the family vineyards, on mountain slopes of 1,500 to 2,000 feet in altitude.

Typical of newly-legislated DOC zones, this area produces a wide range of wine, including three blended wines (a white, red, and rosé) and 15 varietally-labeled wines. Contea di Sclafani Bianco is a dry white that's at least 50 percent Catarratto and/or Inzolia and/or Greganico, with the optional use of other white varieties. The Rosso is a dry red from at least 50 percent Nero d'Avola and/or Perricone, with the optional addition of other red varieties; the Rosato is a dry rosé from at least 50 percent Nerello Mascalese. The 15 Contea di Sclafani varietal wines include seven whites and eight reds. The whites are Inzolia, Catarratto, Chardonnay, Grecanico, Grillo, Pinot Bianco, and Sauvignon. The red varietal wines are Cabernet Sauvignon, Merlot, Nerello Mascalese, Nero d'Avola, Perricone, Pinot Nero, Sangiovese, and Syrah. All the white wines can also be made as *dolce* (sweet) wines, and as *vendemmia tardiva* (late-harvest) wines; the white or rosé wines can be *spumante* (sparkling); and the reds can be made in *novello* versions.

Sicily's most famous winery

The name "Duca di Salaparuta" would probably draw a blank stare from most wine buyers, but the name "Corvo" brings quick recognition. Corvo is the brand name of wines from the gigantic, ultra-modern Duca di Salaparuta winery, about 10 miles east of Palermo. This winery is one of Italy's largest, producing 10 million bottles of wine annually. Just about every wine shop and Italian restaurant in the U.S. carries Corvo White (made from Inzolia, Trebbiana, and Catarratto grapes) and Corvo Red (from Nerello Mascalese, Perricone, and Nero d'Avola); both retail for about $11 or $12. The winery makes a very good, premium Corvo White named Colomba Platina, which costs $15 to $16. Under the Duca di Salaparuta label, the winery's top-of-the-line wine, and possibly Sicily's best dry red, is the powerful, complex Duca Enrico (entirely Nero d'Avola), which costs about $60.

Other Sicilian wine zones that specialize in dry wines, from west to east, are the following:

- **Alcamo** (or **Bianco Alcamo**) *(AHL cah mo):* A dry, light-bodied white wine that's at least 80 percent Catarratto, with Trebbiano Toscano and/or Damaschino and/or Grecanico optional. Its zone is in northwest Sicily, west of Palermo. Rapitalà is a leading winery in the zone.

- **Delia Nivolelli** *(DAE lee ah nee vo LEL lee):* A new wine zone in southwest Sicily, within the Marsala area; some varietal wines carry this DOC designation, but most of the local dry white and red wines are not DOC wines (yet).

- **Menfi** *(MEN fee):* Menfi Bianco is a dry white, 50 to 70 percent Inzolia and 25 to 50 percent Grecanico, Catarratto, and Chardonnay, with other white varieties optional. Three white varietals, all at least 90 percent from the named grape, are Chardonnay, Grecanico, and Inzolia. Two wines, a white and a red, come from specific Menfi sub-zones: Feudi dei Fiori is a dry white from 50 to 75 percent Inzolia and 25 to 50 percent Chardonnay, with other varieties optional; Bonera is a dry red from 50 to 70 percent Nero d'Avola and 25 to 50 percent Sangiovese and/or Cabernet Sauvignon and/or Frappato di Vittoria, with other varieties optional. The Menfi wine zone is along the coast of southwest Sicily. The Settesoli cooperative is the predominant winery of the area.

- **Contessa Entellina** *(con TEHS sah en tel LEE nah):* Ten DOC wines take their unusual name from the village of Contessa Entellina. These wines include seven dry varietals: the white Inzolia, Chardonnay, Grecanico, and Sauvignon; and the red Cabernet Sauvignon, Merlot, and Pinot Nero. Blended wines include a dry Bianco (at least half Inzolia, with seven or more optional white grapes); and a dry Rosso and Rosato (both at least half Nero d'Avola and/or Syrah). This area is north of the Menfi zone, and is dominated by the Donnafugata winery (owned by the Rallo family of Marsala fame).

- **Santa Margherita di Belice** *(SAHN tah mar geh REE tah dee beh LEE chae):* Seven local wines include five varietals: Catarratto, Grecanico, Inzolia, Nero d'Avola and Sangiovese. A dry Bianco is 50 to 70 percent Grecanico and/or Catarratto and 30 to 50 percent Inzolia, with other varieties optional; a dry Rosso is 50 to 80 percent Sangiovese and/or Cabernet Sauvignon and 20 to 50 percent Nero d'Avola, with other varieties optional. All these wines come from a small area in southwest Sicily, between the Contessa Entellina and Menfi zones

✔ **Sambuca di Sicilia** *(sahm BOO cah dee see CHEE lee ah):* These fairly new DOC wines from southwest Sicily, from an area overlapping part of the Menfi zone, take their name from the town of Sambuca di Sicilia — not from Italy's anise-flavored liqueur! They include a blended white, red and rosé, along with a varietal Chardonnay and Cabernet Sauvignon. The dry Bianco is mainly Inzolia, with 25 to 50 percent Catarratto and/or Chardonnay, and other varieties optional; the dry Rosso and Rosato are mainly Nero d'Avola, with 25 to 50 percent Nerello Mascalese and/or Cabernet Sauvignon, and/or Sangiovese, and other varieties optional. A peculiarity of the DOC regulations for these wines is that they explicitly forbid the use of Trebbiano Toscano, the mainland's uninspiring white grape that has gained a foothold in Sicily. A new winery here, Planeta, has already achieved quite a reputation for its varietal wines.

✔ **Sciacca** *(SHOCK cah):* A brand new DOC zone in southwest Sicily, around the coastal town of Sciacca, in Agrigento province. The wines are similar to those of nearby Menfi.

✔ **Faro** *(FAH ro):* Faro is a dry red wine from the extreme northeast corner of Sicily, around the slopes of the city of Messina. Its historic vineyard area is now attempting a revival, after decades of desolation caused by phylloxera (the louse that wiped out many of Europe's vineyards 100 years ago). A few wineries make Faro, but production is a fraction of what it once was. Faro is mainly Nerello Mascalese, with Nerello Cappuccio, some Nocera, and Nero d'Avola, Gaglioppo, and/or Sangiovese optional. The definitive Faro is made by Palari, whose concentrated, limited-production wine retails for about $55. This winery is in the village of Palari, between Messina and the beautiful hilltop town of Taormina, which is a must-stop for every tourist in Sicily.

✔ **Etna:** Etna's vineyards on the volcanic slopes of Mount Etna in northeast Sicily, as high as 2,300 feet, are the coolest in Sicily. (Ironically, they overlook Catania, on the east-central coast, often Italy's hottest city.) Like Faro's, Etna's vineyards are a shell of what they were a century ago, having never recovered from the phylloxera blight. A few valiant winemakers struggle on, as do some 80-year-old vines. Etna Bianco is a dry wine that's mainly Carricante, with Catarratto and/or Trebbiano and/or Minella Bianca; the delicately-perfumed Carricante variety is especially suited to volcanic soil. A dry Rosso and Rosato are mainly Nerello Mascalese, with Nerello Cappuccio and white varieties optional. Benanti is a leading Etna winery; its Rosso "Rovitello" retails for about $22.

✔ **Cerasuolo di Vittoria** *(cher ah SWO lo dee veet TOR ee ah):* This a powerful, dry red from southeast Sicily has a fairly light cherry color that belies its strength (at least 13 percent alcohol); it's best when young. The wine is 40 percent Frappato and up to 60 percent Nero d'Avola, with Grosso Nero and/or Nerello Mascalese optional. Valle dell'Acate is a leading producer; its Cerasuolo di Vittoria is about $20.

✔ **Eloro** *(eh LOH ro):* Eloro wines are all red or rosé, and include three varietals: Nero d'Avola, Frappato, and Pignatello, all at least 90 percent from the named variety. Eloro Rosso and Rosato are dry wines from the same three grapes, with other varieties optional. A Rosso Pachino, from the Pachino sub-zone, also derives from the same varieties, but with emphasis on Nero d'Avola; it's an intensely flavored, dry red that's the area's most renowned wine. The new Eloro zone is in the extreme southeast corner of Sicily.

Sicily also boasts four sweet DOC wines that derive either from Moscato or the white Malvasia varieties. (If ever there was a place for good dessert wines, it's Sicily, where you can find some of the best pastries and desserts in the world!)

Sicily's IGT zones

IGT wines from Sicily can carry the following regional names, depending on vineyard location and the producer's preference: Camarro, Colli Ericini, Fontanarossa di Cerda, Salemi, Salina, Sicilia, and Valle del Belice.

Moscato di Pantelleria *(mohs CAH toh dee pan tel leh REE ah)* comes from the volcanic island of Pantelleria, about 25 miles southwest of the main island of Sicily — actually closer to Tunisia in North Africa. The hot African winds and blazing sun make grape growing difficult, to say the least, but the hardy Zibibbo (Muscat of Alexandria) manages to survive these conditions, and makes a concentrated, rich, peachy-tasting dessert wine that's one of Italy's best. Two broad types of Moscato di Pantelleria exist: Moscato Naturale, which can be *dolce*, *spumante*, or *liquoroso*; and the exotic Passito di Pantelleria. The high sugar content of the *passito's* dried grapes produces a wine with 14.5 percent alcohol, but the wine can also be made in a *liquoroso* style, which is at least 21.5 percent alcohol; when the wine is labeled *Extra*, it must be 23.9 percent alcohol. Marco De Bartoli, the Marsala producer, makes a superb Moscato Passito, called Bukkuram, which retails for about $50; other good Pantelleria wines sell for as little as $20.

The coastal hills around the ancient Greek city of Siracusa, in southeast Sicily, is the territory of the renowned **Moscato di Siracusa** *(mohs CAH toh dee sir ah COO sah)* made from Moscato grapes, partially dried. This dessert wine has an old-gold, slightly amber color, and at least 16.5 percent alcohol. This wine almost disappeared ten years ago, but a recent slight increase in interest for dessert wines has caused a revival of sorts. Another sweet wine from southeast Sicily is **Moscato di Noto,** from hills south of the Moscato di Siracusa zone. Moscato di Noto Naturale is a dessert wine from Moscato Bianco grapes — quite similar to Moscato di Siracusa; it's also made as a sweet *spumante* and as a powerful (22 percent minimum alcohol) *liquoroso*.

Sicily's final dessert wine is a Malvasia from the Lipari Islands, including the volcanic island of Stromboli, in the Straits of Messina, about 25 miles north of northeastern Sicily's mainland. One man, the late Carlo Hauner, revived the wine business on the islands, and preserved one of the most haunting, captivating dessert wines in the world. **Malvasia delle Lipari** *(mahl vah SEE ah del lae LEE pah ree)* wine, mainly Malvasia, with 5 to 8 percent of the red Corinto Nero, takes on unique characteristics from the volcanic soil of the islands. One of our personal favorites, this wine, light-bodied, with just a touch of sweetness, has almost indescribable floral and herbal aromas, combined with hints of dried or ripe apricots and dried figs. A sweeter *passito* version and a rarer, fortified *liquoroso* version also exist. Carlo Hauner's son, Carlo Jr., and his three sisters now carry on the work of their father. Hauner Malvasia delle Lipari retails for about $36 or $37; Hauner *passito* costs about $45. Another good producer is Colosi, whose Malvasia delle Lipari retails for $22 to $23.

A Sicilian wine shopping list

We list alphabetically our recommended wine producers from Sicily:

Abbazia Sant'Anastasia
Benanti
Cantine Torrevecchia
Colosi
Cooperativa Interprovinciale
   Elorina
COS
D'Ancona
De Bartoli
Donnafugata
Duca di Salaparuta (Corvo)
Firriato
Florio
Hauner

Morgante
Salvatore Murana
Palari
Pellegrino
Planeta
Pupillo
Rallo
Rapitalà
Regaleali (Tasca d'Almerita)
Settesole
Spadafora
Valle dell'Acate
Vitivinicola Avide

Sardinia Stands Alone

If you ask a native of Sardinia (or, *Sardegna*) what his nationality is, he'll reply, "Sardinian" — not Italian. While this scenario might play out the same with citizens of many of Italy's independent-minded regions, nowhere would your answer be more emphatic than in Sardinia. (Sicily would be a close second!) But who can blame Sardinians for feeling independent? Sardinia is the most remote, isolated part of Italy. The nearest point of mainland Italy is 111 miles east, across the Tyrrhenian (Mediterranean) Sea. Ironically, the closest land is French-owned Corsica, seven or eight miles north.

Sardinia, like Sicily, was invaded by most of the major Mediterranean powers at some time during the past 3,000 years (even the Piedmontese!), but never truly conquered. It has been a part of Italy only since 1860. Although the island has Italy's longest coastline, most of the people of Sardinia remain in the hills, farming, tending sheep, and logging, instead of fishing.

Sardinia's vineyards and wines

Wine plays a role in the Sardinian life and economy, but not nearly as large a role as you'd expect — considering the sunny, dry climate much of the island enjoys, and the predominantly hilly terrain. Sardinia, the second-largest island in the Mediterranean after Sicily, is Italy's third-largest region, but it produces only 2 percent of Italy's wine — about 11 million cases annually, one-tenth (!) of Sicily's output.

Ironically, considering Sardinia's small wine production, the emphasis had been on quantity rather than quality, until very recently. The change started slowly when Sella & Mosca, a winery that's a Sardinian institution, began its own revival in the early 1970s. When enologists such as Giacomo Tachis, the dean of Italian wine consultants, started working in Sardinia, we knew that it would only be a matter of time before this region began producing quality wines.

Sardinia makes slightly more white wine than it does red; it still has a few excellent dessert wines, but a declining market for sweet wines has decreased production, as in Sicily. Sardinia's most planted variety — occupying about one-third of all the vineyards — is the prolific white grape, Nuragus, which makes rather bland, neutral-tasting wine. But Vermentino, a grape of Spanish origin that's now a distant second to Nuragus in white grape plantings, is on the increase.

Vermentino from Sardinia is a quite distinctive and characterful wine, yet blessedly inexpensive; it very well might become a big success story for Sardinia. One Vermentino wine, Vermentino di Gallura, from a wine zone in Sardinia's northeast corner (see Figure 11-2), has even earned the island's first DOCG. Considering that only 21 DOCG wines exist in Italy (as of this writing), the elevation of Vermentino di Gallura to DOCG is quite an honor for this remote outpost in the middle of the Mediterranean.

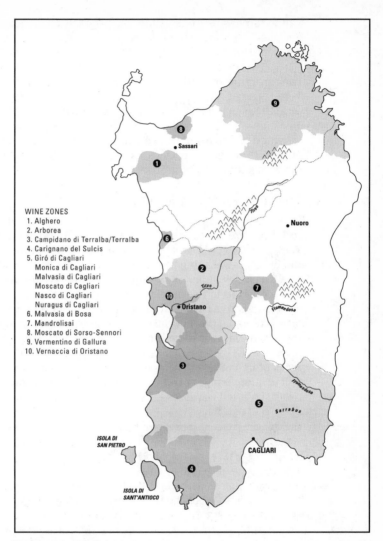

WINE ZONES
 1. Alghero
 2. Arborea
 3. Campidano di Terralba/Terralba
 4. Carignano del Sulcis
 5. Giró di Cagliari
    Monica di Cagliari
    Malvasia di Cagliari
    Moscato di Cagliari
    Nasco di Cagliari
    Nuragus di Cagliari
 6. Malvasia di Bosa
 7. Mandrolisai
 8. Moscato di Sorso-Sennori
 9. Vermentino di Gallura
10. Vernaccia di Oristano

Figure 11-2: Sardinia's wine zones.

The Spanish occupation of Sardinia in the Middle Ages brought more than just Vermentino to the island. The Spaniards planted three of their native red varieties, which together now account for 40 percent of Sardinia's plantings and most of its best red wine. Those grapes are Cannonau, which is Spain's Garnacha (and France's Grenache); Carignano, the Spanish Carignan, a variety now more common in France than in Spain; and Monica.

Cannonau has become especially popular as an inexpensive but pleasant Sardinian varietal wine — the red equivalent of Vermentino.

The structure of Sardinia's wine zones is somewhat different from those of other Italian regions. Sardinia has five region-wide DOCs, whose territory covers the whole island; six province-wide DOCs, whose territory covers all of the province of Calgari in the south; and eight other, more specific DOC wine zones. DOC/G wines account for about 14 percent of Sardinia's total production.

Sardinia's region-wide DOC wines

Two of Sardinia's five island-wide DOC wines are red varietals, and three are white varietals. **Cannonau di Sardegna** *(cahn no NOW dee sar DAEN yah)* is the star performer of the group, and Sardinia's leading red wine. It's now made almost exclusively as a dry wine, but sweet and fortified Cannonau wines were common in the past. Grapes grown in the vineyards of three sub-zones (the best areas for Cannonau) may carry the sub-zone name on their labels: Oliena (or Nepente di Oliena) and Jerzu in the eastern hills of Nuoro province, or Capo Ferrato in Calgari province. Cannonau is best within a few years of its vintage date. A Cannonau Rosato also exists, as well as increasingly rare, dry, fortified *(liquoroso secco)* and sweet, fortified *(liquoroso dolce naturale)* Cannonau.

Comeback in Cagliari

If ever there was a province dedicated to quantity production and industrial winemaking, it's Cagliari. But two things have helped change the picture. Italy's renowned winemaker, Giacomo Tachis, returned to his native Sardinia after retiring from the Antinori firm (where he created Antinori's two great Super-Tuscan wines, Tignanello and Solaia, as well as the wine of Antinori's uncle, Marchese Incisa della Rocchetta — Sassicaia). He now consults at the Santadi cooperative in Cagliari and at the excellent Argiolas winery; both firms make some of the best wines in Sardinia. The other force of change is the Argiolas winery itself. A family-run business, it's the only other producer besides Sella & Mosca to have achieved international acclaim as an exceptional Sardinian winery. Argiolas has gone from one success to another, to the point that you can trust any wine made by this winery.

The Monica variety makes a softer, lighter-bodied red wine than does Cannonau. Although the grapes for **Monica di Sardegna** *(moh nee cah dee sar DAEN yah)* can grow anywhere on the island, they grow mainly in the Campidano plains in western Sardinia. The wine is usually dry (whereas Monica di Cagliari is typically sweet) — but it can be *amabile* (semi-sweet) or *frizzante* (spritzy). Most Monica wines, including the Cagliari version, stay on Sardinia.

Vermentino di Sardegna is a dry white made mainly in the north. *Amabile* and *spumante* versions also exist. Because of the large crops that DOC regulations generously allow this wine, it's seldom as good as the DOCG Vermentino di Gallura (described later this chapter), unless it comes from the Alghero area, as Sella & Mosca's does. The obscure white variety called Semidano, seldom found outside Sardinia, makes **Sardegna Semidano** *(sar DAEN yah seh mee DAH no)*, which is usually a dry, soft, flavorful white wine. Sardegna Semidano can also be *amabile*, *dolce*, or *passito* (from semi-dried grapes). The sub-zone name Mogaro applies to Semidano wines whose grapes grow around the village of Mogaro in western Sardinia. The final wine in the regional category, **Moscato di Sardegna,** is a sweet *spumante* that's at least 90 percent Moscato Bianco. Very little of this delicately flavored bubbly (quite similar to Asti, described in Chapter 4) is made, with most of it coming from the Anglona and Gallura hills in the north; Tempio Pausania (or Tempio) and Gallura are Moscato sub-zones in the Gallura hills.

Cagliari's copious wine list

Cagliari, on the south coast of Sardinia, is the region's capital, and one of Italy's hottest cities in the summer months; Cagliari province occupies the southern third of Sardinia. This entire area, plus a part of Oristano province on the west-central coast, is the vineyard territory for five wines, most of which have been traditionally sweet and/or fortified. Four of these wines are unblended varietals that come in a similar range of styles: Their prevalent form is as a *dolce naturale* (sweet) wine, but they can also be made as a *secco* (dry) wine, and sometimes they are fortified to make a *liquoroso dolce* or *liquoroso secco* style. These four wines include two reds — **Girò di Cagliari** *(gee RO dee CAH l'yah ree),* from another Spanish variety, and **Monica di Cagliari** *(MO nee cah dee CAH l'yah ree)* — and two whites — **Malvasia di Cagliari** and **Nasco di**

Cagliari, from an indigenous variety. The fifth wine, **Moscato di Cagliari** *(mohs CAH to dee CAH l'yah ree)*, is a sweet *(dolce naturale)* or sweet, fortified *(liquoroso dolce naturale)* white wine made from Moscato Bianco. The Campidano di Cagliari area, in Oristano and Cagliari provinces, is the main vineyard zone.

Cagliari's sixth wine, **Nuragus di Cagliari** *(noo RAH goos dee CAH l'yah ree)*, is the largest-production wine in Sardinia, and the one most consumed throughout the island. Its zone extends into villages in a third province, Nuoro, in east-central Sardinia. It's mainly a dry, light, rather neutral-tasting white wine entirely from Nuragus variety; it's also made *amabile* and *frizzante*.

Vermentino di Gallura DOCG

The windswept Gallura hills in northeastern Sardinia have grown Vermentino for centuries; cool breezes from the Adriatic Sea and the rocky, granitic soil create an ideal environment for Sardinia's first DOCG wine (granted in 1996). Vermentino di Gallura is at least 95 percent Vermentino. Restricted crop levels, plus a fine group of wineries in the area, assure the excellence of this wine; it's generally richer and more concentrated than most Vermentino di Sardegna. And this fine DOCG white retails for around $10! Producers to look for are Cantina del Vermentino, Cantina Gallura, and Tenute Capichera.

Other Sardinian wines

Many other Sardinian wines come from eight vineyard zones of more restricted size, mainly along the western coast. The fairly small but prolific **Alghero** *(ahl GAE ro)* zone in northwestern Sardinia was approved for DOC wines in 1995, thanks basically to the work of one exceptional winery, Sella & Mosca — a leader for its modern viticultural practices, state-of-the-art-winery, and research. Sella & Mosca proved that it *is* possible to make a fine Vermentino di Sardegna by controlling crop size; its "La Cala" is the wine of choice at the nearby coastal resort, Costa Smeralda, and is doing well on international markets. Another exceptional Alghero winery, Santa Maria La Palma, was responsible for draining local marshlands to make the Alghero zone suitable for vineyards.

Alghero Bianco, Rosso, and Rosato are dry, still wines that can be made from any of the authorized varieties in Sassari province (a whole range of local and international varieties).

The latitude that producers have in choosing their grapes extends to the styles of wines they make: The Bianco can also be *frizzante, spumante,* or *passito;* the dry Rosato can also be *frizzante*; and the Rosso can be *frizzante, novello,* or *liquoroso.* Varietal wines? Sure, seven of them: Torbato and Torbato *Spumante,* which can be dry, *amabile,* or *dolce* (Torbato, a rare grape brought in from Spain, but probably French in origin, is considered Sardinia's finest dry white variety); Sauvignon; Chardonnay and Chardonnay Spumante, which can be dry, *amabile,* or *dolce*; Vermentino Frizzante, which can be dry or *amabile*; Sangiovese; Cagnulari (or Cagniulari, a dry red); and Cabernet (made from Cabernet Franc and/or Cabernet Sauvignon and/or Carmenère).

Sardinia's remaining DOC wines are limited in the scope of styles made as well as in their production zones. These are the seven wines:

- ✔ **Moscato di Sorso-Sennori** *(mohs CAH toh dee SOR so sehn NO ree):* A sweet wine (or fortified *liquoroso dolce)* made entirely from Moscato Bianco grapes in the small wine zone around the communities of Sorso and Sennori on the northwest coast, north of the Alghero zone. The wine name can use Sorso, or Sennori, or both.

- ✔ **Malvasia di Bosa** *(mahl vah SEE ah dee BOH sah):* This rarity is made around the village of Bosa on the west coast, between Alghero in the north and Oristano. Entirely from Malvasia di Sardegna grapes, it can be *secco* (the most prized form, resembling a fine, dry Madeira), *dolce naturale, liquoroso secco* or *liquoroso dolce.*

- ✔ **Vernaccia di Oristano** *(ver NAHTCH cha dee oh ree STAH no):* Besides Malvasia di Bova, this is the other great apéritif/dessert wine of Sardinia, once very popular, but now falling out of favor. It's made entirely from Vernaccia di Oristano, probably an indigenous variety not related to any other Vernaccia. This dry, Sherry-like wine is best as an *apéritif* wine, like Sherry; it's also made as a *liquoroso* wine, either *secco* and *dolce.*

- ✔ **Mandrolisai** *(mahn dro lee SYE):* The Mandrolisai zone lies in the barren center of the island. Mandrolisai is a dry Rosso or Rosato from Bovale Sardo (another Spanish red variety), Cannonau, and Monica, with other grapes.

↙ **Campidano di Terralba,** or **Terralba** *(cahm pee DAH no dee ter RAHL ba):* Terralba is a dry red made mainly from Bovale Sardo and/or Bovale di Spagna, with up to 20 percent Pascale di Cagliari and/or Greco Nero and/or Monica. This large zone is in the Campidano plains in southwest Sardinia. The wine sells only locally.

↙ **Arborea** *(ahr bo RAE ah):* A large zone in Oristano province making light Sangiovese Rosso and Trebbiano (also made *frizzante*).

↙ **Carignano del Sulcis** *(cah ree N'YAH no dee SUHL chees):* The Sulcis zone is in extreme southwest Sardinia, including two islands off the southwest coast, in Cagliari province. Dry Rosso and Rosato Carignano are varietal wines; *novello* and *passito* versions of the Rosso are also made. One good producer, Santadi, makes a soft, fleshy Rosso with enough richness to outweigh Carignano's tough tannin; it sells for $12.50.

Sardinian wines to seek

We list alphabetically our recommended wine producers from Sardinia:

Argiolas	Antici Poderi Jerzu
Tenute Capichera	Pala
Giovanni Cherchi	Santadi
Attilio Contini	Santa Maria La Palma
Cantine Dolianova	Sella & Mosca
Giuseppe Gabbas	Cantina del Vermentino
Cantina Gallura	

Sardinia's IGT zones

Any Italian wine that carries one of the following regional IGT names is from Sardinia: Barbagia, Colli del Limbara, Isola dei Nuraghi, Marmilla, Nurra, Ogliastra, Parteolla, Planargia, Provincia di Nuoro, Romangia, Sibiola, Tharros, Trexenta, Valle del Tirso, and Valli di Porto Pino.

Part V
The Part of Tens

In this part . . .

Unfortunately, Italian wines can be very complicated. What exactly *is* a Super-Tuscan wine? And have Italian white wines improved in quality, or should you stick to Italian reds? Isn't *spumante* always sweet, and what really is it with DOC wines? We tackle these issues and more in our last two chapters: quick answers to typically confusing questions and myths about Italian wines.

Chapter 12

Ten Commonly-Asked Questions about Italian Wines

. . . .

In This Chapter
▶ Super-Tuscans, food wines, and big government
▶ The toss-up between traditional and modern wines
▶ The best all-purpose Italian red wine
▶ The Franco-Italian prestige stakes

. . . .

I talian wines are delicious, fascinating, and food-friendly — but they're also confusing, no doubt about it! The ten questions that we answer in this chapter are those that we are most frequently asked when we teach classes on Italian wines or conduct Italian wine tastings.

Why Are Italian Wines So Much Better with Food?

Italy's wines come alive with food — it's true. That's because Italians always drink their wines with meals (lunch *and* dinner), and the style of wine that has evolved in Italy is therefore a meal-friendly style. The lack of sweetness, crisp acidity, and fairly subtle flavors of most Italian wines enable them to accommodate and compliment food, rather than compete with it.

Some new-style Italian wines have rich, fruity intensity and soft, dense texture that makes them enjoyable even without food — for example, in wine-tastings, when you compare wines in a clinical ambiance. With time, more Italian wines will probably move in that direction, because that's the style of wine that's most popular in major international markets such as the U.S. In the meantime, if you want to experience Italy's wines the way they're meant to be experienced — *mangia!*

What Are Super-Tuscan Wines?

Super-Tuscans are expensive wines, with proprietary, often fanciful names, and heavy bottles. They're always from the region of Tuscany, they're usually (but not necessarily) high-quality wines made in an international style — often with lots of oaky flavor from French oak barrels, for example — and they're fairly new-fangled (most of them didn't exist 20 years ago). Chapter 8 explains the anti-establishment, counter-culture attitude that gave birth to this category of wines: They were outlaw wines that flagrantly circumvented DOC regulations. But some Super-Tuscan wines have now become DOC wines (does that make them "inlaws"?), which has blurred the definition of the category a bit. Not that it ever was an official category — just a collection of good, innovative, pricey wines from independent Tuscan producers.

Why Does the Italian Government Tell Producers How to Make Their Wines?

Actually, Italy's wine regulations work the other way around: The producers of a certain type of wine tell the government what their wine is — which grape varieties, growing where, produced in which style(s), and so forth — and then the government agrees to act as their watchdog, to make sure no one else makes a different sort of wine using the same name (by protecting that type of wine with a DOC or DOCG designation; see Chapter 3). Sometimes, some producers of a certain type of wine disagree with their fellow producers regarding what the wine should be like, and they make their wine differently. They're free to do that, as long as they don't use the protected, DOC/G name for their wine. (They're also free to convince the majority of their colleagues to formally modify the production requirements for that DOC/G designation.)

What's the Difference Between DOC and Non-DOC Wines?

Wines that carry a DOC or DOCG name (explained in Chapter 3) are wines that conform to the official local practices in the area where the wine is made, in terms of their grape varieties, aging, general taste style, and so forth. Non-DOC wines either don't conform to local practices, or come from a vineyard area that has no formalized local regulations, or (less frequently) are made by anti-establishment producers. Whether a wine is DOC or not has nothing to do with its quality. (Some DOC areas have high standards, while others don't; likewise, some non-DOC wines are excellent, and some are mediocre.)

What's the Best All-Purpose Italian Red Wine?

Now you're forcing us to get personal. Research (our own drinking habits!) proves that Barbera is the most versatile Italian red for everyday enjoyment, at least with the kinds of food *we* like to eat. The acidity of Barbera can stand up to the acidity of tomatoes and tomato sauce — which makes it great with pizza, red-sauced pastas, eggplant parmigiana, and similar dishes. Barbera's fresh, vibrant fruitiness stands up well to spicy dishes like chili and bland dishes like roasted chicken breasts. Barbera even comes in some Sunday-dress styles, capable of impressing the most sophisticated wine drinkers. You can read more about Barbera in Chapter 4.

Isn't Southern Italy Too Hot for Making Wine?

Southern Italy (and the islands) are indeed southerly enough to have a very warm climate. (Palermo, Sicily's capital, is about the same latitude as Raleigh, North Carolina.) But latitude doesn't tell the whole story. Once you factor in the proximity of the Mediterranean Sea to all of Italy's southern regions, the constant presence of mountains, and the high altitudes that many of the vineyards have, the climate is temperate enough for fine wine production. Southern wines are generally fuller-bodied, gutsier, and less delicately perfumed than cooler-climate wines from Northern Italy, but they're no less good.

Which Are Better: "Traditional" or "Modern" Italian Wines?

We hate to hedge, but we can't give a simple answer to this question. Obviously, modern knowledge and technology have eliminated many winemaking faults, and modern grape growing expertise has improved the quality of the grapes tremendously. On the other hand, a boring sameness has crept into many "modern" wines, with so many of them aged in small oak barrels, with the mandatory Cabernet Sauvignon, Merlot, and/or Syrah in the red wines, and Chardonnay (what else?!) in the white wines. We regret this disturbing trend in too many of today's wines. To give just one example that's close to our hearts, give us a traditionally-made Giacomo Conterno Barolo any time over the so-called modern Barolos.

What Are Barriques, and Why Are They Controversial?

Barriques are small (60-gallon) barrels made of French oak that some Italian winemakers use for aging their wines, instead of the much larger casks of Slavonian (Croatian) oak that are traditional in Italy. Because of their small size (which creates a higher oak-to-wine ratio) and because they are generally no more than three years old (as opposed to 25 years old, or more, for traditional casks), *barriques* contribute much more oaky flavor and wood tannin to wines that age in them than casks do. Critics say that *barrique*-aged Italian wines taste like *barrique*-aged wines from anywhere, and are not typically Italian; proponents say that *barriques* are a useful tool for achieving better color, fruitiness, and approachability in their wines, and that the international market prizes such wines. They're both right, depending on which example of *barrique*-aged Italian wine you're talking about.

Why Do Italian Wines Have Such Strange Names?

Most Italian wines are named after the places they come from — just as are most French wines and other European wines. The names sound strange only to those who lack familiarity with the Italian language and the Italian countryside (which includes most American wine drinkers, of course). Many French wine names — such as Bordeaux, Burgundy, and Champagne — have long become a part of wine lovers' vocabularies, and they have lost their foreign ring. Eventually, the same will happen for Montalcino, Montepulciano, Montefalco, and other prestigious Italian wine names.

Why Are Italian Wines Less Prestigious Than French Wines?

French wines had a big head start internationally; they've been popular in England for hundreds of years, and in the U.S. since the 19th century. England, across the Channel from France, was always a big customer of French wines — because its own climate couldn't support grape growing, and because it once owned parts of France; Italy's wines were less familiar to the English, and harder to get. Also, the Italian wines that first made it big abroad were inexpensive, everyday wines rather than the country's elite wines. (The Italians, not being French, saw nothing wrong with that picture.) There's another issue, also: Only in the last 15 to 20 years have Italian wines achieved the over-all quality which they now possess, generally speaking.

Chapter 13

Ten Common Italian Wine Myths Exposed

In This Chapter

▶ What *spumante* really means

▶ Chianti's new quality

▶ Pinot Grigio's greater-than-life reputation

▶ Montepulciano versus Montepulciano

Sometimes ideas or stories take on lives of their own, and innocent wine lovers become unwitting believers in what are the wine equivalent of urban legends. Here are some examples that we've come across — and the real story about each myth, to set you straight.

Chianti Is an Inexpensive, Commercial Wine

Some very fine Chianti wines have always existed, but — in the days of straw-covered flasks — they used to represent a tiny minority of all Chianti. Now the red-checkered-tableclothed tables have turned, and the majority of Chianti wines (at least in major export markets such as the U.S.) are high quality wines. Chianti Classico, the type of Chianti most commonly found outside of Italy, is particularly fine. Prices have risen with the quality, and now you can easily find $25 and $30 bottles of Chianti Classico in good wine shops. Inexpensive, $10 bottles of Chianti do still exist — including some in the nostalgic straw packaging — but the category as a whole has moved uptown.

Italian Wines Should Be Enjoyed with Italian Food

Any time we drink the wine of a particular wine region with the food of the same region, we find the combination apt and harmonious. In the case of Italian food, no wines taste better than Italian wines (to our taste) — even if we drink a lusty wine of the South with a dish that's typical of a northern region. But Italy's wines are so incredibly food-friendly that their pairing talent extends far beyond *la cucina italiana*. The crisp acidity of Italy's white wines cuts through the richness of classic French dishes, and the tanginess of many reds provides thirst-quenching relief with Tex-Mex. We could go on and on. Italian wines are the most food-friendly on earth.

Pinot Grigio Is One of Italy's Best Wines

We wish that were true, because then we'd know that the thousands of wine drinkers who drink Pinot Grigio are experiencing Italian wine at its finest. But in reality, the average quality of Pinot Grigio wines is . . . well, average. They're dry and refreshing, they don't clash with most foods, and they're perfectly fine if you want an inexpensive wine — but they lack the character and intensity that the French Pinot Gris grape (in Italy, Pinot Grigio) is capable of, and they are not Italy's answer to great white wine. Naturally, a few exceptions exist. Look over our lists of favorite producers in Chapter 6 to find the better examples.

Italy's Best Wines Are All Red

An understandable misunderstanding. After all, Italy makes about twice as much red wine as white wine, and most of Italy's most famous wines — Chianti, Barolo, Brunello di Montalcino, and so forth — are red. (In fact, the statement might even have been true 30 years ago.) But certain parts of Italy definitely have what it takes to make fine white wines, and producers in those areas are doing just that. The region of Friuli-Venezia Giulia makes many excellent white wines, as does Alto Adige (both covered in Chapter 7). Campania has two terrific whites, Fiano di Avellino and Greco di Tufo (see Chapter 10). Piedmont and Tuscany — the red wine capitals of Italy — even make some fine whites, such as Gavi, Arneis, and Vernaccia di San Gimignano. (See Chapter 4 for Piedmont, Chapter 8 for Tuscany.) And some traditional Italian white wines, such as Soave (Chapter 7), Verdicchio (Chapter 9), and Vermentino (Chapters 5 and 11), are now better than ever.

Marsala Is Cooking Wine

We have to give credit to the producers of Marsala, Italy's famous fortified wine (see Chapter 11), for tightening production regulations for their wine and upgrading quality. The ridiculous, flavored Marsalas no longer exist, and the top wines — the *Vergine* and *Soleras* styles — are now regaining their rightful place among the world's classic *apéritif* wines. The lower tiers of Marsala might still be more appropriate for cooking than sipping — depending on the brand, the cook, and the sipper — but the category as a whole is more genuine than it has been in recent history, and will probably improve further. (After all, Palermo wasn't built in a day.)

White Italian Wines All Taste Alike

Add a few words to that statement, and it *is* true: (Inexpensive, mass-market) white Italian wines all taste (pretty much) alike. They're light-bodied, un-oaked, dryish, crisp, and not particularly flavorful. But Italy does have some very distinctive white wines: Tocai Friuliano, Vernaccia di San Gimignano, Gavi, Fiano di Avellino, Moscato d'Asti, Alto Adige Sauvignon, and Vermentino di Gallura, to name a few. Italy also makes some white wines that are manifestly un-Italian in style — oaky Chardonnays, for example. Once you leave the mass-market segment, you can find variety among Italy's whites.

Non-DOC Wines Are Better Than DOC Wines

This statement is a myth — as is its corollary: DOC wines are better than non-DOC wines. Just because a producer follows local practice in making his wine (and naming it as a DOC wine) doesn't mean that the wine is necessarily great. And just because a producer shuns local practice to make what he considers a better wine (without a DOC name) doesn't mean that the wine is any greater, or less great, except in his own mind. (See Chapter 3 for more info on DOC.) A producer's winemaking ability, the quality of the vineyards, and the weather in a given year all have much more influence on the quality of the wine than the wine's legal status does. Great wines and clunkers exist within and outside the DOC category.

Spumante Is Sweet

The word *spumante* means "sparkling" — just that. Because Asti Spumante (the sweet, sparkling wine of Asti; see Chapter 4) is so famous, however, wineries in California and Italy have borrowed the term *spumante* for sweet bubblies that imitate Asti, and millions of people now think that the word applies only to sweet, sparkling wines. The connotation of sweetness is so strong, in fact, that Italy's best dry sparkling wines, such as Franciacorta, don't use the word *spumante*. And you rarely see the word even on bottles of Asti these days, because producers of this classic want to distance themselves from their imitators.

Soave and Valpolicella Are Low-Quality Wines

Soave, a white wine, and Valpolicella, a red wine — along with their red companion wine from the Verona area, Bardolino — have received a bad rep in the U.S. and elsewhere. Not that it wasn't somewhat deserved: Many bottles of these wines are mass-produced, unexciting stuff. But all three of these wines can be delightful, if you seek out a good producer, and you are willing to pay a few dollars more than normal. Try a Gini or Pieropan Soave, for example, an Allegrini Valpolicella, or a Guerrieri-Rizzardi Bardolino, and you discover that these wines have character and charm in the hands of a quality-conscious producer. (For more info on these wines, see Chapter 7.)

Montepulciano d'Abruzzo and Vino Nobile di Montepulciano Are Made from the Same Grape

We can understand the confusion, but these two wines are definitely different wines made from different grape varieties. Vino Nobile is a dry red wine made primarily from the Prugnolo Gentile variety (a type of Sangiovese) around the town of Montepulciano in southeastern Tuscany. (See Chapter 8 for more info on Vino Nobile.) Montepulciano d'Abruzzo is also a dry red wine, but made mainly from the Montepulciano variety, which grows in the region of Abruzzo on the Adriatic coast, southeast of Tuscany. The Montepulciano variety is believed to be native to the Abruzzo region, and it has no connection to Sangiovese or to the town of Montepulciano in Tuscany. (See Chapter 9 for more info on Montepulciano d'Abruzzo.)

Part VI
Appendixes

In this part . . .

One of the big stumbling blocks in getting to know, and buying, Italian wines is pronouncing their names. Our pronunciation guide comes to the rescue here. And the next time you *are* thinking about buying a Barolo or Brunello, check our Vintage Chart to determine how good the vintage is, and whether the wine is ready to drink yet.

Appendix A

Pronunciation Guide to Italian Wine Names and Terms

● ●

*I*talian wine names are real mouthfuls — but once you get the hang of them, they're actually fun to say. Here's a quick key for pronouncing the major types of Italian wine and the most common label terms. Chapters 4 through 11 contain more pronunciations — even for the names of obscure wines.

abboccato	*(ahb boh CAH toh)*
Abruzzo	*(ah BROOT zo)*
Aglianico del Vulture	*(ahl YAHN ee co del VUL too rae)*
amabile	*(ah MAH bee lae)*
Amarone	*(ah mah RO nae)*
Arneis	*(ahr NASE)*
Barbaresco	*(bahr bah RES co)*
Barbera d'Alba	*(bar BAE rah DAHL bah)*
Bolgheri	*(BOHL gheh ree)*
Brindisi	*(BREEN deh see)*
Brunello di Montalcino	*(brew NEL lo dee mahn tahl CHEE no)*
Calabria	*(cah LAH bree ah)*
Campania	*(cahm PAH nee ah)*
Cannonau di Sardegna	*(cahn no NOW dee sar DAEN yah)*

Carema	*(cah RAE ma)*
Carmignano	*(car mee NYAH no)*
Chianti Classico	*(key AHN tee CLAHS see co)*
Chianti Rufina	*(ROO fee nah)*
Chiaretto	*(kee ah REHT toh)*
Cirò	*(chee ROH)*
Cortese	*(cor TAE sae)*
Denominazione di Origine Controllata	*(dae no mee naht zee OH nae dee oh REE gee nae con trol LAH tah)*
Denominazione di Origine Controllata e Garantita	*(. . . ae gah rahn TEE tah)*
Dolcetto di Dogliani	*(dohl CHET toh dee doh L'YAH nee)*
Emilia-Romagna	*(ae MEE lee ah ro MAH n'yah)*
fattoria	*(fah toh REE ah)*
Fiano di Avellino	*(fee AH no dee ah vel LEE no)*
Franciacorta	*(frahn cha COR tah)*
Frascati	*(frah SKAH tee)*
Freisa d'Asti	*(FRAE sah DAHS tee)*
Friuli-Venezia Giulia	*(FREE oo lee veh NET zee ah JHOO lee ah)*
frizzante	*(fritz ZAHN tae)*
Gattinara	*(gah tee NAH rah)*
Ghemme	*(GAE mae)*
Greco di Tufo	*(GREH co dee TOO foh)*
Grignolino	*(gree n'yoh LEE no)*
Indicazione Geografica Tipica	*(in dee caht zee OH nae gee oh GRAF ee cah TEE pee cah)*
Lacryma Christi del Vesuvio	*(LAH cree mah CHREE sti de veh SOO vee oh)*
Lagrein	*(lah GRYNE)*

Lambrusco	*(lam BREWS coh)*
Lazio	*(LAH t'zee oh)*
Liguria	*(lee GOO ree ah)*
Malvasia delle Lipari	*(mahl vah SEE ah del lae LEE pah ree)*
Marche	*(MAHR kae)*
Molise	*(mo LEE sae)*
Montepulciano	*(mon tae pull chee AH noh)*
Morellino di Scansano	*(moh rael LEE no dee scahn SAH no)*
Moscato d'Asti	*(mo SCAH toh DAHS tee)*
Nebbiolo d'Alba	*(nehb bee OH loh DAHL bah)*
Negroamaro	*(NAE grow ah MAH roh)*
Nero d'Avola	*(NAE roh DAHV oh lah)*
Nuragus di Cagliari	*(noo RAH goos dee CAH l'yah ree)*
Oltrepó Pavese	*(ohl trae POH pah VAE sae)*
Orvieto	*(or vee AE toh)*
Passito	*(pahs SEE toh)*
Pinot Bianco	*(pee noh bee AHN coh)*
Pinot Grigio	*(pee noh GREE joe)*
podere	*(poh DAE rae)*
Puglia	*(POO l'yah)*
Ribolla Gialla	*(ree BOWL lah JAH lah)*
Riesling Italico	*(REES ling ee TAHL ee coh)*
Roero	*(roh EH roh)*
rosato	*(ro SAH toh)*
Rosso Cònero	*(ROHS so COH nae ro)*
Rosso Piceno	*(ROHS so pee CHAE no)*
Sagrantino	*(sah grahn TEE no)*
Salice Salentino	*(SAH lee chae sah len TEE no)*

Sangiovese	*(san joe VAE sae)*
Sant'Antimo	*(sahnt AHN tee mo)*
Schiava	*(skee AH vah)*
Soave	*(so AH vae)*
spumante	*(spoo MAHN tae)*
Superiore	*(soo peh ree OH rae)*
Taurasi	*(touw RAH see)*
tenuta	*(teh NOO tah)*
Teroldego	*(teh ROHL dae go)*
Tocai Friulano	*(toh KYE free oo LAH no)*
Torgiano	*(tor gee AH no)*
Trebbiano d'Abruzzo	*(trehb bee AH no dah BREWTZ zo)*
Trentino-Alto Adige	*(tren TEE no AHL toe AH dee jhae)*
Valle d'Aosta	*(VAH lae dah OHSS tah)*
vendemmia	*(ven DEM mee ah)*
Veneto	*(VEH neh toe)*
Verdicchio dei Castelli di Jesi	*(ver DEE key oh dae cahs TEL ee dee YAE see)*
Vermentino	*(ver men TEE noh)*
Vernaccia di San Gimignano	*(ver NAHCH cha dee san gee me NYAH no)*
vigna	*(VEE n'yah)*
vigneto	*(vee N'YEH toh)*
vino da tavola	*(VEE no dah TAH vo lah)*
Vino Nobile di Montepulciano	*(VEE no NO bee lae dee mahn tae pool chee AH no)*
vitigno	*(vee TEE n'yoh)*

Appendix B

Italian Wine Vintage Chart: 1980 to 1999

• •

*H*ere is our 20-year Italian wine vintage chart. Any vintage wine chart must be regarded as a rough guide — a general, average rating of the vintage year in a particular wine region. Remember that many wines will always be exceptions to the vintage's rating. For example, some wine producers manage to find a way to make a decent — even fine wine — in a so-called poor vintage.

Because it would not be feasible to give an accurate rating for all the various regions in Italy, we list two general ratings, focussing on the two most important wine regions, which are the following:

✔ Piedmont and Northern Italy

✔ Tuscany and Central-Southern Italy

The ratings give a picture of the best wines of the vintage; this is especially true for vintages prior to 1990.

WINE REGION	1980	1981	1982	1983	1984	1985	1986	1987	1988
Piedmont and Northern Italy	75c	70c	90b	75c	65d	95b	85c	80c	85b
Tuscany and Central-So. Italy	70d	80d	80c	85c	60d	95c	85c	75c	90b

WINE REGION	1989	1990	1991	1992	1993	1994	1995	1996	1997	1998	1999
Piedmont and Northern Italy	95b	95b	80c	70c	80b	75b	85a	95a	90b	95a	90a
Tuscany and Central-So. Italy	70c	90c	75c	70d	75c	85c	85a	75b	95b	85b	85a

100	=	Outstanding
95	=	Excellent
90	=	Very Good
85	=	Good
80	=	Fairly Good
75	=	Average
70	=	Below Average
65	=	Poor
50-60	=	Very Poor
a	=	Too young to drink
b	=	Can be consumed now, but will improve with time
c	=	Ready to drink
d	=	May be too old

Recent Past Great Vintages

WINE REGION	
Piedmont	1964, 1971, 1978
Tuscany	1970 and 1975 (Brunello di Montalcino only), 1971

Index

• *A* •

abboccato, 33
Abruzzo, 188–191
Acininobili wine, 127–128
aging
  barriques, 256–257
  Marsala wine, 237
  riserva, 34
Aglianico del Vulture DOC zone, 226
Aglianico grapes, 19
Alba
  Barbaresco, 47–51
  Barbera d'Alba, 52–53
  Barolo, 42–47
  Dolcetto d'Alba, 52, 54
  Dolcetto delle Langhe
    Monregalesi, 57
  Dolcetto di Diano d'Alba, 57
  Dolcetto di Dogliani, 57
  geography, 41
  Langhe Bianco, 58
  Langhe Freisa, 58
  Langhe Nebbiolo, 58
  Langhe Rosso, 58
  Nebbiolo d'Alba, 52, 54–55
  restaurants, 55, 60
  Roero Arneis, 56
  Roero Rosso, 55–56
  Verduno Pelaverga, 57
Alba-Asti area, 58–59
Albana DOCG, 107
Albugnano DOC, 68
Alcamo DOC, 239
Aleatico di Gradoli DOC, 198
Alezio DOC zone, 220
Alghero DOC, 248–249
Allegrini Valpolicella DOC, 263
Alto Adige DOC, 66, 112–113
amabile, 33

Amarone della Valpolicella wine,
  123–124
Anderson, Burton, 79
annata, 33
Annia DOC, 139–140
annual wine production in Italy,
  9–10, 12
Ansonica grapes, 234
Antinori, Marchese Piero, 50
Aosta Valley, 77–83
Aprilia DOC, 200
Apulia
  Alezio, 220
  Brindisi, 219
  Cacce'e Mmitte di Lucera, 224
  Castel del Monte, 222
  Copertino, 219
  Galatina, 221
  geography, 216–217
  Gioia del Colle, 221–222
  Gravina, 223
  Levorano, 220
  Lizzano, 220
  Locorotondo, 221
  Martina Franca, 221
  Matino, 220
  Moscato di Trani, 223
  Nardò, 220
  Orta Nova, 224
  Ostuni, 221
  Primitivo di Manduria, 218–219
  Rosso Barletta, 223
  Rosso Canosa, 223
  Rosso di Cerignola, 224
  Salice Salentino, 218
  San Severo, 223
  Squinzano, 220
Aquileia DOC, 139–140
Arborea wine, 250
Arnad-Montjovet wine, 81
Arneis grapes, 24, 41, 56

Asprinio di Aversa DOC, 212
Assisi DOC, 181
Asti
  Asti, 61–62
  Barbera d'Asti, 62–64
  Brachetto d'Acqui, 66
  Cortese di Alto Monferrato, 67
  DOCG status, 61
  Dolcetto d'Acqui, 64
  Dolcetto d'Asti, 64
  Dolcetto di Ovada, 65
  Freisa d'Asti, 65
  Freisa di Chieri, 65
  Grignolino d'Asti, 65
  Grignolino del Monferrato
    Casalese, 66
  Malvasia di Casorzo d'Asti, 66
  Malvasia di Castelnuovo Don
    Bosco, 66
  Moscato d'Asti, 62–63
  Quorum, 62
  restaurants, 59–60
  Ruché di Castagnole Monferrato, 67
Asti DOCG, 61
Asti Spumante, 262
Atina DOC, 200
Avellino, 208

Bianco Alcamo DOC, 239
Bianco Capena DOC, 199
Bianco dell'Empolese DOC, 174
Bianco di Custoza DOC, 26, 122
Bianco di Pitigliano DOC, 173
Bianco di Valdinievole DOC, 173
Bianco Pisano di San Torpè DOC, 174
Bianco Vergine Valdichiana DOC, 174
Biferno DOC, 193
Bivongi DOC, 230
Blanc de Morgex DOC, 79–80
Boca DOC, 73
Bolgheri DOC, 170–171
Bologna, Giacomo, 63
Bonarda grapes, 41
Bonarda DOC, 94
Bosco Eliceo DOC, 107
Botticino DOC, 99
Brachetto d'Acqui DOC, 66
Bramaterra DOC, 73
Breganze DOC, 127
Brescia DOC, 99
Brindisi DOC, 219
Brunello di Montalcino DOCG, 144,
  160–162
Bukkuram DOC, 242
Buttafuoco DOC, 94

• B •

Bagnoli DOC, 128–129
Barbaresco DOC/G, 47–51
Barbera d'Alba DOC, 52–53
Barbera d'Asti DOC, 62–64
Barbera del Monferrato DOC, 68
Barbera grapes, 16, 19, 41, 52
Barbera wine, Oltrepó Pavese, 94
Barco Reale di Carmignano DOC, 167
Bardolino DOC, 120–122, 124,
  262–263
Barolo DOC/G, 42–47
barriques, 256–257
Basilicata, 225–226
Berlucchi Cuvée Imperiale wine, 96
Bernabei, Franco, 95
Bianchello del Metauro DOC, 186
bianco, 33

• C •

Cabernet Franc grapes, 16, 19–20
Cabernet Sauvignon grapes, 16–17,
  20, 41, 145
Cacce'e Mmitte di Lucera DOC, 224
Cagliari, 246–248
Cagnina di Romagna DOC, 107
Calabria
  Bivongi, 230
  Cirò, 227–228
  Donnici, 229
  geography, 226
  Greco di Bianco, 230
  Lamezia, 230
  Melissa, 228
  Pollino, 229
  San Vito di Luzzi, 229

Sant'Anna di Isola Capo
    Rizzuto, 228
Savuto, 229
Scavigna, 230
Verbicaro, 229
Caluso DOC, 71
Caluso Passito wine, 71
Campania
    Asprinio di Aversa, 212
    Avellino, 208
    Campi Flegrei, 211
    Capri, 211
    Castel San Lorenzo, 213
    Cilento, 212–213
    Costa d'Amalfi, 211
    Falerno del Massico, 213
    Fiano di Avellino, 209
    Gallucio, 213–214
    geography, 205–206
    Greco di Tufo, 209–210
    Guardiolo, 214–215
    Ischia, 210
    Lacryma Christi del Vesuvio, 211
    Penisola Sorrentina, 212
    Sannio, 215
    Sant'Agata dei Goti, 214
    Solopaca, 214
    Taburno, 214
    Taurasi, 208–209
    Vesuvio, 211
Campi Flegrei DOC, 211
Campidano di Terralba DOC, 250
Canavese DOC, 71
Candia dei Colli Apuani DOC, 173
Cannonau di Sardegna DOC, 246
Cannonau Rosato DOC, 246
cantina sociale (C.S.), 33
Capalbio DOC, 172
Capri DOC, 211
Capriano del Colle DOC, 99
Carema DOC, 70
Carignano del Sulcis DOC, 250
Carignano grapes, 245
Carmignano Rosso DOCG, 145,
    166–167
Carso DOC, 138–139
Castel del Monte DOC, 222

Castel San Lorenzo DOC, 213
Casteller DOC, 118
Castelli Romani DOC, 196
Catarratto Bianco grapes, 234
Cellatica DOC, 99
Cerasuolo di Vittoria DOC, 241
Cerveteri DOC, 198–199
Cesanese di Affile DOC, 200
Cesanese di Olevano DOC, 200
Cesanese di Piglio DOC, 200
Chambave DOC, 81
characteristics of Italian wines, 13–14
Chardonnay grapes, 17, 24–25, 41
Chianti Classico DOCG, 144, 147–152
Chianti DOCG, 144, 147–148, 153–156
Chianti wine
    history, 150
    myths, 259
    prices, 259
    straw-covered flasks, 259
chiaretto, 33
Chiaretto wine, 98, 121
Chiavennasca grapes, 92
Cilento DOC, 212–213
Cinqueterre DOC, 84–85
Circeo DOC, 200
Cirò DOC, 227–228
classico, 33
Colli Albani DOC, 196
Colli Altotiberini DOC, 181
Colli Amerini DOC, 182
Colli Berici DOC, 128
Colli Bolognesi DOC, 105–106
Colli del Trasimeno DOC, 181
Colli della Sabina DOC, 199
Colli dell'Etruria Centrale DOC,
    158–159
Colli di Bolzano (Bozner Leiten)
    DOC, 114
Colli di Conegliano DOC, 130–131
Colli di Imola DOC, 107
Colli di Luni DOC, 84, 87
Colli di Parma DOC, 105
Colli di Rimini DOC, 107
Colli di Scandiano and di Canossa
    DOC, 106
Colli Etruschi Viterbesi DOC, 198

Colli Euganei DOC, 128–129
Colli Lanuvini DOC, 197
Colli Maceratesi DOC, 187
Colli Martani DOC, 181
Colli Morenici Mantovani del Garda
    DOC, 99
Colli Orientali del Friuli DOC,
    135–136
Colli Perugini DOC, 181
Colli Pesaresi DOC, 186
Colli Piacentini DOC, 103–105
Colli Tortonesi DOC, 69
Colline di Levanto DOC, 84, 87
Colline di Lucchesi DOC, 173
Colline Novaresi DOC, 74
Colline Saluzzesi DOC, 75
Collio Goriziano DOC, 134–135
Colomba Platina DOC, 238
Consorzio, 33
Contea di Sclafani Bianco DOC, 238
Contea di Sclafani DOC, 237–238
Contessa Entellina DOC, 239
Controguerra DOC, 191
Copertino DOC, 219
Cori DOC zone, 199
Cortese di Alto Monferrato DOC, 67
Cortese grapes, 25, 41, 67
Corvina grapes, 20, 121, 123
Corvo Red, 238
Corvo White, 238
Costa d'Amalfi DOC, 211–212
Costa dell'Argentario DOC, 172
Coste della Sesia DOC, 74
Croatina grapes, 41

Moscato di Pantelleria, 242
Moscato di Siracusa, 242
Moscato di Sorso-Sennori, 249
Moscato Naturale, 242
Muffato della Sala, 178
Passito di Pantelleria, 242
production, 14
Sciacchetrà, 85
Torcolato, 127–128
Vernaccia di Oristano, 249
Vin Santo di Chianti Classico, 158
DOC/G designation
    authenticity, 32
    explanation, 28
    quality, 32, 255, 262
    Super-Tuscans, 254
    types of DOC wines, 31
    types of DOCG wines, 31
    wine laws, 29–30, 32, 254–255
dolce, 33
Dolceaqua DOC, 84
Dolcetto d'Acqui DOC, 64
Dolcetto d'Alba DOC, 52, 54
Dolcetto d'Asti DOC, 64
Dolcetto delle Langhe Monregalesi
    DOC, 57
Dolcetto di Diano d'Alba DOC, 57
Dolcetto di Ovada DOC, 65
Dolcetto grapes, 20, 41, 54, 79
Dolomites, 10
Donnas DOC, 79, 81
Donnici DOC, 229
Duca Enrico DOC, 238
Durello DOC, 126

• D •

Delia Nivolelli DOC, 239
dessert wines
    Acininobili, 127–128
    Bukkuram, 242
    Caluso Passito, 71
    Malvasia delle Lipari, 242–243
    Malvasia di Bosa, 249
    Moscato d'Asti, 62–63
    Moscato di Cagliari, 248
    Moscato di Noto, 242

• E •

Elba DOC, 174
Eloro DOC, 241
Emilia-Romagna, 89, 100–108
Enfer d'Arvier DOC, 80
enologists. *See* winemakers
Erbaluce di Caluso DOC, 71
Erbaluce grapes, 41
Esino DOC, 186
Est! Est!! Est!!! di Montefiascone, 197
Etna DOC, 240–241

• F •

Falerio dei Colli Ascolani DOC, 187
Falerno del Massico DOC, 213
Fara DOC, 73
Faro DOC, 240
fattoria, 33
Favorita grapes, 41
Feudi dei Fiori DOC, 239
Fiano di Avellino DOC, 209
Fiano grapes, 25
food and wine, 253–254, 260
Franciacorta DOCG, 90, 95–98
Frascati DOC, 195
Freisa d'Asti DOC, 65
Freisa di Chieri DOC, 65
Freisa grapes, 41, 65
French wines, 257
Friuli-Venezia Giulia, 134–140
frizzante, 34

• G •

Gabiano DOC, 69
Gaja, Angelo, 50
Galatina DOC, 221
Gallucio DOC, 213–214
Gamay grapes, 79
Gambellara DOC, 128
Gambero Rosso Italian Wine
    Guide, 39
Garda Orientale DOC, 126
Garganega grapes, 25
Gattinara DOCG, 72
Gavi DOCG, 67–68
Genazzano DOC, 197
geography of Italy, 9–12
Ghemme DOCG, 72
Gioia del Colle DOC, 221–222
Girò di Cagliari DOC, 247
Golfo del Tigullio Bianchetta
    Genovese DOC, 87
Golfo del Tigullio DOC, 84, 87
government regulation, 254–255
grape varieties
    Aglianico, 19
    Ansonica, 234

Arneis, 24, 41, 56
Austrian varieties, 16
Barbera, 16, 19, 41, 52
Blanc de Morgex, 79–80
Bonarda, 41
Cabernet Franc, 16, 19–20
Cabernet Sauvignon, 16–17, 20,
    41, 145
Cannanou, 20, 245–246
Carignano, 245
Catarratto Bianco, 234
Chardonnay, 17, 24–25, 41
Chiavennasca, 92
Cortese, 25, 41, 67
Corvina, 20, 121, 123
Croatina, 41
Dolcetto, 20, 41, 54, 79
Erbaluce, 41
Favorita, 41
Fiano, 25
Freisa, 41, 65
French varieties, 16
Gamay, 79
Garganega, 25
German varieties, 16
Greco, 25
Grignolino, 41
Grillo, 234
internationally known varieties, 17
Inzolia, 15, 234
Lagrein, 20
Lambrusco, 16, 21, 100
Malvasia, 25
Malvasia di Candia, 105
Malvasia Nera, 41, 66
Merlot, 16, 21, 41
migration within Italy, 17
Molinara, 121, 123
Monica, 245, 247
Montepulciano, 21, 189, 263
Moscato, 25, 41, 61
names of wines, 23, 33
native varieties, 16
Nebbiolo, 16, 18–19, 39–40, 42–43,
    47, 52, 69, 90, 92
Negrara, 121
Negroamaro, 16, 21

grape varieties *(continued)*
Nerello Mascalese, 235
Nero d'Avola, 16, 21, 235
new varieties, 16
Nuragus, 244
Pelaverga, 41, 57
Perricone, 235
Petit Rouge, 79
Piedmont, 40–41
Pigato, 85
Pinot Bianco, 26
Pinot Blanc, 16, 26
Pinot Grigio, 23
Pinot Gris, 16, 23
Pinot Nero, 16, 21
Pinot Noir, 16, 21, 79
Primitivo, 16, 21–22
Prugnolo Gentile, 263
red grape varieties, 17–22
Refosco, 22
Riesling, 16, 26
Rondinella, 121, 123
Rossese, 84
Sagrantino, 22
Sangiovese, 15–16, 18, 145
Sangiovese Grosso, 18
Sangioveto, 18
Sauvignon, 26
Sauvignon Blanc, 41
Schiava, 22, 112
Spanish varieties, 16
Syrah, 16
Teroldego, 22, 116
Tocai Friulano, 24
Torbato, 249
Trebbiano, 16, 22–23, 145
Trebbiano Toscano, 234
Verdicchio, 16, 24
Vermentino, 26, 244
Vernaccia, 24
Vernatsch, 112
Vespolina, 41
Viognier, 16
white grape varieties, 22–26
Grave del Friuli DOC, 139–140
Gravina DOC, 223

Greco di Bianco DOC, 230
Greco di Tufo DOC, 209–210
Greco grapes, 25
Grignolino d'Asti DOC, 65
Grignolino del Monferrato Casalese
DOC, 66
Grignolino grapes, 41
Grillo grapes, 234
Grosseto, 171
Grumello wine, 92
Guardiolo DOC, 214–215
Guerrieri-Rizzardi Bardolino DOC, 263
Gutturnio DOC, 104

• *I* •

IGT designation, 30–31
imbottigliato all'origine, 34
Inferno DOC, 92–93
Inzolia grapes, 15, 234
Ischia DOC, 210
Isonzo del Friuli DOC, 138–139

• *L* •

La Grola wine, 123
La Poja wine, 123
labels
common words and phrases on
labels, 33–34
DOC/G designation, 28–32
grape variety, 33
IGT designation, 30–31
names of wines, 28–30
proprietary names, 33
table wines, 30
vineyard names, 33
vino da tavola, 30–31
Lacrima di Morro d'Alba DOC, 186
Lacryma Christi del Vesuvio DOC, 211
Lago di Caldaro DOC, 114
Lago di Corbara DOC, 182
Lagrein grapes, 20
Lambrusco DOC, 101–103
Lambrusco grapes, 16, 21, 100
Lambrusco Mantovano DOC, 99

Lamezia DOC, 230
Langhe DOC, 57–58
Latisana DOC, 139–140
Latium, 194–200
Lessona DOC, 73
Levorano DOC, 220
Liguria, 77, 83–88
liquoroso, 34
Lison-Pramaggiore DOC, 131–132
Lizzano DOC zone, 220
Loazzolo wine, 69
Locorotondo DOC zone, 221
Lombardy, 89–99
Lugana DOC, 90, 98–99

• *M* •

Malvasia delle Lipari DOC, 242–243
Malvasia di Bosa DOC, 249
Malvasia di Cagliari DOC, 247
Malvasia di Candia grapes, 105
Malvasia di Casorzo d'Asti DOC, 66
Malvasia di Castelnuovo Don Bosco
    DOC, 66
Malvasia DOC, 105
Malvasia grapes, 25
Malvasia Nera grapes, 41, 66
Mandrolisai DOC, 249
Mantovano wine, 99
Marche, 183–187
Maremma, 170
Marino DOC, 195–196
Marsala wine
    aging, 237
    cooking wine image, 236, 261
    history, 236
    hues, 236–237
    imitation Marsalas, 236
    prices, 237
    producers, 236–237
    sweetness levels, 237
Martina Franca DOC, 221
Matino DOC, 220
Melissa DOC, 228
Menfi DOC, 239
Meranese di Collina (Meraner Hügel)
    wine, 113

Merlot grapes, 16, 21, 41
metodo classico, 95
modern Italian wines, 256
Molinara grapes, 121, 123
Molise, 192–193
Monferrato DOC, 68
Monica di Cagliari wine, 247
Monica di Sardegna wine, 247
Monica grapes, 245, 247
Montalcino, 159
Montecarlo DOC, 173
Montecompatri Colonna DOC, 196
Montecucco DOC, 172
Montefalco DOC, 180
Montello e Colli Asolani DOC, 131
Montepulciano d'Abruzzo DOC,
    190, 263
Montepulciano grapes, 21, 189, 263
Monterosso Val d'Arta wine, 104
Montescudaio DOC zone, 174
Montuni del Reno DOC, 103
Morellino di Scansano DOC, 172
Moscadello di Montalcino DOC, 162
Moscato d'Asti wine, 62–63
Moscato di Cagliari wine, 248
Moscato di Noto wine, 242
Moscato di Pantelleria DOC, 242
Moscato di Pantelleria wine, 242
Moscato di Sardegna wine, 247
Moscato di Siracusa DOC, 242
Moscato di Sorso-Sennori wine, 249
Moscato di Trani DOC, 223
Moscato grapes, 25, 41, 61
Moscato Naturale wine, 242

• *N* •

names of wines
    DOC/G designation, 28–32
    grape varieties, 33
    IGT designation, 30–31
    pronunciation guide, 267–270
    proprietary names, 33
    table wines, 30
    vino da tavola, 30–31
Naples, 210–212

Nardò DOC zone, 220
Nasco di Cagliari wine, 247–248
Nebbiolo d'Alba wine, 52, 54–55
Nebbiolo grapes, 16, 18–19, 39–40,
  42–43, 47, 52, 69, 90, 92
Negrara grapes, 121
Negroamaro grapes, 16, 21
Nerello Mascalese grapes, 235
Nero d'Avola grapes, 16, 21, 235
Nino Negri, 93
noble rot, 14
Novara, 71–73
novello, 34
Nuragus di Cagliari wine, 248
Nuragus grapes, 244
Nus wine, 81

● *O* ●

Oltrepó Pavese DOC, 93–95
Ormeasco Sciac-trà wine, 85
Ormeasco DOC, 85
Orta Nova DOC, 224
Orvieto DOC, 177–179
Ostuni DOC, 221

● *P* ●

Pagadebit di Romagna DOC, 107
passito, 34
Passito di Pantelleria wine, 242
Pelaverga grapes, 41, 57
Pelaverga DOC, 75
Penisola Sorrentina DOC, 212
Pentro DOC, 193
Perricone grapes, 235
Petit Rouge grapes, 79
Piave DOC, 131
Piedmont
  Alba, 41, 58–60
  Albugnano DOC, 68
  Asti DOC, 58–62
  Barbaresco, 47–51
  Barbera d'Alba, 52–53
  Barbera d'Asti, 62–64
  Barbera del Monferrato, 68

Barolo, 42–47
Boca, 73
Brachetto d'Acqui, 66
Bramaterra, 73
Caluso, 71
Canavese, 71
Carema, 70
Colline Novaresi, 74
Colline Saluzzesi, 75
Cortese di Alto Monferrato, 67
Coste della Sesia, 74
cuisine, 38
DOC/G wine zones, 39
Dolcetto d'Acqui, 64
Dolcetto d'Alba, 52, 54
Dolcetto d'Asti, 64
Dolcetto delle Langhe
  Monregalesi, 57
Dolcetto di Diano d'Alba, 57
Dolcetto di Dogliani, 57
Dolcetto di Ovada, 65
Fara, 73
Freisa d'Asti, 65
Freisa di Chieri, 65
Gabiano, 69
Gattinara, 72
geography, 60
Ghemme, 72
grape varieties, 40–41
Grignolino d'Asti, 65
Grignolino del Monferrato
  Casalese, 66
Langhe Nebbiolo, 58
languages, 38
Lessona, 73
Loazzolo, 69
Malvasia di Casorzo d'Asti, 66
Malvasia di Castelnuovo Don
  Bosco, 66
Monferrato, 68
Moscato d'Asti, 62–63
mountains, 38
Nebbiolo d'Alba, 52, 54–55
Novara, 71–73
people, 38
Piemonte, 75–76

Pinerolese, 75
Po River Valley, 38, 60–61
Quorum, 62
restaurants, 58–60
Roero, 55–56
Rubino di Cantavenna, 69
Ruché di Castagnole Monferrato, 67
Sizzano, 73
Valsusa, 75
Vercelli, 71–73
Verduno Pelaverga wine, 57
vineyards, 38, 41, 69–71
wine production, 39
wine zones, 39–40
Piemonte DOC, 75–76
Pieropan Soave wine, 263
Pigato grapes, 85
Pigato wine, 85
Pinerolese DOC, 75
Pinerolese Rosso wine, 75
Pineroloese Ramie wine, 75
Pineroloese Rosato wine, 75
Pinot Bianco grapes, 16, 26
Pinot Blanc grapes, 16, 26
Pinot Grigio grapes, 16, 23
Pinot Grigio wine, 260
Pinot Gris grapes, 16, 23
Pinot Nero grapes, 16, 21
Pinot Nero wine, 94
Pinot Noir grapes, 16, 21, 79
Po River Valley, 11, 38, 60–61, 89–90
Pollino DOC, 229
Pomino DOC, 157–158
prestige of Italian wines, 12–13, 257
Primitivo di Manduria DOC, 218–219
Primitivo grapes, 16, 21–22
producers
    A. Vicentini Orgnani, 140
    Abbazia di Novacella, 114
    Abbazia Sant'Anastasia, 243
    Adami, 130
    Agricole Vallone, 224
    Agricoltori del Chianti
        Geografico, 153
    Albino Rocca, 51
    Aldo Conterno, 47, 53
    Allegrini, 123, 125

Alois Lageder, 113, 115
Altesino, 161
Anfossi, 88
Angelo Gaja, 51
Angelo Negro e Figli, 56
Angelo Nicolis e Figli, 125
Anselmi, 126
Anteo, 95
Antica Masseria Venditti, 215
Antichi Vigneti di Cantalupo, 72, 74
Antici Poderi Jerzu, 250
Antoine Charrére et Fils, 83
Antonelli, 182
Antonio, Carlo e Pietro
    Mastroberardino, 208
Antonio Caggiano, 215
Antonio Vallana, 73–74
Antoniolo, 72, 74
Anzillotti Solazzi, 188
Argiano, 161
Argiolas, 246, 250
Armando Martino, 226
Arnaldo Caprai-Val di Maggio, 182
Ascevi-Luwa, 137
Astoria Vini, 130
Attilio Contini, 250
Attilio Fabrini, 188
Avignonesi, 166
Azienda Agricola Rigoli, 171
Badia a Coltibuono, 152
Barberani-Vallesanta, 182
Baron von Widmann, 115
Baroncini, 157
Barone Cornacchia, 191
Barone Ricasoli, 152
Baroni a Prato, 117
Bartolo Mascarello, 47, 53
Basilium, 226
Bastianich, 137
Bava, 64
Belisario, 188
Bellavista, 97
Bellucchi, 96
Benanti, 241, 243
Bertani, 121, 125–126
Bigi, 182
Biondi-Santi, 161

producers *(continued)*
Bisci, 188
Bisson, 126
Boccadigabbia, 188
Boffa, 64
Bolla, 125–126
Bonci, 188
Borgo Conventi, 137
Borgo del Tiglio, 137
Borgo Magredo, 140
Borgo San Daniele, 139
Borin, 129
Bortolomiol, 130
Botromagno, 224
Braida, 62, 64
Bricco Asili, 51
Bricco Rocche, 47
Brigaldera, 125
Broglia, 68
Brovia, 47
Bruna, 88
Brunelli, 125
Bruno Giacosa, 47, 51, 94
Bruno Rocca, 51
Brunori, 188
Ca' Romé, 51
Ca' Bolani, 140
Ca' Bruzzo, 128
Ca' del Bosco, 97
Ca' del Monte, 125
Ca' Lustra, 129
Ca' Marcanda, 171
Ca' Ronesca, 137
Ca' Rugate, 126
Ca' dei Frati, 99
Cabert, 140
Calzetti, 105
Camigliano, 161
Camillo Montori, 191
Campagnola, 125–126
Campogiovanni, 161
Canalicchio di Sopra, 161
Candido, 224
Canevel, 130
Cantalupo, 74
Cantele, 224

Cantina Cooperativa di
  Cerveteri, 201
Cantina del Locorotondo, 224
Cantina del Vermentino, 248, 250
Cantina Gallura, 248, 250
Cantina Grotta del Sole, 215
Cantina Monrubio, 182
Cantina Oleificio Sociale di
  Gradoli, 201
Cantina Sociale Copertino, 224
Cantina Sociale dei Colli
  Amerini, 182
Cantina Tollo, 191
Cantine Dolianova, 250
Cantine Lamezia Lento, 231
Cantine Lungarotti, 182
Cantine Torrevecchia, 243
Capanna, 161
Caparra & Siciliani, 231
Cardeto, 182
Carpenè Malvolti, 130
Carpineto, 152
Casal Thaulero, 191
Casale del Giglio, 201
Casale Marchese, 201
Casale-Falchini, 157
Casalfarneto, 188
Casanova di Neri, 161
Cascina Ca' Rossa, 56
Cascina Chicco, 56
Cascina delle Terre Rosse, 88
Cascina du Fèipu, 88
Cascina La Barbatella, 64
Cascina La Pertica, 98
Case Basse of Soldera, 162
Castel de Paolis, 201
Castel Schwanburg, 115
Castelgiocondo, 162
Castellare di Castellina, 152
Castellari Bergaglio, 68
Castell'in Villa, 152
Castello Banfi, 161
Castello Brolio, 151
Castello d'Albola, 153
Castello dei Rampolla, 152
Castello della Sala, 178, 182

Castello di Ama, 152
Castello di Brolio, 152
Castello di Cacchiano, 153
Castello di Farnatella, 155
Castello di Fonterutoli, 152
Castello di Gabbiano, 153
Castello di Lilliano, 153
Castello di Neive, 51
Castello di Querceto, 153
Castello di Spessa, 137
Castello di Verrazzano, 153
Castello di Volpaia, 151–152
Castelluccio, 108
Castelvecchio, 139
Cataldi Madonna, 191
Cavalchina, 121–122
Cavalleri, 97
Cavalotto, 47
Cecchi-Villa Cerna, 153
Cerbaiona, 162
Ceretto, 47, 51, 63
Chigi Saracini, 156
Ciacci Piccolomini, 162
Cinzano, 62
Claudio Vio, 88
Clerico, 47, 54
Col d'Orcia, 162
Col Vetoraz, 130
Colacicchi, 201
Collavini, 137
Colle dei Bardellini, 88
Colle Picchioni-Paola Di Mauro, 201
Colombaio di Candia, 71
Colonnara, 188
Colosi, 243
Còlpetrone, 182
Comincioli, 98
Concilio, 118
Conte Attems, 137
Conte D'Attimis-Maniago, 137
Conte Leopardi, 188
Conte Zandotti, 201
Conterno-Fantino, 47, 54
Conti da Schio, 128
Conti Formentini, 137
Conti Martini, 117

Conti Zecca, 224
Contucci, 166
Cooperativa Agricola di Cinqueterre, 88
Cooperativa Interprovinciale Elorina, 243
Coppo, 62, 64
Cordero di Montezemolo, 47
Corino, 47
Cornaleto, 97
Cornarea, 56
Corte Gardoni, 122
Corte Gardoni's Le Fontane, 121
Corte Rugolin, 125
Corte Sant'Alda, 125
COS, 243
Cosimo Taurino, 224
Costanti, 162
Costaripa, 98
Co.Vi.O., 182
D'Alfonso del Sordo, 224
D'Ambra Vini d'Ischia, 215
D'Ancona, 243
D'Angelo, 226
Dal Forno, 125
Dante Rivetti, 63
De Bartoli, 243
De Concilus, 215
De Forville, 51
De Lucia, 215
Decugnano dei Barbi, 182
Dei, 166
Deltetto, 56
Desiderio Bisol & Figli, 130
Dessilani, 73–74
Dievole, 153
Donnafugata, 243
Doria, 95
Doro Princic, 137
Duca di Salaparuta, 238, 243
E. Pira & Figli, 47
Eddi Luisa, 139
Edi Kante, 139
Edoardo Valentini, 190
Elio Altare, 47, 53–54
Elio Grasso, 47

producers *(continued)*
Elvio Cogno, 47, 53–54
Emidio Pepe, 191
Emiro Cav. Bortolusso, 140
Enoteca Bisson, 88
Enrico Gatti, 97
Enzo Mecella, 188
Ezio Voyat, 82
Falesco, 201
Fassati, 166
Fattoria Coroncino, 188
Fattoria dei Barbi, 161
Fattoria del Casato, 161
Fattoria del Cerro, 166
Fattoria di Basciano, 155
Fattoria di Cusona, 157
Fattoria di Felsina, 152
Fattoria di Manzano, 156
Fattoria di Petrolo, 156
Fattoria Il Paradiso, 157
Fattoria Mancini, 188
Fattoria Paradiso, 108
Fattoria San Francesco, 231
Fattoria San Quirico, 157
Fattoria Selvapiana, 156
Fattoria Zerbina, 108
Fausto Maculan, 127
Fazi Battaglia, 188
Felline, 224
Ferrari, 116, 125
Feudi di San Gregorio, 208, 210, 215
Filippo Gallino, 56
Fior d'Arancio of La Montecchia, 129
Fiorano, 201
Fiorenzo Nada, 51
Fiorini, 188
Firriato, 243
Florio, 236–237, 243
Fontana Candida, 201
Fontanachiara, 95
Fontanafredda, 47, 62, 94
Fontodi, 152
Foradori, 117
Forchir, 140
Forlini e Cappellini, 88
Francesco Pecorari, 137
Francesco Rinaldi, 47

Francesco Sessa, 226
Franco Martinetti, 64
Franz Haas, 115
Fratelli Adanti, 182
Fratelli Bucci, 188
Fratelli Cigliuti, 51
Fratelli Coos, 137
Fratelli Grosjean, 83
Fratelli Speri, 125
Fratelli Sportoletti, 182
Fratelli Tedeschi, 125
Fratelli Vagnoni, 157
Fratelli Zeni, 121, 125
Frecciarossa, 95
Fuligni, 162
Funtanin, 56
Gaierhof, 117
Gaja, 47, 53
Galardi, 215
Gancia, 94
Garofoli, 188
Giacobazzi, 103
Giacomo Borgogno, 47
Giacomo Conterno, 47, 53–54
Gianni Vescovo, 139
Gianni Voerzio, 47
Gini, 126
Giobatta Mandino Cane, 88
Giovanni Cherchi, 250
Giovanni Dri, 137
Giovanni Palombo, 201
Giovanni Panizzi, 157
Giralamo Dorigo, 137
Giuseppe Bianchi, 73–74
Giuseppe Calò, 224
Giuseppe Cortese, 51
Giuseppe Gabbas, 250
Giuseppe Mascarello, 47, 53
Giuseppe Rinaldi, 47
Giuseppi Rinaldi, 53
Gorelli, 162
Gotto d'Oro, 201
Gradnik, 137
Grattamacco, 171
Gravner, 137
Gregoletto, 130
Gualdo del Re, 171

Guerrieri Gonzaga, 117–118
Guerrieri-Rizzardi, 121, 125–126
Guicciardini Strozzi, 157
Hans Rottensteiner, 115
Hastae, 62
Hauner, 243
Hirshprunn, 115
I Paglieri, 51
I Vignaioli Elvio Pertinace, 51
Il Greppone Mazzi, 162
Il Macchione, 166
Il Marroneto, 162
Il Poggiolo, 162
Il Poggione, 162
Il Torchio, 88
Illuminati, 191
Inama, 126
Instituto Agrario Provinciale, 117
Isidoro Polencic, 137
Isole e Olena, 152
J. Hofstätter, 115
J. Tiefenbrunner, 115
Jacopo Banti, 171
Jermann, 137
Josef Brigl, 115
Josef Niedermayr, 115
Kettmeir, 115
La Biancara, 128
La Boatina, 137
La Braccesca, 166
La Brancaia, 152
La Calonica, 166
La Cappuccina, 126
La Caprense, 215
La Carraia, 182
La Castellada, 137
La Cave du Vin Blanc de Morgex et
    de La Salle, 83
La Chiara, 68
La Colombiera, 88
La Crotta di Vegneron, 83
La Fiorita-Lamborghini, 182
La Gerla, 162
La Giustiniana, 68
La Lastra, 157
La Massa, 152
La Monacesca, 188

La Muiraghina, 95
La Pieve di Santa Restituta, 162
La Poderina, 162
La Scolca, 68
La Spinetta, 51, 63
La Spinona, 51
La Stoppa, 104
La Toledana, 68
La Torre, 162
La Tosa, 104
La Vecchia Cantina, 88
La Viarte, 137
La Vis, 116–117
Lamberti, 121–122, 126
Lamoretti, 105
Lanari, 188
Le Caniette, 188
Le Case Bianche, 130
Le Colline, 74
Le Corti, 153
Le Due Terre, 137
Le Fraghe, 121
Le Ragose, 125
Le Tende, 122
Le Terrazze, 188
Le Vigne di San Pietro, 121–122
Le Volpaiole, 171
Leone de Castris, 224
Les Crêtes, 82
Librandi, 231
Lino Maga, 95
Lis Neris-Pecorari, 139
Lisini, 162
Livio Felluga, 137
Livon, 137
Lodola Nuova, 166
Lomazzi & Sarli, 224
Lorella Ambrosini, 171
Luciano Sandrone, 47
Luigi Bianco, 51
Luigi Einaudi, 47
Luigi Ferrando, 70–71
Luigi Maffini, 215
Luigi Perazzi, 73–74
Luigi Pira, 47
Lupi, 88
Machiavelli, 153

producers *(continued)*
Maison Alberto Vevey, 82
Malvirà, 56
Mangilli, 140
Manzone, 47, 53
Marcarini, 47, 53–54
Marchesi Antinori, 152, 155
Marchesi de' Frescobaldi, 156
Marchesi di Barolo, 47
Marchesi di Gresy, 51
Marchetti, 188
Marco De Bartoli, 242
Marco Felluga, 137
Maria Donata Bianchi, 88
Mario Lucchetti, 188
Mario Schiopetto, 137
Marisa Cuomo, 215
Marramiero, 191
Martini & Rossi, 62, 94
Masciarelli, 191
Masciarelli and Emidio Pepe, 190
Masi, 125–126
Masi's La Vegrona, 121
Maso Poli, 117
Masseria Di Majo Norante, 193
Masseria Monaci, 224
Masseria Pepe, 224
Massimi Berucci, 201
Massimo Romeo, 166
Mastroberardino, 208, 210, 215
Mastrojanni, 162
Masut da Rive, 139
Matteo Correggia, 56
Mauro Drius, 139
Mazzioti, 201
Melini, 153, 157
Miani, 137
Michele Calò, 224
Michele Castellani, 125
Michele Chiarlo, 47, 62, 64
Michele Moio, 215
Mionetto, 130
Moccagatta, 51, 53
Monchiero Carbone, 56
Monsanto, 152
Monsupello, 95
Monte del Vigne, 105

Monte Rossa, 97
Monte Schiavo, 188
Montenidoli, 157
Montepeloso, 171
Montevetrano, 215
Monti, 191
Montresor, 122, 125–126
Morgante, 243
Morgassi Superiore, 68
Mormoraia, 157
Moroder, 188
Mottura, 201
Mulino delle Tolle, 140
Mustilli, 215
Nervi, 72, 74
Nicola Bergaglio, 68
Nino Franco, 130
Nino Negri, 93
Nittardi, 153
Nozzole, 153
Nugnes, 224
Ocone, 215
Octaviano Lambruschi, 88
Oddero, 47
Odoardi, 231
Ornellaia, 171
Orsolani, 71
Pala, 250
Palagetto, 157
Palari, 240, 243
Paolo Caccese, 137
Paolo Rodaro, 137
Paolo Saracco, 63
Paolo Scavino, 47, 53
Parroco di Neive, 51
Parusso, 47
Pasqua, 126
Paternoster, 226
Pelissero, 51
Pellegrino, 236–237, 243
Pertimali di Angelo Sassetti, 162
Pertimali di Livio Sassetti, 162
Perusini, 137
Pervini, 224
Peter Zemmer, 115
Petrucco, 137
Piero Gatti, 63

Pieropan, 126
Pierpaolo Pecorari, 139
Pieve del Vescovo, 182
Pighin, 137, 140
Pio Cesare, 47
Planeta, 240, 243
Plozner, 140
Podere Colla, 47
Podere Il Palazzino, 152
Podere San Michele, 171
Poderi Boscarelli, 166
Poggerino, 153
Poggio al Sole, 153
Poggio Antico, 162
Poggio Salvi, 162
Pojer & Sandri, 117
Poliziano, 166
Pra, 126
Prà di Pradis, 137
Produttori del Barbaresco, 51
Produttori Nebbiolo di Carema, 70
Prunotto, 47, 53, 62, 64
Puiatti, 137
Pupillo, 243
Querciabella, 153
Quintarelli, 125
Radikon, 137
Rainoldi, 93
Rallo, 236–237, 243
Rapitalà, 243
Ratti, 54
Redi, 166
Regaleali, 238
Regaleali (Tasca d'Almerita), 243
Renato Anselmet, 83
Renato Ratti, 47
Ricci Curbastro, 98
Riecine, 153
Riseccoli, 153
Riunite, 103
Rivera, 222, 224
Roagna, 51
Roberto Voerzio, 47
Roberto Zeni, 117
Rocca Bernarda, 137
Rocca di Castagnoli, 153
Rocca di Fabri, 182

Rocche Costamagna, 47
Rocche dei Manzoni, 47
Roncada, 137
Ronchi di Cialla, 137
Ronchi di Manzano, 137
Ronco dei Rosetti, of Zamò, 137
Ronco dei Tassi, 137
Ronco del Gelso, 139
Ronco del Gnemiz, 137
Ronco delle Betulle, 137
Rosa del Golfo, 224
Ruffino, 152
Ruggeri & C., 130
Russiz Superiore, of Marco
    Felluga, 137
S. Molettieri, 215
Saladini Pilastri, 188
Salcheto, 166
Salvatore Murana, 243
Salvioni-La Cerbaiola, 162
San Biagio, 188
San Donato, 157
San Fabiano Calcinaia, 153
San Felice, 153
San Giovanni, 215
San Giusto a Rentennano, 152
San Michele Appiano, 115
Sandrone, 54
Sant' Elena, 139
Santa Barbara, 188
Santa Margherita, 132
Santa Maria La Palma, 248, 250
Santa Sofia, 121–122, 125–126
Santadi, 250
Santi, 122, 125–126
Sartarelli, 188
Scarpa, 64
Scrimaglio, 64
Secondo Pasquero-Elia, 51
Seghesio, 47
Sella, 73–74
Sella & Mosca, 244, 246, 248, 250
Settesole, 243
Signano, 157
Silvio Grasso, 47
Silvio Jermann, 135
Sinfarosa, 224

producers *(continued)*
Siro Pacenti, 162
Sorì Paitin, 51
Spadafora, 243
Specogna, 137
Stefano Accordini, 125
Stefano Ferrucci, 108
Stefano Mancinelli, 188
Stelio Gallo, 138
Suavia, 126
Talenti-Pian di Conte, 162
Tavignano, 188
Tenuta Beltrame, 140
Tenuta Bonzara, 106
Tenuta Caparzo, 161
Tenuta Carretta, 47, 55–56
Tenuta Cocci Grifoni, 188
Tenuta di Blasig, 139
Tenuta di Capezzana, 155
Tenuta di Salviano, 182
Tenuta Friggiali, 162
Tenuta Giunchio, 88
Tenuta Guado al Tasso, 171
Tenuta La Palazza, 108
Tenuta La Tenaglia, 64
Tenuta Le Quinte, 201
Tenuta Le Velette, 182
Tenuta Mazzolino, 95
Tenuta San Guido, 171
Tenuta San Leonardo, 118
Tenuta Trerose, 166
Tenuta Valdipatta, 166
Tenuta Villanova, 137
Tenute Capichera, 248, 250
Tenute Silvio Nardi, 162
Terre Bianche, 88
Terre Cortesi Moncaro, 188
Terre Rosse, 106
Terredora, 210, 215
Terredora di Paolo, 208
Teruzzi & Puthod, 157
Tilli, 182
Tommasi, 125
Torre Rosazza, 137
Torrevento, 224
Travaglini, 72, 74
Tre Monti, 108

Trinchero, 64
Tua Rita, 171
Uberti, 98
Uccelliera, 162
Umani Ronchi, 188
Umberto Cesari, 108
Umberto Fiore, 74
Umberto Portinari, 126
Val di Suga, 162
Valentini, 190–191
Valle dell'Acate, 241, 243
Valle dell'Asso, 224
Vallona, 106
Vecchie Terre di Montefili, 153
Velenosi, 188
Venegazzù, 131
Venica & Venica, 137
Venturini, 125
Vi.C.Or., 182
Vie di Romans, 138–139
Vietti, 47, 53–54, 62–64
Vignalta, 129
Vignamaggio, 153
Vigne dal Leon, 137
Vigneti del Sud, 224
Villa Cafaggio, 153
Villa dal Ferro, 128
Villa Era, 74
Villa Matilde, 215
Villa Monte Rico, 171
Villa Pigna, 188
Villa Russiz, 137
Villa San Michele, 215
Villa Sant'Anna, 166
Villa Simone, 201
Villa Sparina, 68
Villamagna, 188
Vincenzo Cesani, 157
Vinicola Savese, 224
Visconti, 99
Vistorta, 140
Viticcio, 153
Vitivinicola Avide, 243
Vittorio Boratto, 71
Volpe Pasini, 137
Walter De Battè, 88

Walter Filliputti, at Abbazia di Rosazzo, 137
Wilhelm Walch, 115
Zaccagnini, 191
Zamò & Zamò, 137
Zardetto, 130
Zenato, 125–126
Zonin, 128, 130
produttore, 34
pronunciation guide, 267–270
proprietary names, 33
Prosecco di Conegliano-Valdobbiadene DOC, 129–130
Prugnolo Gentile grapes, 263
Puglia. *See* Apulia

• *Q* •

Quagliano DOC, 75
quality of Italian wines, 1, 13, 32, 255, 262
Quorum wine, 62

• *R* •

Rainoldi DOC, 93
Refosco grapes, 22
Riesling grapes, 16, 26
riserva, 34
Riviera del Garda Bresciano DOC, 98
Riviera del Garda Bresciano Rosso DOC, 98
Riviera Ligure di Ponente DOC, 84–85
Roero DOC, 55–56
Romagna Albana *Spumante* wine, 107
Rondinella grapes, 121, 123
rosato, 34
Rossese di Dolceacqua DOC, 84
Rossese di Dolceacqua wine, 84–85
Rossese grapes, 84
rosso, 34
Rosso Barletta DOC, 223
Rosso Canosa DOC, 223
Rosso Cònero DOC, 185
Rosso di Cerignola DOC, 224
Rosso di Montalcino DOC, 162–163
Rosso di Montepulciano DOC, 165

Rosso Orvietano DOC, 179
Rosso Pachino DOC, 241
Rosso Piceno DOC, 185
Rubino di Cantavenna DOC, 69
Ruché di Castagnole Monferrato, 67

• *S* •

Sagrantino di Montefalco DOCG, 180
Sagrantino grapes, 22
Salice Salentino DOC, 218
Sambuca di Sicilia DOC, 240
San Colombano DOC, 95
San Gimignano DOC, 156–157
San Martino della Battaglia DOC, 99
San Severo DOC, 223
San Vito di Luzzi DOC, 229
Sangiovese di Romagna DOC, 107
Sangiovese grapes, 15–16, 18, 145
Sangiovese Grosso grapes, 18
Sangioveto grapes, 18
Sangue di Guida wine, 94
Sannio DOC, 215
Sant'Agata dei Goti DOC, 214
Sant'Anna di Isola Capo Rizzuto DOC, 228
Sant'Antimo DOC, 163–164
Santa Maddalener (St. Magdalener) wine, 113
Santa Margherita di Belice DOC, 239–240
Sardegna Semidano wine, 247
Sardinia, 243–250
Sassella wine, 92
Sauvignon Blanc grapes, 41
Sauvignon grapes, 26
Savuto DOC, 229
Scavigna DOC, 230
Schiava grapes, 22, 112
Sciacca DOC, 240
Sciacchetrà wine, 85
secco, 34
Sfursat wine, 93
Sicily, 233–242
Sizzano DOC, 73
Soave DOC, 120, 125–126, 262
Soave wines, 263

Solopaca DOC, 214
Sorni DOC, 118
Sovana DOC, 172
Spanna, 71
sparkling wines
　Asti, 61–62
　Asti Spumante, 262
　Berlucchi Cuvée Imperiale, 96
　Blanc de Morgex, 80
　Bruno Giacosa Brut, 94
　Ferrari, 116
　Franciacorta, 95–98
　Moscato di Sardegna, 247
　Pinot Nero, 94
　production, 14
　Prosecco, 129–130
　Romagna Albana *Spumante*, 107
spumante, 34, 262
Squinzano DOC, 220
Südtiroler DOC, 112
Super-Tuscan wines, 167–169,
　254–255
superiore, 34
sweet wines. *See* dessert wines
Syrah grapes, 16

• T •

table wines, 30
Taburno DOC, 214
Tarquinia DOC, 199
taste of Italian wines, 261
Taurasi DOCG, 208–209
tenuta, 34
Terlano (Terlaner) wine, 114
Teroldego grapes, 22, 116
Teroldego Rotaliano DOC, 117–118
Terralba wine, 250
Terre di Franciacorta DOC, 96
Tocai Friulano grapes, 24
Torbato grapes, 249
Torcolato DOC, 127–128
Torgiano DOC, 179–180
Torgiano Rosso Riserva DOCG, 179
Torrette wine, 81
Tre Venezie, 112

Trebbianino Val Trebbia wine, 104
Trebbiano d'Abruzzo DOC, 190–191
Trebbiano di Romagna DOC, 107
Trebbiano grapes, 16, 22–23, 145
Trebbiano Toscano grapes, 234
Trentino DOC, 116–117
Trentino-Alto Adige, 109–118
Trento DOC, 117
Tuscany
　Barco Reale di Carmignano, 167
　Bianco dell'Empolese, 174
　Bianco di Pitigliano, 173
　Bianco di Valdinievo, 173
　Bianco Pisano di San Torpè, 174
　Bianco Vergine Valdichiana, 174
　Bolgheri, 170–171
　Brunello di Montalcino, 144,
　　160–162
　Candia dei Colli Apuani, 173
　Capalbio, 172
　Carmignano Rosso, 145, 166–167
　Chianti, 144, 147–148, 153–156
　Chianti Classico, 144, 147–152
　climate, 144
　Colli dell'Etruria Centrale, 158–159
　Colline di Lucchesi, 173
　Costa dell'Argentario, 172
　Elba, 174
　geography, 144
　Grosseto, 171
　history, 143
　Maremma, 170
　Montalcino, 159
　Montecarlo, 173
　Montecucco, 172
　Monteregio di Massa Marittima,
　　171–172
　Montescudaio, 174
　Morellino di Scansano, 172
　Moscadello di Montalcino, 162
　Pomino, 157–158
　Rosso di Montalcino, 162–163
　Rosso di Montepulciano, 165
　San Gimignano, 156–157
　Sant'Antimo, 163–164
　Sovana, 172
　Super-Tuscan wines, 167–169, 254

Val d'Arbia, 158
Val di Cornia, 171
Vernaccia di San Gimignano, 145,
    156–157
Vin Santo di Chianti Classico, 158
Vin Santo di Montepulciano,
    165–166
vineyards, 144
Vino Nobile di Montepulciano, 145,
    164–165
wine history, 144
wine zones, 146

• U •

Umbria, 175–182

• V •

Val d'Arbia DOC zone, 158
Val di Cornia DOC zone, 171
Valcalepio DOC zone, 99
Valdadige (Etschtaler) DOC zone, 118
Valgella wine, 92
Valle d'Aosta DOC zone, 77–83
Valle Isarco (Eisacktaler) wine, 114
Valle Venosta (Vinschgau) wine, 114
Valnure wine, 104
Valpolicella DOC zone, 120, 123–124
Valpolicella wine, 262–263
Valsusa DOC zone, 75
Valtellina DOC zone, 92–93
Valtellina DOCG zone, 90–93
Velletri DOC zone, 197
vendemmia, 34
Veneto, 120–131
Verbicaro DOC zone, 229
Vercelli, 71–73
Verdicchio DOC zone, 183–185
Verdicchio grapes, 16, 24
Verduno Pelaverga wine, 57
Vermentino di Gallura wine, 244, 248
Vermentino di Sardegna wine,
    247–248
Vermentino grapes, 26, 244
Vermentino wine, 85

Vernaccia di Oristano wine, 249
Vernaccia di San Gimignano DOCG
    zone, 145, 156–157
Vernaccia di Serrapetrona DOC
    zone, 187
Vernaccia grapes, 24
Vernatsch grapes, 112
Verona, 122
Vespolina grapes, 41
Vesuvio DOC zone, 211
vigna, 34
Vignanello DOC zone, 198
vigneto, 34
Vin Santo di Chianti Classico DOC
    zone, 158
Vin Santo di Montepulciano DOC
    zone, 165–166
vino, 34
vino da tavola, 30–31
Vino Nobile di Montepulciano DOCG
    zone, 145, 164–165
Vino Nobile di Montepulciano
    wine, 263
vintage chart, 271–272
Viognier grapes, 16
vitigno, 34
Voyat, Ezio, 82

• W •

Wine Atlas of Italy, The, 79
wine laws
    DOC/G designation, 28–32, 254–255
    history, 32
    IGT designation, 30–31
    vino da tavola, 30–31
    wine taste, 28
winemakers. See also producers
    Antinori, Marchese Piero, 50
    Antinori, Piero, 155
    Bernabei, Franco, 95
    Bologna, Giacomo, 63
    Cotarella, Riccardo, 62
    Gaja, Angelo, 50
    Grai, Giorgio, 115
    Hauner, Carlo, 242

winemakers *(continued)*
  Lungarotti, Giorgio, 179
  Schiopettok, Mario, 134
  Tachis, Giacomo, 244, 246
  Tasca d'Almerita, Giuseppe
      (Count), 238
  Valentini, Edoardo, 190
  Voyat, Ezio, 82
  Zanella, Maurizio, 97
  Ziliani, Franco, 96

• Z •

Zagarolo DOC zone, 197

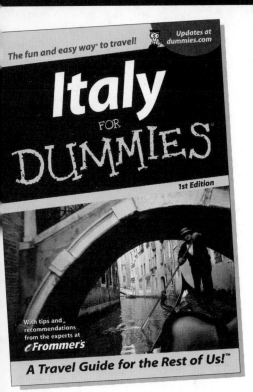